Waiheke Pioneers

Waiheke Pioneers

Dixie Day

Waiheke Island Historical Society Inc

The Waiheke Island Historical Society gratefully acknowledges the generous support of the Waiheke Local Board and Auckland Council for the publication of this edition of *Waiheke Pioneers*.

Published by the Waiheke Island Historical Society, Inc.
Second Edition
Published by The Waiheke Island Historical Society Inc
in association with Lasavia Publishing Ltd
Waiheke, Auckland, New Zealand

ISBN: 978-1-99-115199-5

Table of Contents

Preface to the Second Edition

Nearly a third of a century has passed since Dixie Day published her now-standard reference on the early Pākehā settlers of Waiheke Island. The first printing of *Waiheke Pioneers* in 1989 sold out quickly, with the proceeds used to establish what is now the Museum of Waiheke and Historic Village on Onetangi Straight. A much larger second printing in 1991 supplied the Waiheke Island Historical Society with enough copies to sell for twenty-five years. The addition of a full-name index by Arnie Aretz guaranteed the popularity of the book amongst people researching their own family histories.

Today the first edition is out of print, and with the advances in digital publication technology the cost of reprinting it would actually be higher than that of creating a new edition. That is why the Historical Society has chosen the latter course.

Most of Dixie Day's original text remains untouched, but a second edition has given us an opportunity to address two gaps that Dixie herself acknowledged in her original Preface. First, the pre-European history of the island had been treated in much too brief a manner. The present edition now includes a fuller introduction to Māori settlement, written by island historian Paul Monin with additional information supplied by Glen Tupuhi and Morehu Wilson of Ngāti Pāoa. Although the focus of the book remains on the early European settlers, which was Dixie Day's own expertise, the new overview of the much longer period of Māori occupation offers a sharp context into which to place Dixie's stories.

Second, some important early Pākehā families received only cursory mention in the first edition. Prime among these is the Isaac Merrick family, whom Dixie left out at the request of a Merrick descendant who was writing her own history of that family. Sadly, the Merrick book never saw the light of day, so we have remedied that large gap in our second edition from Dixie Day's own notes, with further information provided by Wendy Gordon and Paul Monin.

Another family about whom some new and colourful information has come to light since 1989 is that of Charles De Witte. Annie Terlinck, a Belgian genealogist who became fascinated by the De Witte story during a visit to the island in 2014, has written a 63-page monograph (in French) describing her findings, which she has kindly allowed us to translate and summarise in a new section on the De Wittes. Jan Scott has also contributed information on Charles De Witte.

Apart from those additions, we have confined our editorial changes to corrections of minor errors in names and dates, and to clarifications of timeframe (references to "early this century", for example, are now "early 20th century"). A few anachronistic statements have also been touched up where, for example, a building that was "still standing today" (in 1989) is now gone.

Such alterations to the original text have, we are pleased to report, been very few. Dixie Day's extensive research and her engaging story-telling style have stood the test of time, and those are the very assets that have made *Waiheke Pioneers* the authoritative reference that it remains today.

The Waiheke Island Historical Society (2021).

Preface

It was September 1940 when I was married in the Day homestead at Ōmaru Bay. Our altar was an oak table under a window that looked out over golden kowhai to the sparkling waters of the Hauraki Gulf.

This marriage to Edsell Day not only made Waiheke my home but made me part of an island heritage that dated back to the 1860s when Martin Day and his young wife decided to settle here. As I adapted to life on an isolated farm, learned how to care for sick cows and make my own butter, I became more and more interested in the stories I heard over the kitchen table of those first Waiheke settlers who had to adjust to island life.

Who were they? What brought them to this remote and beautiful island? How did they cope, wresting their living from the land with no stores, no welfare, no doctors and limited communication with mainland settlements? When time allowed, I started to find out.

I began research in Auckland and found treasure in the Auckland Diocesan office and the journals of Anglican clergy. I contacted descendants of early settlers through a network of family relations, cross-checking where possible.

The result is this book, which doesn't pretend to be a definitive history of Waiheke. The pre-European history is referred to only briefly and further research here is a task better done by descendants of the Ngāti Pāoa settlers. Nor does it cover the more recent and equally colourful history of Waiheke's western settlements, and I regret that it has not been possible to include the stories of all the early settlers.

Waiheke Pioneers looks primarily at the period from the 1840s through to the 1920s when farmland subdivision paved the way for the creation of settlements at Ostend, Onetangi, Palm Beach, Surfdale and Oneroa. It is about those European families who first carved a living for themselves out of the resources this island offered: its seas, forests and land. Hopefully it conveys something of the hardships and joys of their lives. It is, above all, my tribute to Waiheke's pioneers.

Acknowledgements

I would like to thank all the following families who have helped me, by letter, telephone or personal interview, to tell the pioneers' stories: Brown, Carey, Connell, Croll, Day, Gordon, Hooks, Insley, Kennedy, Lang, McLeod, O'Brien, Parris, Pegler, and Powell. Mrs R I Shultz shared the memories of her grandfather, Captain Joseph Hodgson. Mrs M McIntosh and Mr J Watson contributed stories, as did the late Don Croll, and the late Miss Ivy Smytheman who wrote of early Ostend. The late Miss Burgess gave me the early history of the former Alison homestead at Matiatia and the late Mr R Ross supplied information on the Maxwells.

I am also indebted to Mr D Ray who generously gave me notebooks used for his own research. The work of Mr P Monin and Mrs N Robinson assisted me, as did early maps given by Mrs Joyce Barton who has researched the history of the Merrick family on Waiheke which is being written separately.

The following have also helped with research for which I am deeply grateful: Mrs Cheryl Bedggood, Mrs M Coatsworth, Mrs Errol Jones, Mrs A Pegler, Mrs J Vingoe, Mrs B White, and Mrs Kay Clark (who planned and executed the Waiheke map). Some others who shared in the Waiheke story are: Dr Godfrey Armitage, Mr J Ashwin, Mrs L E Drummond, Mr and Mrs Bert Foster, Mr and Mrs F Hookey, Mr J H Kean, Mrs E O'Flaherty, Mr D Pert, Miss Philson, Lady Richmond and Mrs L Smith.

There has been warm interest in this project both on and off the island, particularly among members of the Waiheke Historical

Society for whom the book is written. It would not have been finished without the encouragement and advice of my friend and typist, Peggy Edwards who has supported me in every way.

The photographs in the book are all contained in the Waiheke Museum Archives and are reproduced with thanks to those who took them and those who kindly donated them to the Museum.

Dixie Day (1989).

The First Pioneers
(by Paul Monin)

Located alongside some of the busiest waterways of pre-European Aotearoa, Waiheke Island was destined for an eventful Māori history. Its earliest name, Te Motu Ārai Roa, The Long Sheltering Island, relates to the shelter that the Waiheke Channel and the Tāmaki Strait offered canoe traffic in bad weather. This major waterway directed canoes from as far away as Northland and the East Coast straight to the Tāmaki River and the portage connecting the Waitematā and Manukau Harbours, and onwards to the Waikato. It was a place where diverse peoples met, traded, intermarried, occasionally fought, and periodically displaced one another.

Ngāti Pāoa tradition and modern archaeology differ on the time of first settlement on the island, but these two knowledge systems should be seen as being complementary, not conflicting. To Ngāti Pāoa, the first settlers were Maruiwi from the Pacific, arrivals in about 950. A story of violence and bloodshed from these times has come down to us, through George Graham, who interviewed Ngāti Pāoa elders at the eleventh hour, in the early 20th century. In about 1200 a party under their chief Maeāea was invited by Maruiwi to a feast at Ōmaru (Woodside Bay), where they were enmeshed in hand nets and speared to death. Today this place still carries the name Te Rore a Maeāea, the Snaring of Maeāea, most likely the oldest Māori name on the island.

Archaeology offers a more prosaic account of first settlement. The islands of Tīkapa Moana, the Hauraki Gulf, were well placed geographically to be among the first places to be settled by East Polynesians in Aotearoa, between the late 1200s and the early 1300s. The funnel formed by Northland and the Coromandel Peninsula directed canoes straight down the Mahurangi coast to the islands of the inner Gulf, amidst abundant fisheries. Waiheke also had permanent fresh water and an abundance of quality timber. Evidence of Archaic Polynesian settlement (1300-1500) has been found on a number of our beaches, pre-eminently Ōwhiti Bay, where finds include the one-piece bone bait hooks characteristic of very early settlement, along with rich evidence of the island's pre-human biota.

First settlement in small numbers was followed by settlement in far greater numbers, consequent upon the visit of the waka *Te Arawa*, in about 1350. Commanded by the famous Tama Te Kapua, the great waka landed at Pūtiki inlet for rest and repairs at the end of its great voyage from Hawaiki. Here the waka was re-lashed, hence the naming of the stream that flows through today's Onetangi Sports Park, Te Rangihoua (The Day of Renewal). Returning to Waiheke, Kahu Mata Momoe, a son of Tama, took possession with the name Te Motu nui o Kahu, (The Great Island of Kahu). His whānau occupied the hill south of the stream naming it Pūtiki-o-Kahu (Kahu's Topknot). At times of migration, such naming established the rights of ownership and mana of the new residents. Several other places at Pūtiki acquired Arawa names: Princess Kura, another member of the crew, chose to live at Pūtiki next door to Wharetana, at Ō a Kura (Sigh of Kura). The inlet and wetland straddling today's Ostend causeway is named Ō Kahu iti (the small natural feature of Kahu). The name Omiha at Rocky Bay may also be Arawa in origin.

Coincidentally, at the time of *Te Arawa*'s sojourn at Pūtiki, another great waka also showed up in Waiheke waters, *Te Tainui*, under the command of Hoturoa. They stopped at Gannet Rock, where water lapping on the rocks reminded the crew of their tearful departure from Hawaiki; hence their naming of the rock Horuhoru, uncontrollable sobbing. (On a fine day Horuhoru is clearly visible from Oneroa.) They then tracked along the north coast of Waiheke to Rangitoto. After its Pūtiki sojourn, *Te Arawa* also proceeded to Rangitoto, to take a look at Te Waitematā. There the two commanders Tama Te Kapua and Hoturoa, came to blows, ostensibly over the former's unwanted attentions to the latter's senior wife. Tama Te Kapua got the worse of the altercation, which became the basis of the Tainui name for Rangitoto, the day that the blood of Tama Te Kapua flowed.

Te Arawa then proceeded to its final resting place, Maketū in the Bay of Plenty. Other members of the crew chose to remain at Moehau (Coromandel), in time taking the name of Tama Te Kapua's grandson Huarere. Ngāti Huarere went on to exercise dominion over much of Hauraki, including Waiheke, until the late 1600s. These are the founding traditions of Waiheke Island.

It is important to note that Ngāti Pāoa's links to both the *Arawa* and *Tainui* waka, through whakapapa, project their connections to Waiheke Island right back to the 1300s, if not before. Other Hauraki iwi have like claims, but Ngāti Pāoa's remain pre-eminent. Pāoa himself, the iwi's eponymous ancestor, was a grandson of both Pikiao, a *Te Arawa* chief, and Rereiao of *Tainui*. Pāoa married three times and had at least ten children; over time his enterprising descendants spread their influence over a broad stretch of the western Hauraki Gulf, including its islands.

The 50 or so pā sites on the island — fortified places of food storage and habitation — are mostly on headlands, with two on summits and perhaps three on islets. In Aotearoa widespread pā building began in about 1500, prompted by increasing competition over natural resources. They were not built at the same time and may have been occupied for only short periods. Māori were a highly mobile people, moving from place to place to tend gardens, harvest them, catch birds, to fish and so on. We can only guess the Māori population of Waiheke in these times. However, when threatened by external enemies, large numbers would have had to be marshalled at one or other of its two summit pā, Pūtiki o Kahu and Maunganui.

After several centuries of relatively peaceful occupation, Ngāti Huarere of Waiheke suffered three successive onslaughts, the last of which ended their dominion. First, Maki of Ngāti Awa, while on a northern expedition, swept through from Tāmaki to Kaipara, on the way unsuccessfully besieging Pūtiki o Kahu. Then in about 1680, Kawharu of Ngāti Wairere, Ngāti Mahanga, Ngāti Mahuta and Ngāti Pāoa descent, with assistance from Ngāti Whatua, scoured Tāmaki, Waiheke and Takapuna. Again Pūtiki was besieged, this time the defenders opting for a costly peace in surrendered slaves and goods.

The final onslaught came from Ngāti Pāoa in about 1700, on account of Ngāti Huarere's alliance through marriage with Waiohua of Maungawhau (Mt. Eden) who had murdered several visiting Hauraki chiefs. Ngāti Pāoa vented their wrath on offenders and allies alike. The attack of Kapetaua (ancestor of Te Patukirikiri tribe) on Pūtiki o Kahu is vividly narrated in the minutes of the Māori Land Court, about 170 years later. At this time the Marutūāhu (Hauraki) Confederation of tribes consisting of Ngāti Tamaterā, Ngāti Maru, Ngāti Whanaunga and Ngāti Pāoa challenged and extinguished the mana whenua of Ngāti Huarere (Te Arawa) throughout the Coromandel Peninsula, as well as on Waiheke.

Although tales of war and bloodshed make for memorable stories, it would be wrong to view these events as typical of Māori life on Waiheke. The pā fortifications were there for defence, but the presence of many undefended settlements (kāinga) and the extensive cultivation of kumara and other crops testify to long periods of peaceful relations and mutually beneficial trade between iwi. In fact the absorption of one tribe by another was more often the product of intermarriage than of conquest.

In the 1700s, three Ngāti Pāoa hapū moved to the island from their traditional land bases of the central-east Waikato and the western Firth of Thames — Te Uri Karaka (to the eastern end), Ngāti Hura (to the western end) and Ngāti Kapu. However, it is clear that they did not have the island to themselves, as Ngāti Maru and Te Patukirikiri also claimed considerable land rights here, but for over a century the tribes co-existed amicably. These good relations ended abruptly in about 1815, when Ngāti Pāoa accused Ngāti Maru of defiling the dead body of a Ngāti Pāoa chief drowned off Manaia. Violence erupted on Waiheke and at Coromandel. On the return of the tribes to Waiheke in the 1830s, Ngāti Maru chose to stay away, for fear of rekindling those earlier troubles.

Ngāi Tai ki Tāmaki, neighbours of Ngāti Pāoa on the south-western side of the Firth of Thames, also claimed rights at the eastern end of Waiheke. The union of Thomas Maxwell to Ngeungeu, the daughter of the great Ngāi Tai chief Tara Te Irirangi, facilitated his shift to Man O'War Bay in about 1835. Their story has a prominent place in Dixie's book.

1790 to 1820 were years of increasingly volatile Māori politics in the Hauraki Gulf, exacerbated by the importation of European weaponry. It was the time of the first fishing wars in the Gulf that we know about. However, it was not so much the fish-take that was the problem, for there was plenty to go around, but rather encounters between tribes over issues of mana. The setting was the Mahurangi shark fishery, the richest fishery in the Gulf located between Kawau Island and Whangaparāoa. After

20

1790 the Marutūāhu summer expeditions to the fishery grew in size and participation. Annually, Ngāti Pāoa took some 2000 rig shark (spotted dogfish) known to Māori as mango or kapetā. To minimise troubles with external tribes, Ngāti Pāoa repaired to safe locations to dry and store their catch, before taking it back to home kāinga as a valuable addition to the standard provender. Of these Oneroa Beach may have been the most important — hence the name of the beach's western peninsula, Hā kai Mango. Drying racks would have extended over great lengths of the beach, making known their presence far and wide. Insults traded between Marutūāhu groups and others, on the fishing ground, were causes of conflict.

Of quite a different order was the war from the north, the war that gave the region its name Hauraki, wind from the north. The enemy was Ngā Puhi, with whom Ngāti Maru and the other Hauraki tribes were engaged in a trial of strength at this momentous time. The dress rehearsal came in 1793 when Ngā Puhi, in retaliation for earlier losses to Ngāti Pāoa, hurled its forces at Waiheke's defences. The small pā at Ōkahuiti fell, but Pūtiki o Kahu stood fast. It was another story in 1820 when Hongi Hika crossed to Waiheke, after destroying the two great Ngāti Pāoa pā at Tāmaki, Mokoia and Mauinaina. Having overwhelming superiority in firearms, he laid siege to and destroyed Pūtiki o Kahu. The great age of Ngāti Pāoa had come to an end. Survivors, who escaped captivity, fled to refuges in the middle Waikato (Cambridge). This cataclysmic time is remembered simply and sadly, as 'the time of Hongi'.

Fortunately, Hongi was motivated more by vengeance than by conquest of land. With the end to the Musket Wars and the release of slaves at the behest of the missionaries, the peoples of Hauraki returned to their ancestral lands along the shores of Tīkapa Moana. The return to Waiheke was aided by the marriage of Ngā Puhi chief Eruera Patuone and the Ngāti Pāoa chieftainess, Takarangi (Riria), in 1833. This couple lived at Pūtiki o Kahu for many years.

The arrival of Thomas Maxwell soon after heralded the era of the Pākehā pioneers. Few places in Aotearoa had had a more thorough Māori presence, vestiges of which remained in the landscape, such as the earthworks of our many pā sites. Perhaps it was a sense of this past that led some pioneer families to locate their early burials close by — pioneers such as the Merricks at Graveyard Point, Awaawaroa, and the Careys at Carey

Bay. They set about forging their own connections with the land, while those of the mana whenua remained undiminished and unsurpassed.

The Decline and Re-emergence of Waiheke Māori

By the time of the founding of Auckland in 1840, Ngāti Pāoa had recovered some of the power and prosperity that had been damaged during the Musket Wars. Although the mainland fortress-cities of Mokoia and Mauinaina were never rebuilt, the agricultural and trading centres farther south recovered quickly. There and on Waiheke, vast market gardens were developed for a lucrative trade between Ngāti Pāoa and the new colonial town. As one observer put it, "They have obviously regrouped into a strong and powerful tribe once more as the quantity and variety of their production is mammoth." Māori labour was essential in the exploitation of Waiheke's kauri forests, providing masts for Royal Navy ships and building materials for Auckland.

Yet within two decades the Māori presence in the eastern half of Waiheke had all but vanished, and the western half followed the same path for the remainder of the nineteenth century. In 1924 the last 'Native School' on the island, at Te Huruhi, closed for lack of pupils. What happened?

The principal cause was the loss of land. By 1850, Government Land Purchasing Officers had acquired for the Crown most of the land that became Auckland Province, and much of this came from Ngāti Pāoa. Māori were familiar with land transactions; they had used them between iwi for centuries; but these transactions had involved only the rights of land use and non-exclusive occupancy. British ideas of land ownership, and particularly of vacant possession, were so alien to the Māori worldview as to be almost impossible to translate into te reo Māori.

Thus it was that Ngāti Pāoa families on Waiheke were astonished to find constables arriving from Auckland to evict them from the land the Crown had just sold to their Pākehā neighbours. Officially, the government land agents had instructions to reserve enough land for each tribe to continue to live in its traditional ways; these instructions derived from Article 2 of the Treaty of Waitangi. In practice, however, pressures for colonial expansion were such that these instructions were often ignored, especially around cities like Auckland. No such reserves were ever established on Waiheke. Evicted Ngāti Pāoa families were expected to leave the island for what little remained of Ngāti Pāoa land, in the Firth of Thames area or the Coromandel. Injustices like these were the main cause of the Land Wars of the 1860s.

Two large blocks of land on Waiheke attempted to resist alienation from Ngāti Pāoa. One block remained in Ngāti Pāoa hands until about 1900, while the other represents a reimplantation many decades later.

In western Waiheke, the 2100-acre Te Huruhi block remained in Māori hands into the twentieth century. Early maps suggest that this block was considered for Ngāti Pāoa reserve status — indeed Donald McLean recommended such a designation to the Māori Land Court — but this was never followed through. Nonetheless in 1865 the Māori Land Court recognised Ngāti Pāoa ownership of the Te Huruhi block — not as iwi land, but as belonging to five individuals. The Court was in fact explicitly forbidden to recognise the 'beastly communism' of iwi land ownership.

For two generations the five statutory owners of the Te Huruhi block and their heirs preserved a *de facto* Ngāti Pāoa administration of the land. By 1897, however, the number of legal heirs had grown to 65. Disputes arose among them, and the Māori Land Court divided the block into thirteen parcels, most of which were soon sold off to European farmers and, later, to subdivision developers. The Ngāti Pāoa era in western Waiheke thus came to an end.

Nonetheless a Māori presence has glimmered back to life on a small section of what was once the Te Huruhi block. In 1976 the Waiheke County Council granted a lease of this section to a committee dedicated to establishing a marae on the island. The Piritahi Marae was opened in stages between 1982 and 2016, and today looks proudly over the western end of Te Huruhi Bay.

In the eastern part of the island, Ngāti Pāoa had been induced to relinquish their traditional holdings there to the Crown in 1858. These holdings, amounting to 11,000 acres, were divided into large farms and granted to various European settlers. In 1937, a 1715-acre farm was purchased by Kathleen Hiraani Scott and her husband Charles Te Mangu Scott. Although neither Scott had Ngāti Pāoa ancestry, both were Māori and thus qualified for development assistance from the Department of

Māori Affairs. The Department's involvement grew over the years, to the point where the Scott family sold the land (now 2050 acres) to the Crown in 1972.

For eleven years the Department of Māori Affairs attempted to run the farm as a going concern, providing jobs for unemployed Māori, but without much financial success. In 1983 the decision was taken to sell the land on the open market. Objections quickly arose, especially from Ngāti Pāoa who pointed out that this farm had been part of their rohe or traditional land; that although alienated in 1858 it had effectively reverted to Māori if not Ngāti Pāoa ownership; and that if the Crown were to dispose of the land, it should be to Ngāti Pāoa and not once again on the open (i.e. Pākehā) market.

In early 1984 a group of Ngāti Pāoa and supporters staged a brief but well-publicised occupation of the 'Māori Affairs block', and the following year the iwi filed a claim in the Waitangi Tribunal for ownership of the block, based on Article 2 of the Treaty of Waitangi. Ngāti Pāoa won this case in 1987, and have owned and farmed the land ever since. In a roundabout way, the tribal reserve, which the Government Land Purchase Officers should have established some 140 years earlier, finally came to pass.

European Settlement

The largest island lying inside the waters of the Hauraki Gulf, Waiheke has long attracted settlement. Its 60 miles of coastline contain quiet bays and inlets that provide easy fishing; its distance from the mainland offers a degree of protective isolation that suits the independent spirit but does not sever access to other settlements; its gentle hills, sandy beaches and mild, maritime climate provide a pleasant living environment.

When Captain Cook's *Endeavour* entered the Hauraki Gulf to lie briefly off Waiheke's northeast coast in 1769, the island was the domain of the Ngāti Pāoa. The residents' first contact with European arrivals was with sealers and whalers who stopped off at the island for repairs, and the early missionaries. By mid-19th century, the Pākehā settlement of Waiheke was underway and the process of timber clearance had begun.

A newspaper clipping from 1887 paints the picture of an island just starting to develop its farming potential and yet to realise its possibilities as a holiday resort.

Immense quantities of timber have been cut and left to rot and partially cleared places have, through want of attention and non-sowing of grass, become overgrown again, the former clearers of the bush neither caring for, nor looking forward to the future. The whole upper end of the island is excellent sheep country; the lower end being more rugged and covered in dense bush, is better adapted for the timber trade....

Waiheke possesses a most delightful climate with very picturesque scenery which cannot be equalled by any place situated within such easy distance from town and as a summer resort for business men and their families, it would be difficult to find another place offering so many advantages. There is no doubt that if some enterprising man were to take the matter in hand and build a few houses (cottages to be let during the autumn or summer months) that it would become a fashionable place of resort.

The article notes that islanders were receiving twice weekly visits from the steamship *Transit*, under Captain Niccol, fare 5/-, and estimates the European population at around 150, including children, and the Māori population at around 80.

The *Cyclopedia of New Zealand* 1901 notes the island's development both as sheep farming territory and as a holiday destination.

As a watering place, Waiheke has long been popular and its scenic beauties, rural aspect, fishing grounds in sheltered waters and shores clothed in native bush, attract 100s of townspeople who make it their summer haunt, while 1000s patronise the excursions thither on summer holidays. Cowes Bay on the eastern side of the island, where a jetty meets the steamer in deep water, and where sports are frequently held, is a favourite spot for excursionists and on a summer's day, crowds of pleasure boats and yachts throng the waters of the bay, where a commodious boarding house provides accommodation for visitors and there is a bicycle track in the neighbourhood.

Exploiting Natural Resources

Early Waiheke settlers, like all pioneer families, were dependent for their livelihood on harvesting the wealth of land and sea.

Historical records suggest that the island became a regular stopover point for the white visitors who followed in Captain Cook's wake. At the close of the 18th century, the calmer waters of the Hauraki Gulf attracted the sealers and whalers who wrested a harsh living from the seas around New Zealand. They anchored in the bays of what was then the domain of the Ngāti Pāoa to repair their boats and to buy the potatoes which the Māori now grew for trading.

The Waiheke these early visitors knew was not a land of bare, rolling hills, but of forest that provided an ideal source of the timber needed to patch damaged hulls and decking. It was this forest, with its tall, stately kauri trees that provided the first Pākehā settlers with their livelihood.

A Wealth of Wood

The Ngāti Pāoa, who had hauled totara logs from the forest for their own canoes, adapted their expertise to the task of bringing out the immense kauri logs which were shipped to dockyards in England.

An American settler in Coromandel, William Webster, employed the local Māori people to take kauri from his disputed claim of 865 acres in the northeast. The *Delhi* was also loaded here with timber destined for the Australian market.

Thomas Maxwell settled on nearby land in Man O'War Bay and built houses, a store and saw pits where he cut the planks to build boats including his own schooner, *Sarah Maxwell*. A man called Henry Niccol claimed 113 acres on what is now Kennedy Point. He built his first ship, the 16 ton schooner *Thistle* there and felled both kauri and pohutukawa for use in his Auckland shipyard.

Many early settlers listed their occupation as "sawyer", and men capable of using axe, saw, and timber jack found ready employment.

In 1858, when the Swainsons recorded a canoe trip around the island, they described the beauty of the forest and noted the evidence of kauri felling in Huruhe Bay.

A description of Waiheke's kauri was recorded by J.W. and E. Stack *(Further Māoriland Adventures* published by A.H. and A.W. Reed).

Immediately on landing (Waiheke), we met a little English woman, the wife of a settler engaged in the timber trade who pointed out to us with great pride a road which her husband had made into the finest piece of forest we have yet seen...

We walked up the road until we met the bushmen returning from their day's labour. Some of them kindly offered to take us to the densest part of the forest in order that we might see a huge kauri tree. The remarkable thing about it was its immense size and great girth, and its perfect straightness.... We were told that one of the tallest kauri spars sent from here to England was 60ft long and that, from other forests in the Province, spars 100ft long have reached our naval dockyards. When sawn into boards, no knots or flaws of any sort are found in them and it is that which makes the kauri timber so suitable for ship's decks.

Next day I went alone as far as I could along the forest road... I have never enjoyed anything in my life more than I did that quiet hour or two I spent there. My only living companions were the birds of which the forest seemed to be full. They sang exquisitely and filled the air with sweet melody, whilst the scented aromatic foliage of the trees and plants around filled it with fragrance. There was no sign around me of the presence of man, except the sound made by the strokes of an axe which told of the approaching fall of a giant of the forest.

Much of this felled timber was destined for Auckland, providing house and furniture timber for the growing settlement. It was also used in the building of Waiheke's early homes and farm buildings. Robert McLeod of Te Matuku Bay is said to have sold kauri for spars.

Contractors often brought their wives and camped on the job. One camp was established in a narrow valley at the head of Te Matuku Bay. Provisions for the camp cooks were stored at a homestead about two miles distant where the sawyers also came for first aid treatment.

Remittance men were often to be found in such camps. One popular Waiheke worker had been sent to the colony by his titled family. He was a hard worker but when a cheque arrived from England, he downed tools, tossed his working clothes in the gully and was off to town to quench his thirst. A month later, all his money gone, he found his clothes and started work again.

There was at least one kauri dam on the island, a small one just north of what is now the Goodwin Reserve. Built of pit sawn timber in a rocky gully, the top of its 10ft² gate was 12ft below the top of the dam. The gate was fitted with an iron trigger and when this was tripped, the logs charged through, the men walking quickly ahead of a wall of water. After about one-and-a-half miles, the logs spread out on Day's flat from which they were hauled by bullocks to Rakewau stream and floated into Te Matuku Bay.

To form a raft, a toggle went through a slanting hole in the end of the logs which were then fastened together and towed to the Kauri Timber Co in Auckland by the paddle steamer *Lyttleton*.

An early island resident, Ross Day, remembered an old surveyed track that led from Te Matuku up the valley into Man O'War Bay. A team of 20 bullocks hauled a wagon with an adjustable carriage especially made for moving logs. Kauri, rimu and totara were hauled by bullock to the head of Te Matuku Bay where children at the nearby school heard the splash of logs being rolled down.

On the northern ridge above Hekerua and Sandy bays, hardwood sleepers were evidence of a tramway for logs hauled out along the present bus route. They were sent crashing over a convenient cliff to the beach below.

In 1908, contractors were still cutting out small pockets of kauri. Many hills were scarred, the clay gouged out by the weight of the logs. Old photographs reveal logs waiting on beaches on the north and south coasts. Some kauri did remain and its regeneration is now being encouraged in reserves at Te Matuku, Onetangi and Man O'War Bay farm.

Erosion scars on today's pasture are another effect of the loss of the bush cover, much of which was sold as firewood. Waiheke's vast areas of manuka provided the fuel for Auckland stoves and parlour fires. Men, working on contract, reckoned to cut ten tons a day into 3ft billets. To save time, they lived on the job, sleeping in nikau whares on beds made of mingimingi. An *Auckland Star* of July 1898 advertised 1000 tons of teatree firewood (best dry) at 9/- to 10/- per ton at Auckland wharf.

Teatree piles were used for small jetties and the wood was also reduced to charcoal (by being fired in sod covered stacks for several hours) for ladies' irons, or used for garden stakes. One launch load was shipped to Auckland as late as 1935.

Puriri was felled for house foundations, fence posts and battens. An early *Auckland Star* advertises *puriri posts, large cargoes from Waiheke and the Barrier.* Timber was also cut for mine props in the Coromandel gold mines. Axemen stripped tanekaha bark for use in the tanning trade; the wood was used as walking sticks and fishing rods.

The kauri yielded another source of income for early settlers — kauri gum. Both Māori and Pākehā, equipped with spade and gum spear, searched for the "poor man's gold" that could be traded for supplies or money. Tom Day was one settler who sweated at the job month after month until he had enough money for a deposit on land. It was said on the island that he could smell the stuff in the ground.

Prices were based on quality, colour and firmness with amber coloured gum more highly prized. In 1898, the *Auckland Star* listed prices at £40-£47 a ton for poor ordinary gum, £65-75 for good ordinary gum, and £90-£100 for re-scraped gum. Kauri gum was used for industrial processing particularly in the manufacture of paint and polishes until replaced by synthetics. The gum was also useful for kindling a sluggish fire and most settlers kept a supply of it handy. Golden gum was often polished for gifts.

Harvesting the Sea

There were other natural harvests that could be exploited by the early settlers. The seas around Waiheke yielded a rich harvest. Snapper were so plentiful that bait was taken as soon as it hit the water and up to 60-70 fish were quickly caught.

The old ferry boat *Baroona*, which spent many years seine fishing in the gulf, pulled up snapper by the ton until her decks were awash with fish. Many settlers built smokehouses and at least one sold his smoked fish to the Auckland markets.

Flounder were once easily caught by spear or net in the island's shallow bays. Big sharks were caught and used for garden manure in the days when it was essential to grow vegetables. Sprats were a familiar sight until big hauls for canning depleted the stock.

Rock oysters were a delicacy enjoyed by locals and visitors until an inspector of fisheries was appointed in the early 1900s to police the unlawful taking of shellfish. It was an unpopular prohibition that was evaded by the locals for years. Oyster farms were later established in Awaawaroa and Pūtiki bays.

Mussels were also harvested. Stories are told of a small factory in Mussel Heap Bay between Orapiu and Ōmaru bays where the shellfish were steamed open and packed into casks for export to China. A mussel farm was later established in the Waiheke Channel which, up until recent times, supplied green lipped mussels for export.

A lot of early small-scale fishing was done from mullet boats which were designed around 1880 especially for catching mullet up the shallow tidal creeks and inlets. Generally 22ft-28ft in length, with 8ft-

9ft beam, these were built of a single kauri planking "skin" over a sawn pohutukawa frame. These work boats only needed a small crew and with centreboard lifted had a draught of only two feet.

The sail-powered mullet boats were often seen drifting in the Waiheke Channel waiting for the wind to come up so they could overcome the tidal drift and deliver their catches to the Auckland markets.

Digging In

The discovery of gold on the Coromandel raised hopes that Waiheke would also yield underground wealth. It was not to be.

Early miners searched for copper on the island, apparently with little luck. An item printed in the *Southern Cross* on September 7, 1844, notes: *indications of copper ore on land belonging to Mr Halls at Waiheke, Whitaker and Sinclair are rumoured to be joining Mr Halls to work the mine.*

A Sinclair did claim 144 acres at Pikau Bay (Cowes) and two Halls are listed on the 1857 Electoral Roll but, of copper, no more was heard. There is a hole in the hillside and there were exploratory shafts in other bays, but all were unsuccessful. As for any rumour of gold — that proved to be a hoax.

There was apparently a small manganese mine at the top of the hill above Ōwhiti Bay from which manganese was sent by flying fox to waiting boats. Some may have been sent to Sydney for smelting but it was most frequently used as ballast in sailing ships. Two miner's cottages at Ōwhiti were later moved to Man O'War Bay.

Manganese was certainly discovered in Awaawaroa Valley where a mine operated for several years. Deposits were said to have been found by Donald McLeod and Bill Ashwin on McLeod's land. A report in the *Anglican Gazette* of January 1878 describes the Awaawaroa mine:

Manganese is being worked by a small party of men under the management of Captain Phillips. At the time of my visit to the island, they were short handed and only four or five men being employed.

A later entry notes that the manganese was being worked near the surface and that the ore was being found in other parts of the island which was "most promising". During the 1880s the mine, according to one report, was producing around 40-50 tons weekly.

*Manganese miners in Awaawaroa Valley in the 1880s.
In the background is William Gordon's bullock team.*

The works were bordered on two sides by land belonging to Henry Trace and at one stage there was some dispute when miners trespassed over an unfenced boundary in their search for the manganese.

Mining was mainly pick and shovel work, with tunnels being driven into the hillside. No protective clothing was worn and injury to eyes was always a risk — at least one local man lost the sight in one eye and another carried a supply of horse hair to help remove any metal that got into a miner's eyes.

The heavy ore was hauled in bags by a bullock team to the landing at the head of Awaawaroa Bay where it was collected at full tide by the cutters which carried it to Auckland. Never of high commercial value, the manganese did provide work for local men, as did cutting mine props.

When the mine ceased working, the land it stood on was sold by ballot, going to the Gordon family. One retired farmer retained mining rights on some Waiheke land but when the local manganese was examined by Japanese experts some years ago, it was found to be of little value.

Mining on Waiheke is discussed further in the section on the island's first miner, Isaac Merrick.

Natural Resources

Settlers were not slow to find a dollar where they could, and other island resources that were harvested included beach rushes — one couple camped in Pūtiki Bay made rush brooms with tea-tree handles for sale in Auckland; edible fungus — *Auricularia Polytricha* (Jew's Ear) was collected off old logs and sent to Auckland for export to China; rushes and flax were made into mats and baskets; and wild rabbits were shot for meat and skins during the Depression years.

But those pioneers who came to stay had to earn their living by actively working the land.

Farming the Land

For most of Waiheke's early settlers, their land was also their living. Following early contact with European visitors, the Ngāti Pāoa started growing crops for trade, becoming important food suppliers to Auckland's growing settlement.

Timber cutting and bush cutting, started in the 1800s, accelerated after the 1850s when nearly half of Waiheke's 9324 hectares were bought for the Crown by Donald McLean. Many new settlers eked out a subsistence lifestyle, growing their own fruit and vegetables, keeping a cow to provide milk and butter, bartering or selling excess produce and finding whatever work was available.

By the turn of the century, the island landscape had already begun its gradual transformation from bush covered hills to rolling pastureland, and short-term timber exploitation was being exchanged for a more settled approach to making a living from the land.

An early *Anglican Church Gazette* noted the changing face of Waiheke with favour.

> *During the past 12 months, four new settlers have established themselves on the island, and of a class likely to promote very much the welfare of the place. One of them, a runholder from the South, has purchased a property 4000 acres in extent, besides leasing a quantity more. He is doing a great deal in the way of clearing and laying down grass. He tells me that throughout a life-long experience of sheep farming, he has never known a place more suitable for sheep...*
>
> *The efforts of such settlers as these have the effect of opening the eyes of old identities to the importance of their holdings, and also set an example they cannot fail to see it will be in their interest to follow. I was informed that about 1500 acres of land has been laid down in grass during the year and about 200 chains of fencing erected. There are now upon the island about 5000 sheep and 500 head of horned cattle.*

Clearing the bush was a major task. Some men earned money by contracting for underscrubbing, cutting small trees and vines, completing two acres a week per man and living on the job in a whare. From wages, fencing wire, grass seed and household necessities were bought.

A contract for the clearance of 100 acres for the O'Brien family of Pūtiki in 1904 specified what was to be cleared and a deadline for completion. Scrub and vines were to be cut clean not more than 6in from the ground. All trees felled up to 3ft in diameter were to be taken 4ft from the ground, those up to 2ft in diameter were to be chopped off not more than 2ft 6in from the ground. All the work was to be completed by November 12, 1904, or a fine of £1 a day could be imposed and if the owners did not think the work would be finished on time, they could hire extra workers at the contractor's expense. The contractors were to be paid 20 shillings per acre cleared as instructed.

Once a section was cleared, a burn off took care of remaining sticks and left a good layer of ash. One of the first crops sown was danthonia, a tough grass that grew as a single plant. Established pasture could be shut up and, when over a foot high, cut with a sickle and left to dry in the sun.

Sometimes this was gathered, packed carefully and sold unthreshed. Usually, however, it was threshed — hot, dusty work that carried the risk of damage to eyes from the sharp seeds. One casualty was a Waikopou Bay farmer who in 1909 was admitted to hospital in some distress for a throat operation after threshing danthonia on his property.

Danthonia seed was sold by weight in North Auckland, on the Clevedon hills and as far as the Waikato. The demand for this seed dwindled as new grass varieties were brought in.

The danthonia pastures provided grazing for hardy shorthorn cattle that provided both beef and dairy products. The cattle frequently carried bells so they could more easily be found while foraging in the bush. Milking was by hand, either outdoors or in a makeshift bail. Some of the cattle died from eating poisonous tutu leaves or were bogged in undrained swamps. The first sheep grazed on some blocks among blackened stumps and their wool often became discoloured and tousled. One problem with danthonia was that, if not cut, it grew too long for the sheep to graze in summer and had to be burned off. Plumes of smoke rising over Waiheke pastures were a familiar sight for summer visitors. The burn-offs also killed off the ever encroaching tea-tree, and the green of new grass soon covered the hills again.

The pastures were steadily upgraded. Stumps were blasted out. Farmers spread fine basic slag from Belgian iron works by hand, packing it out by horse and cart. While it certainly improved pastures, the laborious spreading left faces and hands blackened with slag and meant a lot of cleaning up afterwards.

When W J Rutherford acquired the Man O'War block in the early 1900s, he brought with him new ideas on sheep breeding from the South Island and persuaded some farmers to buy Merino rams. These were generally crossed with Romneys and their offspring thrived, producing a wool with long staple and noticeable crimp. This soon topped the Auckland wool sales and Waiheke became renowned throughout the country for its quality wool.

Stock numbers increased so much that Waiheke and Ponui Island farmers formed the Waiheke Co-op Saleyard Company Ltd in 1920. Shares were allotted at £1 producing a paid-up capital of £235. Among the shareholders were the NZ Loan and Mercantile and Alfred Buckland

& Co — the leading stock agents of the day whose auctioneers played a major role in the new enterprise.

The Gray brothers, Will Connell and Ted Day received shares in lieu of wages for building substantial stock yards along the southern foreshore at Man O'War Bay on land leased from Rutherford.

Sale Day at Man O'War was a real occasion with the men turning out in riding pants, leggings, jackets and hats and the women in pretty frocks and shady hats. Sometimes the shipping company laid on special trips for buyers, auctioneers and visitors and here, miles from any store, they were served a delicious lunch of cold meat, vegetables, and dessert, washed down with a cup of tea, all for 1/6d. Catering was done by Dora (Mrs Jack) Gray with help from other local ladies.

Sale day at Man O'War Bay in the early 1920s.

Here, with boats and scows anchored out in the bay, horses grazing and children running round, the auctioneers would go to work. Campbell Mitchell bought for Bucklands and Joe Hardwicke acted for N.Z. Loan and Mercantile. These men wanted the venture to succeed but it was no easy task when the Depression started forcing prices down. One farmer drove home a line of ewes bought for 2/3d and steers priced at 10/- each.

Prices recovered later but costs also increased and much of the island was now subdivided, so the Saleyards Company was wound up in 1937. A community enterprise had served its purpose.

With the threat of war, ships were requisitioned. The old scow *Rahiri* skippered by its owner, Captain Jock McKinnon, continued to carry stock from the Gulf Islands. When higher costs threatened to stop even this run, local farmers were in a dilemma. They decided to form the Rahiri Shipping Co which was chaired by E E Mizen of Great Mercury Island and had an authorised capital of £12,000. McKinnon was retained as skipper. Although the stock were moved, the company ran at a loss and was eventually wound up. The *Rahiri* is now beached in Te Huruhi Bay.

In the 1930s, top dressing provided a means of raising stock numbers on what was mostly fairly marginal farmland. Rocketing wool prices after the war provided the finance. The first airstrip was made for Lumley Ashwin on a rise near the road from Onetangi, followed by one under joint ownership of Days, Connells and McIntosh on an Orapiu headland. One of the first top-dressing pilots to use the strips in his Tiger Moth was Tim Evans-Freke, later a pioneer TV newsreader.

When footrot became a problem in the half-bred sheep, some farmers introduced Perendale and began shearing twice a year. With top dressed paddocks, lambs were shipped away instead of so much dry stock and Waiheke lost its reputation for super half-bred wool.

Some sheep farmers boosted their incomes in lean years by milking cows and shipping cream to the Mt Eden Dairy Co. The Gordons kept a dairy herd for many years on their Awaawaroa Bay farm. Two efficient dairy farms were run in later years by Newton in Ostend and McGrevy in Onetangi. Others supplied local needs until pasteurisation became compulsory in the 1960s.

During the Depression years, home killed meat was sold by several farmers. The sale of eggs and fruit also helped to supplement island incomes. Many settlers had established thriving orchards and excess fruit was picked and packed for the Thomson and Hills jam factory in Auckland.

Education During the Pioneer Period

The Education Act of 1877 made provision for itinerant teachers to give house-to-house instruction in rural areas. Waiheke with its scattered settlements fell into this category but, in the latter part of the 19th century, those settlers who could not afford private tutors were seeing their children grow up illiterate.

It was a state of affairs that a visiting clergyman, Reverend Gould, was determined to change. While he started lobbying the education authorities for a school building, the Gordon family decided to make a room available in their own home and 27 youngsters of all ages crowded into this first pioneer "school".

Heading the list of admissions on February 2, 1882, was Margaret Ashwin of Awaawaroa. Others came from Huruhe, Waikopou, Cowes and Te Matuku Bays. On May 10, the Reverend Gould reports spending an hour at the new district school taken by Mr Hutton and was "much pleased" with what he saw. *The room in a settler's house could hold no more, but there was perfect discipline and order...*

In August, he notes that:

> there is every prospect, thanks to the Board of Education, of having the school room built. It would hardly be possible in summer, to crowd in the number that now attend school... and besides the Gordons urgently need the room.

The schoolroom was erected that same year. A tender of £315 was accepted for a 600ft^2 building on a five-acre block in Te Matuku Valley. The one big room was heated by an open fireplace that used up about two tons of firewood a year. In the back porch was a wash basin and rows of hooks for coats. The original kauri shingle roof was later replaced by corrugated iron.

For many years, the school also served as a hall and church. A service held by Bishop Cowie was the first use of the new building and the first annual church meeting was held there early in 1883. Dances, parties, farewells, and even a Government Poll took place there; waiting horses were tethered or left to crop grass in the paddock.

Te Matuku Central School

One of the first teachers at Te Matuku Central was William McIntosh, a well-educated man who had recently settled at Orapiu and took on the job at the request of the local school committee in February 1883. Other early teachers included a Mr Phillips and Mr Hudson.

The first woman teacher, Jane Eleanor Boxhall, remembered arriving by steamer to take up her new post at the age of 19, in the drenching rain, with sodden paper disintegrating around a gift to her future hostess — a string of sausages that had to be hastily draped around her neck as she descended a rope ladder into the waiting dinghy. No one met her on shore, so she picked up one small bag and walked around to the nearest house, McLeod's. Later the Gordons collected her and she was warmly welcomed. Equal to the difficult conditions in which she worked, Jane was later to ride through from Te Matuku to teach part-time at Brown's home in what is now Surfdale. She later married and settled in an eastern bay.

Some teachers ended up dividing their time between either two or three schools on the island: one established in an old miner's cottage at Huruhe (Man O'War) Bay, Te Matuku, and another which catered for the western Waiheke settlers at Brown's Bay. In 1898, seven Māori and three Pākehā children were taught around the kitchen table at the Browns' house

39

by a Mr Allison who rode through from Te Matuku.

A Charles Boswell (who is thought to have later entered Parliament and become the first ambassador to Russia under the Labour Government) lived for a time at the miner's cottage at Man O'War, teaching there and at the other schools. James S Broun apparently taught at all three schools, boarding for a time at Opopo Bay with the Thomas Days. He eventually married the youngest Day girl, Margaret, and became a lawyer.

Jack Harvey was another early teacher who left a valuable memento of his early days on Waiheke in the form of photos of the old Man O'War Bay school, kauri and other island scenes. A conservationist whose knowledge and interest in New Zealand plant life is revealed in his discovery of a rare orchid near Cowes Bay that now bears his name, Harvey taught botany. This cultured man was a frequent visitor to the Douglas family of Arran Bay whose descendants treasure an autograph book which contains quotations and poems in English, French and Spanish written in exquisite script.

Martin Pegler of Ōmaru Bay, killed in Flanders 1918.

Two teachers left during the First World War: A S Grey returned to farm in Cambridge; his successor W D Voysey, met former pupil Martin Pegler in the muddy trenches of France — neither returned from the war. The money for a memorial tablet to honour these two men was raised by pupils at Te Matuku. This was made in wood by local artist Harry Garrett of Ostend and unveiled by Martin Pegler's mother. Pupils from Te Matuku and Man O'War who enlisted included Lumley Ashwin of Awaawaroa, George, Martin and Stanley Pegler of Ōmaru Bay, Arthur Hooks of Hooks Bay, Henry and Allan Insley of Cowes Bay.

Temporary teachers during the war years included an elderly man called Mr Ainsley and a young man, Shane, who was in later years to become the headmaster of Cornwall Park School. A Reg Molloy, who encouraged local musical talent, also taught during the early 1900s. He was a devout Catholic and a football enthusiast who played for Marist in Auckland at weekends.

In later years, the Te Matuku Central school was virtually forgotten, certainly by school inspectors. Two women were the last to teach there, Marie Turner, a qualified teacher who later married into the Insley family of Cowes Bay, and Romsey Weir, a well-educated but untrained teacher, who carried on, with no help from inspectors, for five years. In 1932, with the population now centred at Waiheke's western end, the School Committee approved the closing of the old school. Will Connell tendered for the building and used much of the kauri timber and windows in a building that still stands in Connells Bay.

The Man O'War Bay school, which had closed after many years in a building described as "unsuited" as a school being old, draughty and poorly lit, had a second burst of life during the Second World War.

In 1939, residents in the area could muster seven children as pupils for a woman teacher appointed that year. By 1941, the roll had crept to 10 and rose still further as a few families lived on the nearby flat during the construction of the Stony Batter tunnels. There are few remaining records of this school — apart from complaints as to its condition. One astonished Education Board member queried: "Is this one of ours?" The Board decided to close the school for a second time on March 20, 1946.

Man O'War Bay School photographed by Jack Harvey around 1907

In western Waiheke, the first school was apparently established by the Church Missionary Society at Pūtiki. It was visited in 1842 by Bishop Selwyn who reported that there were 130 charges, many of whom were adults. He described the classes as "admirable" after hearing a fine and accurate reading of the New Testament.

Chief William Hoete, a staunch Christian, is mentioned as teacher in 1844. It is not known when this school closed, but in the latter half of the 19th century the Māori population on Waiheke declined rapidly and lack of pupils probably prompted its closure.

In 1909, the Education Department received a proposal for the establishment of a Native School at Te Huruhi on two acres leased from its Ngāti Pāoa owners, Te Pokaitara Tamihane and Tareha Te Tairiri.

The following year, a Mr J P Bawden started the construction of school buildings which were to be divided into a school room with two living rooms with a chimney, two fireplaces and kitchen. The school opened on February 6, 1911, with a roll of 21 youngsters from local Māori families being taught by Mrs Lucy Read Smith.

Huruhi School, opened 1911, closed 1924

By 1913, the roll was up to 32 and included both Māori and Pākehā children. The following year, the Department reported a drop in numbers due to Māori parents selling their land and moving elsewhere to find employment. Two years later, in November 1916, the school roll of 17 consisted of 11 Europeans and six Māori. Prospects of its revival as a Native School were not good, according to official records.

In general and in accordance with policy, it has now become European in character and has consequently ceased to fulfil the function of a Native School.

In 1924, this school closed. A Surfdale teacher used the old school residence until 1950. The following year, an order in the Māori Land Court returned the two-acre block occupied by the school to nine Māori owners as tenants in common.

The population of the western end was growing and, even before the closure of Te Huruhi School, Pūtiki residents had petitioned the Education Board for a part-time school at Ostend. Eddie Brown, a son of the family whose kitchen had served as schoolroom for early settlers, continued this family tradition by making a room in his house available.

The native school teacher, R J Martin, provided part-time tutoring. Within four years, on July 31, 1921, the school was closed because of lack of space and did not re-open until April 1 the following year when the three-day-a-week teacher was a Mr McKenna. The Ostend school (site of the present Playcentre) was built in 1923. Later schools were established in Blackpool, Onetangi and Surfdale.

School picnic at Cowes Bay about 1902. Pupils from Te Matuku and Man O'War Bay school. Teacher James Broun is at back left.

Worship in Woolsheds: Waiheke's Pioneer Church

Waiheke's earliest known church was established by the Ngāti Pāoa of Huruhi, on a site at the western end of the island still known as Church Bay.

Records of early visits by Anglican clergy to the island's Māori settlement include Samuel Marsden in 1820, Henry Williams in 1833 and Bishop Selwyn in 1842. Chief William Hoete of Huruhi was an early convert, later becoming a deacon and eventually a priest. It was his people who apparently built the first small raupo chapel in 1833.

John Telford recorded his visit to the Māori village in 1849 when he arrived aboard the Bishop's schooner *Undine* and stayed, while they sailed on, to conduct services and give school lessons outside his tent. His notes reveal his own desire and the villagers' wish for him to stay on, but church resources, already stretched over a wide area, did not allow it.

The 1873 *Church Gazette* describes an 1867 visit to the Hauraki Gulf by Reverend Maunsell and includes the following extract.

...Crossing the Firth from Thames, we reach the island of Waiheke, where there are scattered parties of Maoris who are always willing to receive me: and at some of the settlements prayers are held morning and evening daily. They keep Sunday strictly and were an example to the English, and later collected money toward a church building on the western end of the island.

This church was built in 1881 of kauri boards and measured about 18ft by 12ft. A visit the following year by the Reverend Gould is recorded in the Church Gazette.

Held a service in their little church which is prettily situated and was scrupulously clean... William Marsh has a service here every Sunday and also a Sunday School.

As the population of this settlement dwindled, the church fell into disrepair. It was later blown down in a gale and the remains burned in a grass fire. Rehutai Piopio Karaka, a respected sheep farmer from Church Bay, was last in the line of lay readers at the settlement.

In the early 1840s there were also visits from French Marist Fathers like Father Petit-Jean of St Patrick's in Auckland who ministered to Māori families to the east of Puke Range, including Huruhe (Man O'War).

Auckland Diocesan records for 1863 note the Waiheke (listed as Native Station) services.

Mass, Sermon in Maori language at 11 o'clock on Sundays; after Mass, Baptisms etc; Catechism and Vespers at 3 o'clock. Confessional attended to on Saturdays and Vigils of Great Festivals.

This suggests that a number of Catholic Māori lived on Waiheke in the 1860s. However, after the land was sold, the population dwindled. Suggestions of a clay church in the area cannot be confirmed.

Visits by clergy to the scattered European settlements were spasmodic and welcome. Services were held wherever there was space enough to accommodate a congregation that often had to travel miles by boat or horse to attend. There are records of weddings and christenings held in woolsheds — the old woolshed on Onetangi Straight that was restored and converted to a museum by the local historical society was sometimes used as a place of worship by early settlers in Pūtiki.

O'Brien descendants speak of priests visiting their grandparents' home and of mass celebrated at the homestead in Wharetana Bay. English Benedictines from St Benedict's in Newton were transported across Pūtiki Bay in the O'Briens' boat.

Early Anglican Diocesan missionaries described the help given to them by these early settlers who, whatever their faith, would provide food, shelter, horses and guidance between the isolated homes. An extract from the Journal of Reverend Bolar is typical of the spirit of these early visits and demonstrates the enthusiastic energy needed to tend such a scattered parish.

Started early and walked to Fraser's who accompanied me to Huruhe (Man O'War Bay), held service at Mr Davenport's house Huruhe, over 20 present. He had made arrangements for service in a large room often at much inconvenience. He gave me a mount and I rode over to the school in Te Matuku Valley, calling at Hawthorne's on the way. About 50 were present at the school service, then I walked to Gordons... afterwards walked to Ashwins, our esteemed lay reader. Went on to Trace's where I stayed the night and he went with me next day several miles to show me a better way across to Davenport's. His two boys rowed me across the bay to Mr Laing's. Later I scrambled along the foot of the cliffs... tide so high I had to climb the cliff, scramble through the scrub on the steep slope, my clothes suffered rather severely... I passed on to Mr Gray's, henceforth to Hannah (on the far outer nor'east coast), he walked with me to Mr Cairn's. After rough walk reached Mr Hook's and baptised his little girl. Mr Hook then accompanied me a long way through the bush in the dark on my way to Mr Gray's.

Tuesday: Rode over to Mr Carey's on a pony kindly lent me by Mr Gray. Mr Carey provided me with another horse and accompanied me himself to

Captain Kennedy at Pūtiki calling at Mr Henry Brown's and Mr William Brown's on the way. Mrs Kennedy with her usual kindness made me welcome for the night.

Wednesday: Mr Kennedy's man put me across the bay to O'Brien's, where Mr and Mrs Jenkins received me. Mr Carey had thoughtfully sent a horse over here so that I was able to ride over to Mr Hodgson's whence I rode on to Mr Kissling's. I was pulled out into the Strait waiting for the steamer, which took me on board for Coromandel.

Other clergy based in Coromandel followed a similar route, holding services in Cowes Bay, Awaawaroa or Te Matuku school, and in the Kennedy home at Pūtiki. One such was the Reverend Gilfillan, a very competent rider who aroused new enthusiasm among the settlers and started confirmation classes. Between these busy clerical visits, some settlers conducted their own services. Charles Ashwin, lay reader, held services once a month in Te Matuku school with Lucy Rowbottom (later Watson) playing the harmonium.

Ashwin kept the accounts of the first Anglican Church Committee on Waiheke. Presided over by the Reverend Gould, this committee was set up in the 1880s and represented the populated areas of the time. There was Ashwin of Awaawaroa Valley, Francis of Pūtiki, Gray of Waiti, Hayland of Orapiu and Kissling from Ōmaru Bay. Another 70 years passed before Waiheke's Anglican community had a church in which to worship. Te Matuku school was the venue for a 1915 confirmation service that attracted a large congregation despite teeming rain. Bishop Averill was landed from Kennedy's launch on a very muddy landing to officiate. Transport was ever a problem for the clergy whose diocese stretched across Hauraki Gulf and out to Great Barrier.

Even when the church became more established on the island, transport problems made it difficult for many of the eastern end residents to attend services in populated settlements of the west. Attending a confirmation service in Surfdale for one farmer's wife meant leaving home at 5.00am to catch the *Baroona* at Orapiu and travelling first to Auckland before the ferry returned to the island's western end, attending early communion the following day and then catching the *Baroona* back to Orapiu at noon. Oneroa clergy still had a long walk to hold services in the more distant homesteads like that of the Days in Ōmaru Bay. These would be held in the lounge or on fine days on the lawn overlooking the sea.

For long years on Waiheke, men and women had worshipped in schoolrooms, woolsheds, boarding houses, in farm kitchens or spacious parlours, but the pioneer period was closing. When new subdivisions swelled the island populations, churches were built in the new areas. Notes from the Reverend F L Gardner report that Interdenominational church services were held in the Blackpool school in July 1947. St Paul's Presbyterian Church in Puriri St was built by voluntary labour and dedicated on October 23, 1948. Waiheke's first Catholic Church, Our Lady of the Sea, was opened in the old Ostend dance hall and blessed by Auckland Bishop, James Liston in November 1950. The following year St Peter's was opened in Oneroa. That same year the Anglican Church of the Transfiguration was established in Oneroa on a rise overlooking Alison Park.

Keeping In Touch

In the days before phone and fax brought the outside world much closer, the stretch of water that separates Waiheke from the mainland made communication a chancy business.

The earliest settlers probably relied on passing cutters to take messages to the mainland or post mail overseas. By the late 1870s, a postal service had been established to two Waiheke settlements — Pūtiki, and Ōmaru (based in what is now Woodside Bay). A service to more eastern settlements was established a few years later.

Post office records show that the first Waiheke office was run by Phillip Lloyd Francis at his farmhouse in Pūtiki, on a site occupied later by the Waiheke County Council offices. Established 1876, this was taken over in 1885 by Captain John Kennedy who shifted the office to his new home, "Dunesslin", where it was to remain for nearly 16 years.

Mail was brought in by sea under contract to the Auckland Central Post Office. Listed contractors included J McFarlane in 1879, A R H Swindley in 1881 and the Coromandel Steamship Co in 1885. The local postmaster had to row out to collect the mail from passing steamers which didn't always run to schedule.

In 1878, Charles Frederick Evans-Kissling performed this duty from his home in Woodside Bay. His successor, Beaumont George Hotham continued providing a service for southern settlers until 1884 when this office was closed. The Cowes Post Office had started a year earlier, initially being run by William McIntosh of Orapiu before actually settling in Pikau (Cowes) Bay in 1886. Here the Northern Steamship Co built a long wharf and local postmaster Innes Parres was the first to collect mail dryshod. When Parres sold the guesthouse in 1904, his successor, Harry Insley, also inherited the job of postmaster.

The trek to Cowes was still a long one for many settlers and in 1900 William Gordon was appointed postmaster at the newly established Awaawaroa office. In the early 1900s, before the wharf was built, passengers on a Northern Co steamer might see the Gordon girls rowing out to meet their vessel to collect mail, supplies or passengers. Because the steamer didn't stop, this transfer sometimes did not take place till well past White's Point, giving them a long pull home.

These three offices — at Pūtiki, Cowes and Awaawaroa — were also to become early telephone exchanges. The marine cable connecting Waiheke with the mainland was laid from Motuihe to Cable Bay on Waiheke's western coast. A phone line was then set up to the Pūtiki Post Office which was established at the Kennedy home in a special room with separate outside entry. The first poles were iron rails hauled and erected by local contractors.

Brothers Jim and Ted Day contracted for hauling to the exchanges at Awaawaroa and Cowes and it was fitting that the first message to the Awaawaroa exchange was the announcement of a son to Jim Day in 1901.

The early phones were all battery-powered and manually operated. Poor reception meant that conversations often tended to be short and shouted rather than chatty. The phones did, however, provide a welcome link to mainland medical services.

Settlers maintained their own private lines without P & T supervision, with the wire suspended from trees and neighbours setting up party lines. An unwritten law with such lines was that nobody listened in to other calls and that in sickness or emergency the line was immediately cleared. There was a small charge between the Waiheke exchanges, and calls to Auckland were more expensive.

When Ostend was subdivided in 1916, the Pūtiki Post Office shifted to the newly built guesthouse and store with post and telephone duties now handled by Mrs Hindman. A separate office was opened in 1943 and run, respectively, by Mr Hopkins, Miss Ponsonby, and Marjorie Foster who was still in charge when the name changed to Ostend Post Office in 1960.

The Awaawaroa Post Office was to be continued by successive generations of the Gordon family for 74 years. In 1911, William James took over from his father to earn the princely sum of £21 a year for post and telephone duties. The last Awaawaroa postmaster was Colin Gordon who retired when the office closed in 1974.

The Cowes Post Office continued to be run from the hotel there until 1963 when it shifted to Connells Bay. It retained the same name for three years until confusion as to its whereabouts prompted a name change to Connells Bay Post Office. It continued to operate until Eric Connell sold the store and in 1981 was the last eastern end post office to close.

These chapters have provided a general look at how the early settlers made a living from Waiheke's resources, but the history of an area is primarily its people. The following chapters will tell the stories of some of these people, where they came from, how they came to the island, and what sort of lives they created for themselves.

Huruhe (Man O'War) Bay

A quiet, east-facing bay reputed to have provided a rest and repair haven for early whalers and sealers, Huruhe, or Man O'War, Bay became home in the 1830s to Waiheke's first known European resident, Thomas Maxwell .

Maxwell Family

A Scot from Aberdeen, Maxwell was living and trading in the Bay of Islands when he married Ngeungeu, the beautiful daughter of Chief Tara Te Irirangi whose tribe, Ngāi Tai, claimed control over large areas of the Hauraki Gulf including Maraetai, Motutapu and Waiheke. Ngeungeu had been captured in one of the Ngā Puhi's raids into the gulf and, it is said, saved from being executed by a missionary's wife. Her mother, Maunga Tau Tari, could trace her family back to the Tainui canoe and the tribal lands were at Umupuia near Clevedon. It was there that Thomas Maxwell lived when he brought his bride back to her people and sought out land to buy on the gulf islands.

Although Europeans had been buying land on Waiheke for some time, Maxwell's June 1837 claim to 3000 acres is the first recorded transaction. His claim was disputed according to National Archives records of the 1841 Land Commission hearings at which it became Case 163. Maxwell told the Commission that the 3000 acres extended "from middle Huruhe Harbour along the coast to Opopo and back inland" and said he had paid "in goods, £168 12s".

51

On August 11, 1841, he testified:

I took possession of the land a few months after the purchase was made and I have resided there ever since. I have built several houses, a store and other buildings on the land and made sawpits etc to the value of £150. The natives still reside upon and cultivate this land. I gave them permission to do so and they now deny having sold part of this land.

James Moncur, described as a partner in trade, supported Maxwell's case with evidence that "improvements were dwelling houses, a blacksmith's shop, a shipyard, sawpits, and about five acres in cultivation". Mentioned in payment: "one whale boat".

In defence, Hohepa Te Ruinga of Ngāti Pāoa testified:

I sold Mr Maxwell some land in the island of Wyheke long before the first Governor arrived in the country... I have not given up possession of the land because I have not received full payment.

Although the original survey map of Waiheke shows a 572-acre block at Huruhe in the name of R & J Maxwell (probably sons Robert and James), the dispute was not settled before his death the following year.

While the claim was proceeding, Maxwell, an enterprising and industrious character skilled in the use of tools, was building himself a small trading schooner, the *Sarah Maxwell*, on the shore at Huruhe Bay. The vessel was doomed to a short life, taking her builder and skipper with her when she was lost at sea the following year.

According to a report in *The New Zealander Illustrated* in 1846, the *Sarah Maxwell* was on her maiden voyage when she ran into a northeasterly gale shortly after leaving Auckland. Another account, probably more accurate, said the vessel sank after leaving Wellington on her return voyage. That report came from another Waiheke resident and fellow Scot, Robert McLeod, who told the Land Court on July 29, 1844:

I have lived on Wyheke at the time Mr Maxwell was going to Port Nicholson and he placed his wife and children in my charge during his absence. I engaged to look after them till his return; they lived with me for some time, and then they went to their native friends ... I have lived on the place ever since.

The New Zealander Illustrated reported that Ngeungeu was:

...deeply affected with her loss, and although solicited by more than one European to re-enter the married state, she has declined every offer and still remains a widow. She possesses a considerable estate in land, which circumstances no doubt, rendered an alliance with her an object of ambition to those who aspired to her hand. Since her husband's death, she has generally resided at Umupuia, her native village. She is highly respected for the propriety of her conduct and is very neat in her habits.

A painting by George French Angas, published with the story, shows Ngeungeu and her son, James Maxwell. She is described as *wearing a garland of pendulous blossom of the red Kowhai ... and her dress is one of the finer kinds of flax garments made by herself and ornamented with tufts of scarlet wool...*(A copy of the painting is in the Waiheke Island Historical Society's museum.)

James was one of six sons, all of whom found themselves prevented from claiming their father's inheritance as a result of their mixed parentage. A notice in the *Southern Cross* on September 23, 1843, stated: *Maxwell Thomas: recently drowned. Plight of his numerous family by Maori wife deplored who can't claim his land because there is no legal provision for half-castes.*

An attempt at redress was made by Maxwell's trading partner, James Moncur, who told the Land Court in August 1844:

I am interested in the welfare of Maxwell's children and I am willing to complete the payment [for Motutapu Island] to the satisfaction of Tara [a Ngai Tai chief] and his party provided His Excellency will grant me lease ... till the eldest boy be capable of managing the property ... he is now about 13 years of age.

Direct descendants of Thomas Maxwell and Ngeungeu still living in 1989 on tribal land at Umupuia include Mrs R N Zister and Frederick Taiawhio Maxwell.

The Regans

The home of Waiheke's first known European resident, Huruhe was also the place of the first recorded European birth on the island. Born on Christmas Day 1841 to Irish immigrants John and Ellen Regan from County Cork, Mary Regan was to witness a century in which she would establish a family whose links with Waiheke continue to this day.

Mary was the sixth child of John and Ellen who had first sought a new life in Australia where only one of the first five children, a son, survived infancy. Moving on to New Zealand, the Regans found a home at Huruhe where John bought land and felled its kauri trees for ships' masts. Their land was later handed back to its Māori owners, who were reportedly annoyed because they considered that "Honest John", as he was known, had struck a fair bargain.

On May 4, 1865, Mary married Henry Parker. She was 24, he was 20, and they had at least 12 children. Henry died in 1920, aged 75; a lieutenant-colonel, he was given a military funeral. Mary lived another two decades, surviving into her 101st year and, at one time, the oldest living European in New Zealand. Many of their descendants returned to Waiheke. One of their daughters, Ellen, married John Croll and managed farms on the island, raising six children. The second son, Don, managed Mr Alison's Matiatia property until he retired, and the youngest daughter, Aggie, married a son of Henry Insley who owned the hotel at Cowes Bay where she died in childbirth at the age of 23. Of the Croll grandchildren, Lola M Smith lived all her life at Palm Beach, and Mavis Paulin Evans died in Onetangi at age 90.

Waiheke's First Regatta

Waiheke's first regatta, an event which would become the highlight of social life along the island's southeast coast for many summers to come, was held at Huruhe on December 28, 1882.

Later regattas would be held at Arran and Cowes Bays but the first was planned for Huruhe at a meeting in Martin Day's home attended by the Hooks, Grays, Careys, Ryan, Hanna and J Cairns. Their programme included events for open sailing boats of less than 20ft (first prize: £4), open boats of any length owned by settlers (first prize: a silver cup), a three-mile rowing race for pairs with no cox (first prize: a silver teapot) and a dinghy race (first prize: a butter cooler).

Despite a lack of refreshments and inconsiderate weather on the day, the first regatta was judged a success by a *Weekly News* correspondent in a report published on January 6, 1883:

The SS 'Coromandel' was chartered to carry excursionists to see the regatta and a great number of Aucklanders took advantage of seeing the beautiful scenery and sandy bays situated on the island. They all seemed to enjoy themselves. The only inconvenience to visitors was the absence of refreshment booths. If it had not been for the kindness of some of the settlers there would have been nothing to eat or drink. Although the day was most unsuitable for a regatta, there being a series of rain squalls, the regatta went of very well, and everyone seemed satisfied. A word of praise is due to the officers and men of the 'Coromandel' in the prompt way in which they landed all passengers in number about one hundred.

The Davenports

Also living at Huruhe in the second half of the last century were the Davenports who were related to the Hooks at nearby Te Patu. One of John and Jane Hooks' daughters, Ruth, married Benjamin Davenport at the age of 17 and bore him nine children, five boys and four girls. The Davenport children were among the pupils who attended Waiheke's first school which opened at Te Matuku in 1882. Benjamin Davenport was a member of the first Anglican Church committee in the 1880s.

Little is known of the Davenports' life on Waiheke, although one tragic incident is vividly recalled. One of the sons was out hunting. Perhaps overly-confident after shooting his first pig the previous day, he put his gun in the scrub and, pulling it out, shot himself. The nearest doctor was in Auckland, 20 miles away, and the fastest transport was a boat with two sets of oars for rowing long distances. Placing the boy tenderly in the bottom of the boat, Benjamin Davenport and John Hooks took up the oars and headed out into the Waiheke Passage, past Orapiu and westward into the Tāmaki Strait. They had reached Motukorea (Brown's Island) when Benjamin saw that his son had died. The lad was buried in the Hooks' family burial ground, near his grandfather, Sergeant Major Rawson, and was joined there by his mother after her death on May 26, 1893.

Thomson Family

About this time, a new arrival at Huruhe was building a mansion in the bay. He was a Mr W J A Thomson, a wealthy man who was reputed to have owned Kawau Island at one time. Spending about £25,000 he created Waiheke's finest residence of the period, naming it "Ardrossan" after a town in Ayrshire.

Designed in the prevailing fashion, with ornate ceilings 12ft high and 6ft slip-up windows, "Ardrossan" encompassed about 10 rooms. Inside the front door, large moulded figures with cherubic features welcomed visitors to the central hallway which was about 7ft wide. The reception room had a server and was about 30ft by 20ft. The centrepiece in the wooden ceiling had been gilded and French doors opened on to the garden, a setting for summer parties.

The fireplace, one of four which warmed the large house, was surrounded by a beautiful mantel of soft grey and white marble with curved supporting pieces and a patterned tiled hearth. In the parlour, which had a carved wooden ceiling centrepiece, another marble mantelpiece was complemented by an exquisite hearth with blue and white tiles set in a geometric design.

At the rear, the big kitchen with wood-burning stove opened on to a quadrangle surrounded on three sides by buildings — the house, an immense woodshed, a wash house, a saddle room and a room for the handyman who was employed to look after the firewood, garden, orchard, horses and cows.

The ground had been cleared and levelled, the soil lifted and replaced, to make a garden, and the little creek was bridged. Kauri piles 16in square were used to build a private wharf where Mr Thomson's small steamer berthed with supplies and guests from Auckland.

Visitors to "Ardrossan" used to go boating and fishing, play tennis and enjoy the various social events planned by the three pretty Thomson daughters, one of whom married Henry (later Sir Henry) Horton. Henry Winkelmann, the noted photographer who took many pictures of Waiheke, was a regular visitor to "Ardrossan", sailing there in Horton's yacht.

James Fleming

Around the turn of the century, "Ardrossan" and the Man O'War Bay
Block was bought by James Fleming who had struck it lucky in the
Coromandel goldfields. A daughter, Ivy, was born in 1898 and the Fleming
children attended the Man O'War Bay School in 1904. Evidence that the
property was farmed is contained in records of Northern Steamship
Company vessels calling at the wharf to collect the wool clip.

James Bruce

The next owner was James Bruce, a bearded Scot who is remembered for
his kindly and devout nature. Alf Hooks, in his seventies, recalled
the lavish afternoon teas which lured local children to Sunday School
at "Ardrossan". For the large Hooks family there were gifts of fruit
from the orchard and milk in wine bottles. On returning from an
overseas trip, James Bruce brought a gift for each child in the district.
Even though there was no church in the area, the Sabbath was sacrosanct
and no tennis was played on the "Ardrossan" courts on Sundays while
James Bruce was there.

His strict observance of the Lord's Day was to have its disadvantages
when a drain blocked one Sunday and he called on the Insley boys
from Cowes Bay for help. Their response: "Work on Sunday? Oh no, Mr
Bruce!" And a story was told of the time when James Bruce asked to see
a bullock team in action. Ted Day was doubtful. He knew the devout Scot
would be offended by the strong language bullock drivers used to spur on
their beasts. Nevertheless, a demonstration was arranged and Mr Bruce
watched Jamieson, a contractor, drag kauri from a difficult site. The last
log proved obstinate and Jamieson had modified his language so much
that the bullocks would not move. He had to revert to his usual fluent
style and the bullocks responded, slowly easing out the big log. Observing
the difficulty and the strain on Jamieson, Mr Bruce said: "I forgive the
bullock driver for swearing."

James Bruce employed Thomas Day as farm manager and a
cowman, gardener and assistant to maintain the tennis courts, lawns

and gardens in immaculate order. Tamarix or flowering cypress grew along one border and there was always a spring show of daffodils.

Rutherford

James Bruce sold the Man O'War Block to W J Rutherford, a South Island farmer who knew fine wool and wanted to introduce a Merino strain to Waiheke flocks. On a visit to the Days, he sat in the kitchen and told Mrs Day: "We'll import some rams from the South Island and top the sales with our half-bred wools," adding, as he munched fresh scones, "your husband will be in on it."

His enthusiasm was catching. Local farmers took his advice and topped the Auckland sales, making Waiheke famous for its fine wool. A saleyard was built at Man O'War Bay and Rutherford was a shareholder in Waiheke Co-op Saleyards Co Ltd. At "Ardrossan", a governess was employed to help with the children and Mrs Rutherford began to take in a few paying guests who were delivered in Connell's launch which collected them from the steamer.

When the Rutherfords left the bay, the Grays (see "Waiti" chapter) took over and "Ardrossan" ceased to be a centre of parties and social life. The Grays were followed about 1937 by the Hooks (see "Hooks Bay" chapter). In the 1970s, when John Hooks was living alone in the big house, "Ardrossan" became a target for vandals who attacked its marble fireplaces and kauri timbers. Only drifts of agapanthus and white oleander remained in the once beautiful and orderly garden and a solitary plum tree and an old pear tree marked the place where the orchard had flourished.

By the time the Spencers acquired the property from Arthur Hooks in 1981, "Ardrossan" was desolated, well beyond repair let alone restoration.

The cottage at the southern end of the bay, snug below Nelson's Hill, had also suffered from vandalism and neglect, its verandahs sagging, windows broken, timbers fallen and kitchen ruined. Old apple and peach trees were the only evidence of its garden and small orchard. On a gentle rise of dry ground above the beach, the kauri frame and weatherboards had remained sound and John Spencer's wife, Tytti, who had qualified as an architect at Helsinki in her native Finland, saw the potential for saving the picturesque little cottage.

Using kauri and rimu wherever possible, the cottage was restored in conformity to its colonial design with the addition of some modern conveniences such as a toilet, bathroom and laundry.

A wall was removed from the parlour, one of the two rooms downstairs, to create a more spacious living room and the kitchen at the rear had to be almost completely rebuilt. About 1000ft^2 overall, with verandahs on two sides, the cottage is to the right of the road at the end of the descent from Nelson's Hill into the bay.

The Vesper leaving Man O'War Bay with a load of cattle, about 1912.

Te Matuku (McLeods) Bay

A wide inlet that brought both local and mainland Māori to fish for the plentiful flounder in its shallows, Te Matuku Bay became one of the island's first European settlements when Scotsman Robert McLeod arrived there looking for land in 1839. By the turn of the century, the Bay had also become a centre for the island's scattered eastern end population, a fact marked by the establishment there of an early school and of the pioneer cemetery.

The McLeod Family

Born in Scourie, Sutherlandshire, McLeod had little incentive to stay in an area where the Highland Clearances had deprived many crofters of their land, leaving them with little money and few work prospects. Anxious to find money to support his medical studies, it is rumoured that he left Scotland in some haste to avoid being caught for smuggling, a crime that carried heavy penalties. The move proved to be a good one: comments in a later letter from his brother John showed that things in Scourie did not improve.

> *There was no fishing in the lochs here since more than 20 years back and no work of any kind going on, so that you may understand that leaves the poor of the place in a bad state.*

McLeod lived for a time at Huruhe (Man O'War Bay) on Thomas Maxwell's eastern block where the island's first Pākehā settler had already used his own timber to build several houses and a store. In 1842, after building a schooner which he christened *Sarah Maxwell,* Thomas set sail for Port Nicholson (Wellington) leaving his Māori wife and six children in McLeod's care — and never returned.

McLeod used his time at Huruhe to learn Māori customs and language. He advertised in 1844 that he was prepared to act as land agent in negotiations with the local tribes. Meanwhile his own block of land in Te Matuku had become the subject of claims and counter claims among various Pākehā land purchasers. These disputes were eventually settled in the Court of Claims and in 1856 Robert McLeod became legal owner of 777 acres in Te Matuku. Among those who had an interest in the land were William Brown and (later Sir) John Logan Campbell who were understood to be interested in copper mining.

McLeod was anxious to have title to his land as he planned to settle there with his new wife. Grace Fraser (née Barr) was a Scottish woman whose soldier husband had been killed in India. George Panton, the Presbyterian minister in Auckland called banns for the couple and there being "no objections offered" he duly certified the new union on June 11, 1849.

Grace, with her little son William Fraser, probably started married life in a nikau whare adapting to life on her own while her husband earned a living cutting kauri timber and firewood from the land. The kauri that provided the couple's principal income also supplied building materials for their homestead. This featured wide verandahs on two sides, a central corridor, three bedrooms, a kitchen/living room with large iron stove, family-sized dining table, and French windows looking out across the peaceful bay. The first roof, of kauri shingles, was later replaced by iron.

Robert kept in touch with the Old World, writing occasionally to his brother and also sending an exhibit of locally caught dried fish to the 1851 Crystal Palace exhibition in London, for which he received a medal and certificate of acknowledgement. But his loyalties lay more and more with the Māori people who were frequent visitors to the McLeod homestead. Often they came with wounds to be dressed and Robert's early medical training proved invaluable. His help and understanding of their language and customs strengthened the friendships between Waiheke's existing population and the newcomers.

During Māori/Pākehā conflict in the 1860s, the McLeods were told by Māori friends to stay on their farm. Beacons were set on the hill to call for help from the tribe at Maraetai if there was any trouble. Once, a Māori war canoe paddled swiftly into the bay and the McLeod girls and governess took to the bush. But when Robert met the warriors he found friends among them and the hungry visitors ended up eating the household out of flour as Grace turned out batch after batch of scones for them. Daughter Jane, then living with the Merrick family in Awaawaroa, did the same thing.

In September 1877, the McLeods added a further 368 acres on the eastern side of Awaawaroa Bay to their holding. This land, previously leased to George Proud and on his death to his sister Ann Collingwood, was bought from its owner, Isaac Merrick, for £270.

The couple had five girls (Dollina, Effy, Mary, Jane and Sinclair) when son Donald McLean was born in 1863. An Anglican parson, the Reverend Gould, recalled a visit to Te Matuku in 1884 where he found one McLeod girl teaching the children of Māori farm workers. Young Donald lent him a horse and accompanied him on his visits along the south coast.

When Robert, known locally as "The Governor", died in 1897, he was buried, as he wished, on the farm near the sea. Māori friends arrived by canoes from Te Huruhi and the mainland to hold a tangi for the Pākehā who had understood their customs and treated their ailments and injuries. Grace McLeod died three years later and was buried near her husband.

Son Donald inherited the farm, now mainly cleared of bush but growing an unwelcome crop of gorse. With neighbour Bill Ashwin, Donald had prospected and discovered manganese on the land, but neither farming nor mining held as much interest for him as the world of commerce. He became a member of the Auckland Stock Exchange and during his frequent absences the farm was managed by his neighbour Ted Day. This was the time of Auckland's building boom and scows were coming into Te Matuku to poach sand and shingle from the beaches.

Donald married Caroline Maud Harper in 1894 and bought a house in Auckland where he worked as a sharebroker. The couple with their three sons and one daughter still enjoyed regular holidays on Waiheke. The only drawback of these visits, as far as Caroline was concerned, was the transport. This involved waiting out in the Channel in an open boat, often in a southerly chop, for the steamer to draw alongside and then, in the awkward long skirts and hats of the time, scrambling on board by rope ladder.

One drawback for Donald was the lack of a telephone. During the First World War, the nearest phone to Te Matuku was a half hour's ride away at the Days' farm. A sheet hung at their window was the signal for him to come to the phone and he sometimes waited hours at their house for an important call before heading home, only to be summoned back by the banging of kerosene tins as the call finally came through allowing him to clinch a deal.

A horse racing enthusiast who was President of the Avondale Jockey Club from 1923 - 1935, Donald often spelled racehorses on his island farm and always had good riding horses. He was also a genial host who often invited neighbours over to share the flounder that were so easy to net in the Bay.

For a time, Donald's widowed sister, Dollina (Dolly) Grant, ran the farm with the help of neighbour Harry Ashwin. Her daughter, Grace, later married into the Ashwin family. Dolly was remembered as an experienced musterer and tireless walker. She died suddenly at the age of 59. She had collapsed on Day's Landing after rowing up Te Matuku Bay en route to the funeral of her brother-in-law, William Gordon. The other mourners, surprised by her non-appearance, found her in the boat and hurried her back to the McLeod homestead where she died later that night. She was buried near her parents on the Te Matuku headland.

In the 1920s the old home burnt down after a kerosene heater used when incubating chicks was accidentally overturned. The family lost everything including family records, old swords and muskets and a treasured wooden cradle said to have belonged to Governor Hobson.

When Donald died, the farm passed to his son, Ivan Donald who had followed his father into the stockbroking business. Henry, son of James Day, share-farmed the bay for a while. In 1963, the property finally passed out of the McLeod family. A sale notice described it as a *coastal block, 891 acres approx 1/2 grass, rest scrub, bush, gorse, good water. 2 old houses on waterfront.* The land changed hands again in 1984 for $310,000.

Of the McLeod daughters, only Jane, who married William Gordon, has descendants still living on the island. Donald's elder son, Robert, became manager for New Zealand Insurance in India and retired to live in

England. His brother Kenneth also worked in India but returned to New Zealand where he died in September 1979 and had his ashes scattered over the calm blue waters of the bay where he had played as a little boy.

The Jones Family

Effy McLeod married a Welshman, David Jones, who worked for a while in the manganese mine in Awaawaroa Valley. Jones had emigrated to New Zealand with his brother, Thomas, around 1870. His brother skippered harbour vessels in the Gulf and married Lydia Letitia. The couple had no children.

David (1851-1898) lived with Effy on Jones Point (now part of Day's Flat), a promontory reached from the mangrove-fringed creek of upper Te Matuku Bay. A skilled builder, he used timber felled on the property and milled in Auckland to construct a fine six-roomed dwelling with 11ft high ceilings. Records show a total labour cost of £12.10 for a house which included three fireplaces. Shingle from the bay was used for the concreting.

The Jones family left the island after their first son was born. Despite having lost an eye through his work in the mine, David was to take work in another manganese mine just south of Russell in an area now called Frenchman's Creek. Just before the turn of the century, the family took a block in the Takatu district. Tragedy was to strike the family there when a boating accident drowned both David and his daughter, Laura. A son, Robert, was saved by John Day, a relative who was working in the area at the time. He and brother Edward helped out for a while as Effy continued to run the farm.

John Curley

The house on Jones Point was taken over by a man whose involvement in Waiheke history was brief but interesting. John Curley had been born in the military settlement of Howick and had known lean times for he spoke of searching for eels and puha to provide a meal for his widowed sister and family at Huntly.

On Waiheke, he found work as a carpenter and house painter; he also stripped around 40 tons of tanekaha bark to be used in tanning nets et cetera.

He cut firewood and pea sticks for the Auckland market and took them up by cutter, realising 4/- a ton. It was while working the cutter that John took two girls to Cowes and persuaded Mrs Parris to accept them as guests. The delighted girls were to be the first of a long line of visitors to what became the Cowes holiday guesthouse.

John Curley helped David Jones build the spacious kauri dwelling at the head of Te Matuku Bay and when Jones left he bought the place. He finished and painted the interior, using material from the mudflat to create a pretty blue wash for the hall which still looked fresh after 40 years.

When his mother and his young niece and nephew, Will and Mercie Connell, settled in Waikorariki Bay, John leased the property owned by Dr Coates for them. Apart from painting a number of Waiheke homes, he took an active part in community activities including the role of judge in rowing races at the Cowes Regatta.

A sister, Sarah, lived on Waiheke for some time with her husband Benjamin Thomas, a Crimean War veteran who had been caretaker for Moore at Rosstrevor (Pasadena) Bay.

In the early 1900s, John Curley sold his property to young Edward Day and moved north, finally settling in Silverdale.

Hawthorne Family

Letters from Waiheke settler, William Gordon (see Awaawaroa Bay chapter), could well have prompted his sister Jane and her husband John Hawthorne to leave their home in Ireland and start a pioneer life in Te Matuku Valley.

With their two sons, William and Tom, they sailed on the *Indian Empire* to reach Auckland — and a joyful reunion with brother Will — on October 20, 1862.

When, in the 1870s, the Hawthornes bought 212 acres in Te Matuku Valley, the two families became neighbours. To the left of the present road, in a now scrub covered valley which is still called Hawthornes, a house was built from their own timber and hand-made bricks.

John cut firewood for the Auckland market and mine props for the Coromandel mines. It is said that there were between 14 and 17 children in this family altogether, certainly the eldest girl was in her teens when the new school opened in 1882. The previous year, 1881, saw four of the youngsters baptised when an Anglican parson the Reverend Gould visited the family, staying overnight, on November 15. Another son, Frederick, was also baptised at home in 1888.

The Migans

Another Te Matuku family of Irish descent were the Migans. Born in Northern Ireland, Peter Migan probably came to New Zealand with an Irish regiment to fight in the Land Wars of the 1860s.

He came to Waiheke, married a local girl, Catherine, and lived for a time at the head of Te Matuku Bay. Like the other pioneer families in the area, he cut firewood for a living and also worked at the manganese mine to help support his family of ten children, some of whom were among the first pupils at the valley school. Four of the children were baptised by the Reverend Gould during a visit to the island on November 16, 1881.

The Migans were known for their tame tuis and pigeons. Using muzzle loader guns, with small charge powder and pieces of supplejack in place of shot, they stunned the birds for capture and taming. One son, Jack, was very strong and was never beaten in the local boxing matches which were held on the landing at the head of Awaawaroa Bay. The purse was often three sovereigns — a lot of money in those days.

Another son was appointed oyster inspector and regularly sailed a ketch around the Gulf. Stories of nineteenth century Waiheke recall two Migan girls walking over the hills to Ostend in the 1890s to attend a woolshed dance.

Peter Migan died in 1886 aged 67 and was the first person to be interred at the new cemetery in Te Matuku Valley. It is said that there was some confusion over the siting of this cemetery and that the burial was actually in the wrong place.

Catherine Migan lived long enough to see five sons enlist to fight in the First World War but died in 1916 and is also buried at the Pioneer Cemetery alongside her daughter, Kate, wife of Thomas Bowden.

Edward Day

It was around the turn of the century when young Edward (Ted) Day started farming in Te Matuku. Pushed into an early adulthood after both parents died (see Days Bay chapter), this Waiheke-born son of Martin Day went to work at the age of 13 to help support the family. His first job was splitting posts with a big maul, and with the help of an uncle he also learned to become a competent shearer.

Once his younger brother, Harry, was able to support himself, Ted set out to fulfill an ambition to farm his own land. His only asset was a tenth share in his parents' estate — enough security for surveyor Adam Kelly who helped the young man out by advancing funds to buy a house and 245 acres at the head of Te Matuku Bay.

The kauri had gone but there was some bush left and enough grazing for one cow. It needed a lot of hard work but Ted now had something to offer a future wife. The target of his affections was Mercie Connell, who was living with her grandmother at Waikorariki Bay. On March 16, 1904, the couple were married by Reverend Fortune of Coromandel at the residence of Dr Coates. The simple ceremony was witnessed by the Curleys (then leasing the Coates house) and there was no time for a honeymoon. Instead the young bride found a heap of socks and work trousers to be mended as her husband went to work clearing bush with Will Connell.

Their house, at the head of the bay, was bounded on three sides by mangroves and the Rakewau Stream. Children calling in on their way to the nearby schoolroom were company for Mercie during the week while her husband worked up on Waiheke's eastern coast sleeping in a nikau whare and earning 18d an hour. The men came home at weekends to collect clean clothes and a fresh supply of homemade bread, butter, pies and puddings. One of their last jobs was for the Gray brothers, clearing bush on Stony Batter.

Ted also worked for the Kauri Timber Co which had a work gang camped in the bush just beyond his farm boundary. Most of the stores for this camp were kept in the Days' storeroom and because theirs was the nearest house, Mercie also supplied simple remedies for injured workers.

The establishment of farms at the western end of the island brought more shearing work. The "Pūtiki" season would see Ted Day heading off on his horse "Mug O Beer" with food, cutlery and bed roll to work at the Kennedy and O'Brien sheds. Bed and cooking facilities were provided at a workman's cottage; later on, meals were also provided. There was friendly rivalry between Ted and the Māori shearers. Sheep were only shorn once a year, and with the blades a good shearer could do about 125 sheep a day. No second cuts were allowed and all sheep were closely inspected.

Ted also rowed across to the farm on Ponui Island which offered similar work conditions for its seasonal shear. In this way he saved for grass seed and stock for his own property. Meanwhile, Mercie established the home garden, milked the cow, kept up the endless supplies of butter and bread and cared for the couple's only son Edsell who, born in 1905, inherited his father's blue eyes, fair skin and good sense of humour.

Every year Ted cleared more land, careful when he burnt off to save some lovely stands of puriri, titoki, kowhai, karaka, rewarewa and totara which are still visible from the road today. His first stock consisted of seven yearlings, the best of which broke its neck. The cattle were later swapped for 25 sheep and this was the beginning of the Hallsdale flock.

The first shearing of this little flock took place in 1905. A gate was removed to serve as a shearing table and the wool was clipped off on to a sheet of canvas. The rolled fleece was carried into the spare room where it was baled that night. The first clip amounted to four bales.

By 1915, the Days could afford to build a kauri woolshed and install a hand-powered shearing machine with modern cutters. This machine still required continuous and even turning which left arms aching by the end of the day. A later improvement was a machine powered by a one cylinder, hopper cooled stationary engine which banged away steadily for hour after hour. In the 1950s the kauri woolshed was taken down and rebuilt near the new homestead in Ōmaru Bay.

Finding a ready response to his visits, Anglican clergyman Reverend Gilfillan planned for a confirmation service at the school and James Kennedy transported Bishop Averill to the island in his launch. This 1915 service was to be memorable for the Days, with Ted, Mercie and their ten-year-old son, Edsell all confirmed into the fellowship of the Church. The weather was not kind to the visitors. It rained, and the Days lent the Bishop their one umbrella which he forgot to return.

Close to both school and cemetery, the Days' home became an informal meeting place for island visitors. Ted Day was appointed one of the Trustees of the Waiheke Cemetery. He usually dug the graves and sometimes conveyed coffins to the burial ground using horse and sledge. Mourners generally called into the Days' home for a cup of tea after a funeral — keeping a wary eye on the tide. Once a large funeral party missed the tide and had to wait hours before they could head home again, prompting Ted to ride off to Connell's store for extra food supplies.

Mercie Connell aged 16 and Ted Day aged 19

When the mortgage to Kelly was paid off, Ted was able to buy the block of land facing Ōmaru Bay and employ Māori workers from Te Huruhi. Young Edsell had picked up Māori phrases from the workers on McLeod's farm and remembered being given a pony by Māori workers who were delighted to find a Pākehā boy speaking their language. He was taught how to plant kumara properly by a Mrs Manahi and watched the Te Huruhi Māori gaffing huge eels in the Rakewau Stream, a task that involved both skill and excitement.

When the Waiheke Saleyeards were established at Man O'War Bay in the 1920s, Ted Day helped erect them on land leased from W J Rutherford, and became actively involved in the local farming co-op.

Influenced by his farm neighbour, Rutherford, he started breeding merino cross sheep which thrived on the tough conditions and danthonia grass on the steep hills.

As for other local families, Waiheke's annual Regatta became a focal point of the Days' social life and Mercie, who sometimes joined in the sporting events, once won a ton of coal which had to be hauled back to their homestead by horse and sledge. The farmers needed cheering during Depression years when prices for sheep and cattle slumped and the bottom fell out of the wool market. It became hard to make ends meet, and Ted took on jobs for some of the weekenders in the island's eastern bays.

In Pasadena, the planting of trees and hundreds of daffodils led to a lasting friendship with the owner, William Boucher. It was while lunching there that he met the future King of Tonga, then an agent for the Tongan Government. Boucher was the first to offer help when tragedy struck the Day family.

Ted was alone in the big house asleep when he was awakened by his horse neighing in a nearby paddock. When he opened the bedroom door, flames rushed up the hall. He had no time to save anything.

In gentle rain he watched the fire destroy his home and furniture. When the new constable, Elms, rode through a little later, he saw only a blackened ruin. When Mercie and Edsell returned from their visit to Auckland, they were appalled to find that all their possessions, including a treasured piano, were completely gone. Fortunately there was still the woolshed and the family slept there, cooking over an open fire until a new homestead could be built.

The new house was to be in Ōmaru Bay where Mercie insisted on a kitchen with windows overlooking the sea. Its construction proved to be a family affair with one cousin choosing timber — including beautifully grained rimu for doors and beams, another making the plans, and Eric Connell doing the building.

Many years before, Ted Day and Will Connell had saved a man from drowning and this act resulted in an unexpected bequest. With this, Ted bought his son a baby grand piano which arrived from Auckland by scow to be hauled up to the new house by horse and sledge.

Two years after its arrival, while cruising around Waiheke on my parents' launch, I came ashore at the Day homestead for some milk, talked music with Edsell Day and was invited to play the piano. I still play that piano for at that point the Day family history became my own.

Snobs and Ricketts

The names of some pioneer families in the district were recalled in local placenames. *Snobs Flat* —the name given to a flat at the head of McLeod's farm in Te Matuku Bay — is a Yorkshire term for a bootmaker. The bootmaker in this case was a man called Barrett who came from the Coromandel and started a business repairing saddles, bridles and boots.

Bobbie Dickson's— a name used for a block on the former Day farm — was named after a Robert Dickson who, according to records, sold his allotment to Peter Migan. *Rickett's Paddock* appears to be a corruption of the name J H Rickard whose allotment was also later sold to Peter Migan. *Jones Point* was named for the family of David Jones.

Pioneer Cemetery

The names of some early settlers in the island's eastern bays are recorded in stone at the Pioneer Cemetery which saw its first burial in 1886. It was not until 32 years later that the cemetery was formally gazetted by the Lands and Survey Department and trustees appointed.

These first trustees were named as Frank Annadale, William James Connell, Henry Ingram Insley, John Herbert Watson and Edward Day. The cemetery still stands on a small knoll at the head of the bay, just across the road from the Te Matuku Reserve. Not all the graves have headstones, but the names of those buried there were recorded by Edsell Day, one of the last trustees.

These include Peter Migan (1886), wife Catherine (1916) and daughter Kate Bowden (1931); John and Mary Fraser and daughters Lena, Mary and Lexie; William and Mary Ashwin and daughter Margaret; William and Jane Gordon and daughters Lena, Edith and a grandaughter; a Notman child; Pegler's small son Colin; Anne, wife of Samuel Powell; Gladys Connell (child); Charles Insley; Thomas; Auguste Natzka (father of the famous singer Oscar); Agnes Ann Woolley; Bill Hughes; and Bendick (husband and wife).

The western end of the island had no cemetery in the early days and a number of early settlers on Waiheke were buried on their own property.

There are believed to be six graves at Hooks Bay including those of Major John Rawson; Jane and John Hooks; Jessie, a baby daughter of John and Isabella Hooks; and Jim and Harry Cairns. Seven members of the Gray family were buried on their property at Waiti Bay including Eliezer and Mary, their sons David and John, daughters Mary and Jane and John's wife Dora. A gravestone on the hillside in Days Bay marks where Martin Day was buried. On a hill overlooking Cowes Bay is the grave of Jane Parris. An infant daughter of the McIntosh family, Gertrude, was buried on the family property at Orapiu.

At Te Matuku Bay, the graves of Robert and Grace McLeod, a daughter Dollina Grant and a relative Bill Fraser are believed to be on the headland. In Awaawaroa Valley are headstones for Henry Matthew Trace and wife Isabella Jane. Several members of the Carey family were buried on their land in Wairua Bay, including William and Margaret Carey, their sons and daughters and Margaret's sister Mary Nicol.

There is a promontory in Awaawaroa Bay called Graveyard Point, where David, Abraham, and Samuel Merrick are buried. Members of the Pokai and Webb families may also be buried there. Above Awaawaroa Bay is the grave of Mrs Castle.

A gravestone in Rocky Bay commemorates John Watson and his wife, Lucy. In Wharetana Bay is the grave of Pierre (Peter) De Norre, an elderly manservant of the De Witte family. In Surfdale, on former Kennedy farmland, are the graves of Captain John and Jessie Kennedy and their son James. Also in Surfdale is the grave of William Jackson who was drowned in the bay in 1906.

At Matiatia is a headstone for Ropata Rou who died 1894; there are also Māori graves at Te Wharau Point.

Omiha: A World Apart

Its sheltered waters have long made Omiha a boaties' haven. Lack of road access to the rest of the island meant that, even after subdivision in the 1920s, it remained a settlement apart, reached only by horseback or boat until the late 1950s. Its history is not so much one of isolation, however, but of a self-containment that is typified by its earliest settlers.

The Hodgson Family

A sense of adventure brought Joseph Hodgson to New Zealand but it was love that prompted him to stay and carve out his own destiny far from his English homeland.

The third son of the Lancashire Hodgsons whose family owned sailing barques and brigs which traded stores out to the penal colony in Australia, Joseph served an apprenticeship to qualify as a veterinary surgeon. Before going into practice, he asked his father if he could come to Australia on one of the company ships. Joseph's father granted his wish of a round trip as an adventure before he settled down to his profession in England.

Both his brothers were sea captains and one of them was almost certainly master of the barque he sailed on to Sydney. While the barque was in Australia, an immigrant ship, the *Duke of Marlborough* sailed into Sydney and, as Joseph knew the captain, it was decided he could make the trip to New Zealand and be back in six weeks to catch his father's barque back to England. He never did make that return trip.

Instead, he accepted an invitation to visit the Reverend Henry Williams in the Bay of Islands and met Mary Ann Prouse who was working as a companion help to the Williams family. It was love at first sight and on November 5, 1840, the young couple were married by the Reverend Richard Taylor at Waimate North. Joseph decided not to return to England, a move which so angered his father that he cut his third son off "without a shilling".

Mary was also a newcomer to the Antipodes, having arrived only a few months earlier (in February 1840) on board the *Duke of Roxburgh* with her parents, two sisters and three brothers. The Quaker family, farmers from Devon, had the unusual experience of losing their captain overboard in a storm during their voyage out.

The couple started their married life in the Bay of Islands with Joseph putting his veterinary skills to work as a farm manager for the Reverend Williams. It was here that their first two children, Jane and William, were born in 1841 and 1843.

Soon afterwards the Hodgson family moved to Auckland where Joseph opened the town's first butcher shop at the bottom of Queen St. In the mid-1840s, they bought some land in Omiha Bay from its Māori owners and it was here, possibly in a nikau whare, that their third child, Edward, was born in 1846.

Two years later (June 1848) the fourth baby, Joseph Junior, was born in Auckland. The birth took place in a Swanson St house that overlooked the prison where a man was due to be hanged: a nurse drew the curtains in Mary Ann's room to avoid distressing the young mother. The couple's next three children were all born on Waiheke: Mary-Ann in 1851, Thomas in 1855 and Sarah in 1858. The last son, Richard, was born in Auckland in 1861.

Their Omiha property was gradually developed with tea-tree cut and sold as firewood, and pasture developed for sheep, a few cattle and some pigs. The family made their own butter and kept a big vegetable garden. Fruit trees were planted and, before the days of bottling, fruit was dried for preservation.

A strict but loving man, Joseph's strong sense of duty was often expressed in kindness, as the following story demonstrates. Returning to his farm one day with a few cattle in the cutter, Joseph saw someone waving from Rangitoto Island. He sailed over and found a young boy who, he understood, had jumped ship. Thirteen-year-old Inez or Innes Parres and his mate had slipped overboard in the night while the ship was anchored in Rangitoto Channel. His companion had disappeared, but Inez made it to the barren shoreline of Rangitoto. He was cold, hungry and could speak no English. Seeing his terror, Joseph decided to take him home.

As a member of a ship-owning family, Joseph would be well aware that there was a risk for him in giving shelter to an illegal immigrant. However, when police searched the Gulf Islands and came ashore at the Hodgson homestead, he said nothing. Inez was carefully hidden in a hollow log where young Jane Hodgson brought him food until the search was abandoned. This proved to be the start of life-long partnership as Inez, who stayed to make his home on the island, later married the girl who brought him food and comfort during those days of fear and secrecy (see Parres story in Cowes Bay chapter).

Joseph and Mary educated their own family, Inez included. Mary was both teacher and pupil, being able to teach the young people hymns and songs but, at the time of her marriage, unable to sign her own name.

The family waited years to obtain title to the land overlooking Omiha on which they had built their cottage. However, on August 21, 1868, the following Deed of Sale was recorded:

Te Hoterene Toupari and Mohi Te Hararei to Joseph Hodgson, Conveyance of 125 acres of land being portion of Whakanewha situated at Waiheke, County of Eden and Province of Auckland.

For this acreage, Joseph paid $125.

In a few years, he and Mary had founded their own dynasty on the island, as visiting parson Reverend Gould was to note in his diary on Tuesday, November 22, 1881.

Called on Hodgson, one of the old settlers and a kind of patriarch, having 32 grandchildren many of whom were born on the island. He and his wife are living quite by themselves but are hearty and cheerful.

Two of Joseph's sons, Joe and Edward, followed the family's seafaring traditions running trading cutters, loading firewood out and bringing much needed supplies in as the island population grew.

Edward suffered a heavy loss when the schooner *Susan* loaded with timber was driven ashore and wrecked at Onetangi on February 1, 1876. Edward was not skippering the boat but was its part-owner at the time.

Other members of the family settled on Waiheke. Mary Ann and Sarah married Waiheke brothers Henry and William Brown. Joseph was visiting Parnell when he first saw young Jeane Archibald Wright drawing water from a well there. A year later, dressed in a grey silk frock and aged 18, she married him and they settled in Parnell.

Christmas and New Year holidays brought the rapidly growing family back to the island, with the older Hodgsons playing host for up to 30 grandchildren. Their grandad was very strict; uneaten breakfast was served up again for lunch or tea. It did not take long for the children to change their habits. Such a busy holiday camp had to be firmly organised or it would have been chaos.

The woolshed housed the children's bunks, mattresses were large flour bags filled with native brush and two parents were on duty there at night. Two mothers cooked the midday meal and two others did the washing up and tea towels — each family bringing their own linen. No children were allowed in the dining room, and the men slept in their boats. Every day either breakfast or tea was provided from the sea, all seafood being cooked by two men outside in the shed.

This careful planning extended to washing day, particularly as in those days much of their clothing, including underwear, was made of white cotton. All bed linen was changed on Sunday morning, soaked overnight, boiled outside in the copper, rinsed and laid overnight in a special paddock set aside for bleaching. Next it was brought in for blueing and some starching on the line and then dampened down for ironing on Thursday and Friday using irons heated on the stove.

When the "Christmas family" was in residence, the Thames paddle steamer would bring bread, collected by rowing boat, to save baking. Enough cows were kept to supply the family with milk and butter.

One feature of these family gatherings was music. Granny Hodgson had an organ, but each year the family brought a piano down to the island with them as they were all good singers — an enduring family trait.

A sad loss for the old couple was that of their youngest son, Richard, who was engaged to be married to Maggie Ashwin of Awaawaroa Valley when he was accidently drowned. Both his parents lived to a ripe old age, Mary dying of measles and bronchitis on July 13, 1893, in her 73rd year. She had been visiting in Parnell with her son Edward's family and was buried at Purewa next to two of her grandchildren. Fanny (21) and Henry (19), children of Mary Ann and Henry Brown, had died just two weeks earlier.

Joseph Hodgson also died in Parnell in an accident that was reported as follows in the *New Zealand Herald* on June 15, 1895.

An accident of a somewhat distressing nature occurred to an aged man named Joseph Hodgson near the corner of Queen and Durham Streets. Mr Hodgson had come into town on the bus from Parnell and got out at the corner of Durham St to cross towards the saleyards. While he was crossing the street, one of Rich & Dennery's (grocers) carts came through Durham St and struck Mr Hodgson violently, the shaft striking his temple and throwing him down. The cart wheel passed over his right leg inflicting a fracture of a serious nature. He was carried into J P King & Sons Chemist shop where his more immediate injuries were treated by Dr King and he was conveyed in the ambulance wagon to the hospital.

Just over a week later on June 24, the *Herald* published a follow up to this story.

It will be remembered that an old man named Joseph Hodgson of Parnell, on Friday week, met with an accident at the corner of Queen and Durham Sts, having been inadvertently in crossing the street in front of a dray, been knocked down by the guard iron, one of the wheels of the dray passing over his leg and breaking it. He was taken to hospital but it was feared that, owing to his age, he would probably succumb. Hodgson died yesterday.

There are no Hodgsons living on Waiheke now, but the family line continues in the Brown family (see Okahu Bay/Surfdale story).

The 125-acre property with its old kauri homestead was sold in 1894 to the Watson family who took up residence in the bay. The story of early days in Omiha is continued by Jack Watson — a grandson of John and Lucy whose meeting on Waiheke in the 1890s started a long association with the island.

The Watson Family

Lucy Rowbottom's path to the island started when she set sail from Britain aboard the *SS Kaikoura* in 1886 with her sister Annie and their widowed mother. They were heading for Christchurch to join Mrs Mary Anne Rowbottom's father Henry Burn, a skilled engineer who had emigrated the previous year after the failure of a Derby foundry in which he had invested a lot of money.

Burn, a former engine department superintendent for Midland Rail in Leicester who had made his money supervising various engineering projects throughout Europe, including the construction of British Army huts at Balaklava during the Crimean War, was by then in his seventies. His hope of finding engineering work in the young colony was not to be and the family's income in Christchurch was supplemented by Mrs Rowbottom's piano lessons and Annie's work as a milliner.

During their voyage to New Zealand, the Rowbottoms had befriended a young Scots couple, the Crolls (see Arran Bay chapter), and it was this friendship that brought Annie to the couple's new home in Arran Bay on Waiheke Island in 1892. Delighted by the reunion with her old friends and the beauty of the place in which they lived, Annie persuaded the other members of her family to move north to live at Arran.

A further attraction was the fact that the Crolls had a house available for rent at a considerably lower figure than the Rowbottoms were paying in Christchurch. This house known then as the South House and now, Arran Cottage, is still standing. Annie herself did not move to Arran as she married a Christchurch man, George McFarlane, and settled there.

The same year as the Rowbottoms arrived at Arran, the Crolls had another visitor. John (Jack) Herbert Watson was educated at Westminster School (where he held a Queen's Scholarship) and London University. He practised as a solicitor in the family firm at Kingston-upon-Hull in Yorkshire and later worked in Edinburgh as Company Secretary for the North British Distillery. A series of family troubles prompted his decision to emigrate and he initially set out for Canada. After surviving a shipwreck just out of England, he decided to sail instead to Auckland. With him, he carried a letter of introduction to his first wife's cousin — Andrew Croll of Arran Bay.

Thus it was that Jack and Lucy met. They decided to marry and, in 1893, were looking for somewhere to settle when they heard that Joseph Hodgson was thinking of selling his Omiha property. Jack rode up from Arran to look at the property, a visit later described by his grandson.

Terms of sale were discussed over lunch which consisted of bread and butter and a huge dish of hard-boiled eggs. My grandfather, in his excitement, ate five eggs; he often said afterwards he never before or since ate so many. He finally agreed to buy the property for £650 (just over £5 an acre) thus earning the scorn of the local people, who said he was mad to pay so much.

After their marriage, the Watsons enlarged and renovated the house, divided the 125-acre property into several paddocks and settled down to farm. Despite their apparent isolation, they led quite a social life, exchanging visits with neighbours, particularly on Sundays when Lucy always made a large steamed pudding to cope with any extras that might turn up for dinner. Such visits became less frequent in later years, recalled grandson Jack.

My father has often said that the advent of the telephone shortly after World War One killed social intercourse among the Waiheke farming community. It was so much easier to make a phone call than to ride miles to see neighbours.

Other visitors were yachting friends from Auckland who would anchor in the bay and come up to the house for musical evenings. My grandparents were both accomplished pianists and vocalists. My grandmother used to ride regularly to the old school at McLeod's (Te Matuku) Bay to play the harmonium for Anglican Church services held there.

Henry Burn and his daughter Mary Anne (Lucy's mother) moved from Arran Bay after the Watsons' marriage and lived in a cottage owned by the Kennedy family at Pūtiki which was sited where the Kennedy Point carpark is now. Lucy visited regularly, either rowing up from Rocky Bay in the family's 3.9 metre dinghy or riding sidesaddle. Like other south coast settlers, the family was reliant for contact with the mainland on the steamers that plied the Waiheke Channel, until the wharf at Awaawaroa made life a little easier. Communication improved still further when the family bought a 28ft launch powered by a 5 hp single cylinder petrol engine. The *Elaine* (Lady of the Lake) gave sterling service for many years.

John Herbert Watson never practised as a solicitor in New Zealand, though he was local JP and was always happy to give legal advice to neighbours. Son Neville was born at home in 1898 and because of the distance from any school was taught by his father. Neville took over the running of the farm following the 1914-18 war and began supplying milk to the new settlement of Rocky Bay, as his son recalled.

Every day he rowed across the Bay with the milk in two kerosene tins in the bottom of the dinghy. If the water in the bay became too rough, even for his expert seamanship, he would carry two four-gallon tins round the shore. On arrival at Rocky Bay, the milk was transferred to billies left by customers at a central collection point.

In 1928 Neville Watson married Eva, the daughter of Reverend Greer who had retired to Rocky Bay in 1925 because of ill health and ran services in the Rocky Bay Hall until the late 1930s. A house for the newly-weds was built by Reg Beadnall, reputedly one of the better builders in early Rocky Bay. In those days the only local transport was by horse and cart and the roads were muddy and hazardous. Rocky Bay was not to be connected by road to the rest of the island until 1956.

Neville became President of the Omiha Welfare and Recreation Society which was a focal point for social life in the community, and later served for two terms on the Waiheke Roads Board where he was a staunch advocate of the Kennedy Point port project. He also took on his father's role as local JP and served as Peoples' Warden for the Anglican Church Islands Parochial District.

Son John Neville (Jack) continued the tradition of community service as committee member and Chairman for 14 years of Waiheke's St John Ambulance Association. He was also a lay reader in the Anglican Church.

He and wife, Marie (née Jenkin) also continued farming in the Bay, running a flock of Romneys and a small milking herd. Two motel units were built on the farm in 1970. Their two sons became the sixth generation of Watsons in the Bay.

The property was subdivided in 1973 and by 1980 the remaining Watson home block was sold when the family moved to Auckland. The homestead in the bay was renovated by its new owners, the Reeve family.

Te Patu (Hooks) Bay

A lonely and windswept bay at the far eastern tip of Waiheke, Te Patu is as inaccessible now as it was at the turn of the century and sees a lot less human activity than it did when scows were raiding its shingle beaches for raw materials to fuel Auckland's building boom. Today's most frequent visitors are the gannets that come from their offshore colony to fish in the shallows. Its present isolation echoes that found by the first Pākehā settlers who arrived to farm this distant bay back in the 1860s.

The Hooks Family

John Hooks, an Irishman from Newry, was felling bush on Waiheke in the late 1850s when he met an attractive young widow with three small children. Jane Baker had lived on Waiheke for more than a decade before she met and married John Hooks. A few years after arriving in New Zealand with her father, Sergeant-Major John Rawson, a veteran of the Battle of Waterloo, she married and moved to Waiheke in 1847.

Her youngest child, John Stephen, born in Whakarite Valley in 1857, was just an infant when she was left a widow. Accepting John Hooks' offer of marriage, she moved her young family to the remote Te Patu block at Thumb Point where they lived for some time in raupo huts. By 1864, her enterprising new husband had obtained title to the 610-acre block, paying 5s an acre to its first European owner, A Shepherd, and laying the foundations of a Waiheke family that would remain on the island for more than a century.

85

The following year her father came out to the island to be with his daughter. He was in time for the first (and only) Royal visit to Waiheke.

Hooks Bay, early 1900s , with a scow waiting to load shingle.

In 1869, HMS *Galatea* was sailing through the gulf with the Duke of Edinburgh on board. Although the Lands and Survey map of Waiheke and the Islands records the ship anchoring at Man O'War Bay, the Duke actually came ashore at Hooks Bay and was invited up to the house for a cup of tea. It must have been a great moment for Rawson — an old infantry soldier whose stories of Redcoats in battle formation and troop movements at Quatre Bras made such an impression on his young grandson that John Stephen would later pass them on to his children.

There was no school for young John to attend and he went to work early, growing into a strong, wiry, pioneer farmer, felling bush and cutting firewood for the Auckland market. He certainly caught the eye of 19-year-old Isabella Taylor, the daughter of a Melbourne architect, when she came to visit her relatives, the Trace family, in the Awaawaroa Valley.

She was destined never to return home for she fell in love with the 27-year-old farmer and they were wed in the Auckland office of the

Registrar of Marriages on December 5, 1884. Blue-eyed and town-bred, Isabella became a pioneer legend on Waiheke, cheerfully accepting isolation and hardship in a rustic home built with kauri timber felled on the property. A reminder of how much her life had changed came with the arrival of Janet, the first of her 14 children. Before he could collect the midwife, her husband had to walk over the hills to Waiti to borrow a boat. The remaining children were born into similar pioneering isolation; all except Jessie, who was buried in the family cemetery at Te Patu, survived to adulthood.

Grandmother Jane Hooks lived in her own cabin and smoked a clay pipe, telling stories of the old days to the young ones who were accommodated in lean-to rooms added on to the house as the family steadily grew. When she died on August 16, 1905, at the age of 83, John Stephen was rowed out to meet the Coromandel steamer by the Gray brothers. Climbing aboard the steamer near Ruthe's Passage, he announced: "The old lady's gone, and I'm off to Coromandel to buy a coffin." On his return, his mother was buried in the family plot on Te Patu.

Life continued in Hooks Bay, the arrival of each child followed some time later by a visit from a parson and a christening service in the kitchen, the same little gown probably used for each baby. As well as the formidable tasks of motherhood in those conditions, there was also the duty of education. The new school at Te Matuku Valley was too far away while the one at Man O'War Bay was only open a few years.

One day a trading barque dropped anchor off the bay and the captain came ashore. His home port was Melbourne and he brought news of Isabella's two brothers, and a reminder of what life might have been as she turned again to the inevitable bread making and the daily round of domestic chores and meal preparation.

Meat dishes included the farm's mutton and, occasionally, wild pork. Turkeys were bred and sold, poultry provided eggs, butter was purchased from the Careys a few miles up the coast, and fish and shellfish added variety. Although yeast could be made from potatoes and was often kept in a bottle on the mantlepiece, staples such as flour for baking and salt to preserve meat came from the mainland. John would sail the mullet out past the Thumb Point rocks and on into Auckland where he purchased goods to last many months.

From childhood he had developed a keen weather eye but was

delayed with much needed provisions on one occasion. Food supplies were so low that Isabella had to kill and dress a sheep with the help of one of her sons.

A building boom in fast-growing Auckland brought the Hooks a new source of income — the sale of shingle from their beach. Contractors seeking quality shingle for new buildings and public works such as the Grafton Bridge found a good supply on Waiheke, poaching it from lonely beaches by moonlight, promising payment when tackled but often forgetting — as John Hooks found to his cost. His remedy was to give J G Haddow power of attorney over his affairs. Haddow refused an initial offer of 2d a cubic yard, settled for 6d, and eventually sold sole rights to the beach to J J Craig Ltd for £50 in 1913. After that, shingle boats were frequent visitors to Hooks Bay, sometimes queuing up offshore and even coming in at night to collect their loads. John and Isabella's son Alf later recalled scenes of this time.

Three days a week we walked along our bay, up Stony Batter and down the steep spurs to school (at Man O'War Bay). It took about two hours. On Waiti once, we passed stacks of cut firewood stretching half a mile each side of the track. In mid-winter we arrived home in the dark. It was on such a night I saw the lights flickering all along our bay, the wicks in bowls on stands driven into the shingle. It was such a pretty sight. Five or six boats were working the shingle at our own beach.

Alf's brother, Jimmy, was among the men employed by J J Craig to work the Waiheke shingle deposits. His job was to wheelbarrow the shingle out to the half tide mark where it would be washed by the incoming tide. The boats would come in about two hours after high water and were loaded by their crews, racing their wheelbarrows up and down the narrow planks to beat the tide — hard work for which they were paid by the boat's skipper. He took two-thirds of the shingle's value and paid for fuel, oil and wages; the remaining third went to the boat's owner who provided kerosene for the lights.

The natural elements rather than the profit motive wielded the whip over the loading operation. Hooks Bay, like the rest of that coast, was

Isabella Hooks

exposed to the fierce northerlies that sweep in across the gulf. When boats missed the tide they risked being caught by a sudden change in the weather. Among the victims at Hooks Bay were the *Rimu*, the *Stag* and the *Lizette* — all listed as wrecks although some may have been repaired later.

Rimu and *Stag* were caught in the same northeasterly blow. Spotting their distress, the Hooks raced to Wairua (Careys) Bay where the Careys had a telephone. Their call for help was answered by the tug *Te Awhina* which launched a lifeboat. Watched by the Hooks children on the shore, the lifeboat capsized in the violent seas and the tug retreated to shelter at Pakatoa Island. The men must have all reached the beach safely; the family recalls Mrs Hooks tending to the drenched and cold crews of the two shingle boats and the lifeboat in their home.

Although the shingle brought in a much-needed income, the Hooks were to pay a heavy price for its removal. Freed from its natural boundaries, the sea advanced to engulf 20 acres of foreshore, submerging sheepyards, orchard, vegetable and flower gardens, and eventually threatened their home. A gang of local men came to the rescue, cutting the house in half and lifting it on to braced runners to be towed to higher ground by a team of bullocks brought over by their Waiti neighbour, Dave Gray.

The house was reconstructed by Frank Bell, who had built the original Pakatoa guesthouse, with a larger kitchen and at least four bedrooms. And while the sale of the shingle had cost John Hooks 20 acres of land at one end of the island, it enabled him to buy double the area at the other.

In 1918 he paid £1,267 for 40 acres, a spacious villa and a woolshed close to the beach at Browns Bay (Surfdale). Built in 1899, the house had a roomy kitchen, a parlour and a wide hall dividing the bedrooms; an annexe in 1916 added five more rooms.

For Isabella, the new home represented an end to the hardships and isolation of Hooks Bay and allowed her to enjoy the delayed rewards of motherhood. Her children married and the sounds of their grandchildren filled the house. A photograph of this remarkable woman reveals the serene face of a woman who accepted hardship, living for others as she cared for her many children.

Alf, 11 when the family moved to Surfdale, was able to go to school again, making new friends from a wider circle including the local Māori children, a son and daughter of Rehutai Karaka, the Dick Brown family from Te Huruhi, the Royals, and the Parris children from Park Point. He and his brothers helped to milk up to 20 Holstein, Shorthorn and Jersey cows which grazed the block and, occasionally, nearby vegetable gardens, causing some heated exchanges with neighbours.

After a seemingly tireless life on the land, John Hooks died in his sleep on July 13, 1921, at the age of 65 and was buried at Te Patu on the same sort of stormy day that had bedevilled the shingle boats a few years earlier. After the graveside service, some of the mourners sheltered in the farmhouse while the rest of the party prayed for their safety as Insley's launch bucked and rolled on its way back to Cowes Bay.

Isabella survived him by almost 30 years, dying at the age of 82 in Auckland on January 17, 1949. Two sons lived on in the Surfdale home: Alf, the gentle host, and Phillip (Pally), robust but reserved, an identity as he delivered shingle around the island in his truck.

After Alf died on June 18, 1982, Pally lived alone until he passed away in September 1985 and the house, deserted and vandalised, was demolished. Another brother, Arthur, who died in 1981 aged 87, had carried on the family's presence at Te Patu, taking over from his eldest brother, Jack, and other family members who had leased the eastern farm when their parents moved to Surfdale.

Born in 1894, the eighth in the family, Arthur spent his boyhood at Te Patu, walking to school at Man O'War Bay. Wounded in the Great War, he returned to marry his sweetheart, a beautiful Auckland woman called Linda Marion. After a family wedding in the new family home at Surfdale where the sheltered beach was convenient for the officiating parson, Rev Jasper Calder, who rowed ashore from his boat, the couple moved into the Te Patu home.

Like Isabella before her, Linda was accustomed to city life. Well-educated, she had to learn new skills for a lonelier existence. The nearest neighbours were the Careys and the Grays and she learned to ride so she could visit them and the family in Surfdale.

The isolation was to be a special worry after the birth of her two children, Joan and John. When baby Joan became seriously ill, her distracted mother had to arrange for Connell's launch to collect them from Hooks Beach. After a three-hour boat trip from Cowes Bay to Auckland, the infant was taken to her grandmother's house in the city. A doctor called to attend to her was horrified: "That child has pneumonia and cannot be moved to hospital." She was to recover although the illness would continue to affect her health.

At Hooks Bay, with its exposed shingle beach, life was ruled by the moods of the sea. Supplies could only be delivered by Connell's in favourable conditions and the excitement of a trip to Auckland could quickly change to disappointment at a turn in the weather.

Linda remembered such occasions, her children in their best outfits, noses pressed against the window, waiting and waiting for Connell's launch, concluding as the wind freshened again that it had probably turned back to try again another day. This isolated existence was only to continue for a few more years, ending with an unexpected act of generosity from a neighbour.

The Hooks and the Grays had been friends and neighbours for more than 70 years. When Jack Gray died without heir, he left the Man O'War Bay Block to Arthur Hooks and Allan Insley of Cowes Bay, also giving his brother, Davy, a life interest in the estate. Arthur decided to buy out Allan Insley and transferred his family into the large Man O'War Bay mansion, "Ardrossan", about 1937.

The move was timely for Linda whose eyesight was failing as a result of diabetes and the lack of medical attention, and the children were able to attend the re-opened school. With Arthur out all day running the two properties, Linda was grateful for the company of neighbours, now much closer than at Hooks Bay, and she sometimes went for long walks with Jack's widow, Dora Gray.

Once they were old enough, the children left home. Joan took a job in Auckland and John fulfilled an ambition to go to sea. He was to return, reluctantly, to Man O'War Bay when his father was laid low by a stroke which confined him to a resthome for his final years. During John's short and uneasy tenure at Man O'War Bay, vandals entered "Ardrossan" and smashed the marble fireplaces, starting a gradual destruction of the property that would place it beyond restoration. After his mother, Linda, died in Auckland, John lived alone in the rambling homestead. Although he had no liking for farming, his father wanted to retain the property for his grandson, Joan's boy.

Then, shortly before his death, Arthur was visited in hospital by John Spencer whose father, Berridge, had established the Caxton paper business. John Spencer had known Waiheke from camping and sailing expeditions through the gulf with his parents and had expressed a desire to buy a farm on the island.

When he was told that Arthur Hooks might be willing to sell, he visited the old man in hospital several times, assuring him that the bush would be retained and the farm restored to fertility. Arthur agreed in 1981, the year of his death. The transaction released his son John from his filial duty and he left Waiheke when the farm was sold. Arthur lies buried in the Waiheke cemetery beside other returned servicemen.

A picnic at Onetangi reserve 1913.

Waikopou Bay

As isolated now as it was in colonial times, Waikopou Bay has a history made colourful by the international origin of its inhabitants. Securely remote behind a narrow sea frontage and steep hillside, Waikopou has at times sheltered farmers from Nova Scotia, aristocrats from Czarist Russia, a corn merchant from Dunedin, and an English colonel.

The Fraser Family

The first to arrive were John and Mary Fraser and their four daughters, one of those intrepid Scottish families who came to New Zealand via Nova Scotia. Paying £16 each and taking aboard enough of their own food for the voyage, the Frasers had sailed from Cape Breton on the barque *Ellen Lewin* in December 1859, reaching Auckland five months later. While many other emigrants on the same vessel settled at Waipu where their descendants live today, James Fraser took up land on Waiheke where he was named as original grantee of Blocks 22 to 26.

Accustomed to hard work in Nova Scotia, he cut bush and manuka for an immediate income on his inland valley property before clearing and grassing land at Waikopou. His seaside home became a magnet for fishermen and sailors passing through the Waiheke Passage, keen to barter their freshly-caught mullet in exchange for equally fresh homemade butter. The butter was made by the Fraser girls, Maggie, Lena, Mary and Lexie, whose workload increased as their parents aged.

They pulled scrub, milked the cows, made the butter, cared for the farm animals, tended the orchard and gardens and still found the time to indulge their love of reading.

John Fraser took a lively interest in the school committee and Maggie was an early pupil at the school in the Te Matuku valley. It was a long walk for her, over part of Days' farm with a stiff climb up a ridge which was known locally as "Maggie Fraser's". Rev Gould, the Anglican minister, visiting them in 1881, referred to them as "old settlers".

The little farm with its cows and a few sheep supplied most of their needs, variety in diet supplemented by succulent rock oysters, mussels, flounder, snapper and mullet. The family's income was dedicated to its survival with nothing left over for luxuries, as is evident from the story about the time when the sisters needed new suits for their annual trip into Auckland. They came up with a plan to make the money they needed by selling flowers. There was no demand for the wallflowers, lavender and violets which grew in scented borders around their cottage, so they decided to grow daffodils. The bulbs were bought and planted and, the following spring, yielded their first crop of blooms which were carefully packed and despatched on a steamer to Auckland. It was to take more than one season before they had enough to choose their new costumes from an Auckland store. Well-dressed women at last!

Over the years, the parents followed by their daughters Lena, Mary who had married Charles Ashwin of Awaawaroa Valley, and Lexie were laid to rest in the little pioneer cemetery in Te Matuku Valley. Maggie, a gracious, gentle woman, lived on alone in the old house. Once a year she would walk over her ridge to weed the family plot with its iron fence, calling in on the Ted Day family for a cup of tea in the homestead on Jones Point. After she died in Auckland the Fraser property was sold to one of the Wilsons who owned the Martin Day block.

The Powell Family

The story of Waikopou Bay is taken up by Mr J H Powell whose father, Samuel, bought two-fifths of a 5,000-acre block of land there in 1905. The Powells came from Arapohue near Dargaville and shipped the kauri for their house from Te Kopuru near the head of the Wairoa River.

I remember that the timber was bought as a line of between 30,000 and 40,000 super feet for 5s per 100ft but my father had to pay extra for any of it to be dressed. Dad and my brother did most of the work of building the house. I was going to school at the time.

One week he would attend the school at Man O'War Bay, the next trudging miles over the hills to Te Matuku Central. His education would have been supplemented by reading from the Bible, a living force in the Powell household. An old family photograph includes a visiting preacher.

Sometimes they would row the preacher across to Rotoroa to take a service for the alcoholics in Salvation Army care on the island. In a typical gesture, Samuel Powell gave two dozen bound copies of the New Testament to the Central school as a parting gift after eight years of trying to tame Waikopou's rugged slopes — a tough task, as his son recalled.

The first years we were there my brother did a lot of hard slogging work in cutting tea-tree firewood and sledging it down to the beach where it would be loaded into scows. All we used to get for it was 4s 6d a ton at the beach. After I left school my brother and I and Dad must have done miles of fencing, tea-tree chopping and bush-felling.

On the land they cleared for grazing, the Powells ran mostly Romney and a few half-bred Merino sheep before deciding to move on in the face of what they saw as rather unproductive labour.

It needed an ocean of money spent on it. They did not see much potential in the place so it was sold about the end of 1912 to a Russian named Arapoff.

The Arapoff Family

How Count Arapoff came to live at Waikopou Bay with his beautiful blonde Countess and their young son is something of a mystery. It was said that they were members of the Russian aristocracy who had escaped after one of the uprisings that preceded the Revolution in 1917. A safe refuge from the Bolsheviks, Waikopou's comforts must have seemed primitive to a family who once lived in a castle with servants and were accustomed to chartering a train for private travel. When Count Arapoff came to Waiheke he was accompanied by a partner. Little is known of this second family other than that the partner was married and had two sons and a daughter.

At Waikopou, help in adapting to local customs and tutelage in English came from their nearest neighbour, Maggie Fraser. The children, who had acquired a small vocabulary in their new language, attended the Man O'War Bay School. The boys would ride Cossack-style along the flat, jumping bareback on their racing ponies. The Countess was also to be seen on horseback and was described as a fearless horsewoman who delighted in riding over the surrounding hills. Visitors to the house reported that meals were served on old family silver and comprised exotic dishes — such as soup with cream, a previously unheard-of combination on Waiheke. Count Arapoff, it seems, did not adapt to pioneer life. He remained the aloof aristocrat, leaving farm work to others such as one of the Day family who used to muster and shear the sheep. Eventually, the Count decided that hill country sheep farming held no future for him and the family returned to Auckland.

James Hamilton

Waikopou's next owner, a Dunedin corn merchant named James Hamilton, had the money to develop the property. He set about enlarging the house, building a worker's cottage and employing labour to clear stumps, remove logs and cut the remaining tea-tree.

A man with initiative, he found a way of speeding up the production of firewood by building a chute, made of kauri and 450ft long, from the top of the ridge to the beach far below.

Tea-tree, delivered to the top of the chute on a sledge, was sent hurtling to the bottom where it was cut into stove lengths by an engine-driven saw and bagged for shipment by scow to Auckland. Years later, boys returning from school would throw sticks down the chute although none were game to slide down themselves.

James Hamilton's business experience proved valuable in the

formation of the Waiheke Co-op Saleyard Company in 1920. One of its original shareholders, he kept the accounts for some years before selling Waikopou to another colourful character, Colonel Teddy Nops.

Colonel Teddy Nops

Educated in English public schools and a veteran of the Boer War, Colonel Nops came to New Zealand as a farm cadet. In his Norfolk jacket, knickerbockers and tweed cap, he was a distinctive figure at local sale days and was always ready to join in the fun at picnics and dances. From his Auckland town house, he made regular visits to Waikopou, which was only one of several properties in which he had an interest.

On Kawau Island, he hoped to develop a complete township on 30 acres rising in gentle slopes behind Two Houses Bay. Plans for streets and sections, drawn up in 1911, never left the drawing board and the land, known as the Nops Estate, is now part of the Hauraki Gulf Maritime Park. A heavy loser when cattle prices plummeted during the Depression, Colonel Nops leased the Waikopou farm block to Lumley Ashwin. One result of absentee ownership was inefficient stock control, resulting in incidents during a big cattle muster which Henry Day would never forget:

There was Lum Ashwin, Phil and Terry O'Brien, Cec Brown, Uncle Ted Day, plus horses and dogs. The cattle, Shorthorn Cross, had become wild in the remaining bush on Nops' property. There were no fences out there and the infuriated beasts and maddened bulls went for us. Two men raced for a small leaning tree. One got up and one went behind as the bull charged. Men hauled with ropes to get the beast out, some to pull, others to push. Sometimes those at the back would slip. Then the angry animal would have a go at us. Cows with calves attacked the horses. Eventually we got them out into the open country and fenced off where they could quieten down with other cattle. One cow was crazed with the pain of a twisted horn growing into her eye so Lum, with cool nerve and good aim, hit the horn with a heavy stick, sending it over 20ft into the air.

The farm block was later owned by Kathleen Hiraani Scott (née Blake), a Taranaki Māori who for some years unsuccessfully petitioned

the Department of Māori Affairs to develop the property. It was farmed
during the war years by Kathleen's son Farley and wife Mavis (née Gordon).
In 1965, the Māori Affairs Department established a Development Scheme
on the land which later passed, along with an adjoining 450 acres, into
Crown ownership. In 1985 the land, known locally as the Māori Affairs
Block, was the subject of a claim to the Waitangi Tribunal which resulted
in its transfer into Ngāti Pāoa ownership. The iwi still owns and farms
the land today; its official name is the Waiheke Station.

Outside of the Waiheke Station there are several sections along
Waikopou Bay that have had a series of owners who have built luxurious
holiday homes beside the beach.

Orapiu

This peaceful, scenic bay has had a long history of hospitality. Once a gateway to what was then the more populous end of Waiheke, Orapiu has provided visitor accommodation since the turn of the 20th century.

The McIntosh Family

The first European owner of the bay was Charles Hunter McIntosh. Born at Stirling Castle, Scotland, in 1809, his path to the island was via the penal colony in Sydney where his father, Major Charles McIntosh, was sent to keep order just a year after the baby's birth. His regiment, the 73rd, was the first company to be sent south of the equator.

The Major, who spent 47 years in service (30 of those in America and the East Indies), had married a Frenchwoman, Frances de Cecy (Coutel) in Pondicherry, India. When he died in 1829 his son had to give up law studies to help keep the family which had been left with little money.

Charles and wife, Emily, came to New Zealand in 1840 with Governor Hobson's party after being appointed as surveyor. Throughout the 1840s he was involved in survey work in Auckland and by 1844 was Chief Clerk and Draughtsman. In the same year, he was also appointed Secretary to the Land Claims Commission. He bought his block at the eastern end of Waiheke in the 1840s, and died in Parnell in 1860.

The Orapiu property was taken over by his son, William Nepean McIntosh. He, wife Mary Ellen and their three children moved to the

101

island, to live in more primitive conditions than they were used to. There was no stove on the farm, just a camp oven, and water had to be drawn from a well. Mary Ellen, an Englishwoman accustomed to having servants, had not learned to cook and employed a local girl to help out.

At this time the farming industry was in the doldrums and when McIntosh was asked to swap farming for teaching because the island was having problems with their schoolmaster, he rather doubtfully agreed. He milked the cows night and morning, cut enough firewood at weekends to last the week and spent the rest of his time at the island's small school. He rode over the hills to the Te Matuku Bay schoolroom accompanied by his two older children, Ethel riding with her father and Charles walking alongside.

The couple had eight children, two of whom died as babies. Gertrude Isobel, born in 1883, was buried at Orapiu on the hillside just below the bush. This sad event was recorded by the Reverend Gould in the Church Gazette, Diocese of Auckland 1883.

October 29th. Landed at Mr McIntosh's Orapiu Bay and found the family in great sorrow, having lost their little baby Gertrude Isobel.

She was about six months old, never strong, and her end came suddenly. She was buried last Saturday in a pretty spot near the house and shaded by trees. A cemetery has been granted by the Waste Lands Board, but it is not yet surveyed. Deacon Ashwin read the service and about 50 present at the funeral evinced the general sympathy felt for the bereaved parents.

Although the family later moved from Waiheke, William was to continue teaching, first at Puteke in the Waikato, then in Auckland where he was appointed first headmaster of Epsom School. The family remained in this area for several years during which William was on the vestry of St Andrew's Church. In 1918, he was appointed headmaster at Onehunga High School.

The family retained its ties with Orapiu, spending most of their holidays there. William leased the property out and built the bay's first boarding house to supplement accommodation at the old cottage. In 1918 he had the Orapiu wharf built. When he died in 1932, the property was taken over by his son William Neil (born 1884) and wife Ethel. They worked the farm and operated the guesthouse, with family assistance, until 1950. During that time, more accommodation was added eventually catering for more than 60 guests during the summer.

William McIntosh: Orapiu settler.

Their younger son, John William (Jack) McIntosh, born in 1918, was to carry on the family tradition of hospitality at Orapiu until 1968 when he sold to Ronald and Janet Gay. Jack's wife Marjorie recalls their life at Orapiu where, from Labour weekend to Easter, life revolved around the operation of the guesthouse.

Until power came through in 1957, cooking was done on coal ranges and three-oven oil fired stoves. A large cool room was built operated by a petrol motor and a 240 volt DC generator was installed for lighting and the use of a washing machine and vacuum cleaner. Before that, lighting was provided by a bank of 32-volt batteries.

The launch went out every day on morning and afternoon fishing excursions and, once a week, guests were taken on an all-day fishing picnic to the north end of Ponui Island. An entertainment hall was built for dances and games.

All supplies for the hotel were bought in bulk from Auckland and transported by the *Baroona, Tangaroa, Iris Moana* or *Coromel* (run by Sam Strongman to Coromandel). Apart from bags of flour, sugar etc, there were 44-gallon drums of benzine, diesel for the lighting generator, sacks of coke for boilers, all to be trucked up to the house from the wharf.

The farm itself covered 370 acres and farm work, said Marjorie, was carried out in conjunction with the seasonal work of the hotel. Summer was for guests:

Winters were taken up with house renovations and farm work. Cattle and sheep were culled for transport to Auckland on board the scow Rahiri skippered by Jock McKinnon. These were loaded at Awaawaroa after being driven through from Orapiu.

The only access to Orapiu was by water until Jack bulldozed a road through the farm which made it possible to drive through to Onetangi in the four-wheel-drive army truck. Jack was a member of the Waiheke Roads Board and eventually the Waiheke County Council for 20 years, nine of them as chairman.

When weather conditions made it impossible to drive to meetings in Ostend, he would walk miles or take the launch into Omiha and get a lift from there. He was awarded the Queen's Jubilee Medal and Queen's Service Medal for his services to Waiheke.

In 1965, the road was put through from Onetangi to Cowes Bay, finally providing easy access between East and West Waiheke. "We had our first car and as the road crept closer, so the long walk out to the car lessened," said Marjorie. The road came too late for children's schooling. All four McIntosh youngsters boarded away, even to attend high school at Ostend.

In about 1970, the homestead-guesthouse, then owned by Ron Gay, was destroyed by fire. Jack McIntosh died in 1980.

The Rahiri skippered by Jock McKinnon off Awaawaroa Bay

The Pegler Family

The early success of Orapiu's guesthouse goes back to its first managers, John and Nell Pegler, whose own contributions to life in the bay spanned more than three decades.

The Tasmanian-born Pegler brothers, John and George, first arrived on Waiheke in the mid-1880s (see Ōmaru Bay chapter). Both married into the Day family and lived in adjoining bays for many years.

John was an early landowner on Waiheke having bought 38 acres of Block 7 beyond Arran Bay Hill in 1884. He cut tons of firewood from this land which was still known as "Pegler's Paddock" long after it was sold, in 1924, to Will Connell. A stream running down to Te Matuku Bay is named on an early map as "Nell's Stream" after John's sweetheart and, later, wife.

An expert shearer, John was said to be the fastest and neatest man with the blades on Waiheke, a skill he passed on to his young brother-in-law, Ted Day. He started training the boy at the age of 12 with the warning that he would give him "the tough ones first". For some years he farmed at the "Slip" in Opopo Bay (later selling to Tom Day). Occasionally he rowed his sheep, with legs firmly trussed, across to neighbouring Pakatoa Island for additional grazing.

By 1891, he was leasing about 400 acres at Orapiu from William McIntosh. Three years later, an experienced farmer of 42, he married his 17-year-old sweetheart, Ellen (Nell) Day.

An efficient cook and housekeeper, dark-haired Nell was soon to find herself caring for more than her own growing family. Visitors to the island frequently asked for accommodation in the bay, sleeping in the woolshed, tents, or in the Peglers' cottage. When the McIntoshes decided to build a guesthouse to cater for Orapiu's growing popularity as a holiday resort, the Peglers took charge.

John would row out to meet the Northern Steamship Co vessel, collecting goods and passengers in all weathers. The guesthouse, erected on the flat, featured large windows overlooking the bay; front porch and side verandahs provided a shady resting place for guests. A garden with hollyhocks, pansies, and snapdragons flourished behind the neat picket fence.

In winter the Peglers lived in the guesthouse. In summer they moved out to make way for the guests who also had the choice of sleeping in four large wooden-floored tents. These had four beds apiece and were segregated into male and female sleeping quarters. Using bedrooms in the old house and additional tents, the Peglers were able to put up about 40 guests. There were few vacancies, with the same visitors returning year after year.

Apart from looking after visitors, Nell had her hands full with her own growing family. She had her first three babies on the island; the eldest, Mary, who was later to work as a cook at the guesthouse, inherited her mother's gentle patience. All nine Pegler youngsters were to lend a hand during the holiday season, laying tables and doing dishes as well as collecting kauri gum to sell.

The family grew their own fruit and vegetables. John also collected honey from the wild bees and kept sheep, cattle, pigs, geese and turkeys. The boys milked Jersey Ayrshire cows and cream was kept to make butter. All surplus eggs and butter were sold to Gallaugher, the merchant in Auckland who supplied their stores and provided Christmas treats in the form of large tins of biscuits and boiled sweets.

The deliciously cooked, home-grown produce and fresh seafood were not Orapiu's only drawcards. Five boats were kept for guests to go rowing or fishing; John bought a launch to run fishing and picnic trips to other Gulf islands; and apart from swimming and bush walks, the bay boasted a tennis court and a small bowling green.

Guests also provided their own entertainment. One regular and well-remembered visitor was May Fuller. Daughter of the family which owned Auckland's Opera House, she willingly sang and played the piano while holidaying at the guesthouse.

Other interesting visitors included Justice Speight, Mervyn Adams of the city shoe store, and Canon (later Bishop) Averill. It was Bishop Averill who officiated when the eldest daughter, Mary, was confirmed at Te Matuku school in 1915.

Although both guesthouse and farm were thriving, the Peglers decided not to renew their lease on the Orapiu land. In 1924 eastern Waiheke residents held a farewell gathering to express their affection and appreciation for the family with the presentation of an inscribed silver tea service which is still treasured by John and Nell's descendants. After 20 years as neighbours, the Pegler brothers — George and John — went their separate ways.

John was never to forget his island bay with its crimson pohutukawas and the blue agapanthus he planted along the beach edge. His family ties with the area are noted on an early subdivision map which describes it as *Orapiu Estate, commonly known as Pegler's Bay...*

When John died at Paerata on December 18, 1928, at the age of 77, he was survived by eight children. John, Mary Ann and Esther Margaret were Waiheke-born; Arthur Selwyn who was baptised on the island in 1901 was to manage the farm; Laurence William and Athol Wallace served overseas during the Second World War as did their sister, Eileen Florence, who was a nurse; the other daughter was Edna May. Their mother, Nell, did not live to see her youngsters return from overseas service but died at Paerata on June 6th, 1941, at the age of 63.

In the Pioneer Cemetery on Waiheke a memorial to another Pegler son bears the following incription:

Colin Dudley, Beloved son of John and Ellen Pegler, who died
20th January 1916, aged 10 months.
Suffer little children to come unto me

Of such is the kingdom of Heaven

None of the original buildings are left on Orapiu flat. The cottage, first home of the Peglers and McIntoshes, was burnt down, a fate later suffered by the main guesthouse in the 1970s.

Other popular lessees of the Orapiu guesthouse were the Teutenbergs whose tennis parties were enjoyed by both locals and guests. Mr Teutenberg was the son of a Prussian craftsman whose carving of wood and stone enriched early Auckland buildings, including the Supreme Court.

Orapiu: Subdivision

An early subdivision map of Richard Arthur and Co, Auctioneers, which gives terms for the purchase of land in Orapiu as £1 deposit and £1 per month, describes the attractions of the bay in 1918.

Charming summer resort. Yachtsman's Paradise. New wharf on property handy to sections. Steamer Service... Daily and weekend trips during summer months. Well sheltered bays and good beaches. Good bathing and fishing. Choice sections with water frontage.

It advertises a free excursion to view on Saturday, February 5, 1918, and an auction sale being held at the firm's rooms in Elliot Street the following Monday evening.

Okahu Bay (Surfdale)

Once known as Okahu Bay, Surfdale gained its present name as the result of a contest that earned one island visitor first prize of a section in the new subdivision. Long before then the bay was home to a family whose connection with the island remained unbroken for more than 130 years.

The Brown Family

First members of the Brown family to reach Waiheke were Henry and Mary who arrived in the 1850s. Henry John Brown, from Lower Edmonton, England, applied for a free passage to New Zealand on January 18, 1841, at the age of 30. His occupation was put down then as agricultural labourer. Just three weeks later, he boarded the *Katherine Stewart Forbes* at Gravesend to head for his new life on the other side of the world. He arrived in Wellington on June 11.

It was on board the ship that he married the 34-year-old widow Mary Bell (née Lane), who was from Hadleigh in London. They were married on April 1, 1841, by the captain, John Hobbes.

Henry and Mary settled in Wellington where their first two children were christened, a son Henry John (called Henry Junior) in September 1841 and a daughter Ann Eliza three years later. It appears that Henry initially worked as a butcher before becoming a mariner. In 1844 he is listed as the Master of a schooner called the *Erin* which was wrecked 20 miles east of Cape Palliser on April 22, 1844.

After this loss in the turbulent waters of Cook Strait, the couple decided to move north to the Auckland district where a daughter, Charlotte, was born in 1847. The family settled at the Wade (Silverdale, north of Auckland) and Henry acquired a schooner called the *Ann* which was built there in 1852. In 1850 a second son, William, was born there and it is his descendants who were to enjoy a long-time involvement with Waiheke.

Henry and Mary moved to Waiheke sometime in the 1850s. Henry was still trading in the mid-1850s, sailing the *Ann* to Kawau and the Wade with various cargoes including fish hooks and potatoes. He is listed on the Waiheke Electoral Rolls from 1855 as Master Mariner, house-holder.

He bought land from Ngāti Pāoa along Okahu Bay, the sale recorded at the Deeds Registry Office in Auckland on February 6, 1857. The 233 acres described as "Allot 6, one boundary Okahu Bay", was purchased for the sum of £104.15s. The deed also states that *in accordance with the Regulations of 4 March 1853, Section No.3, Clause No.12, Henry Brown is entitled to an allowance of eleven acres and three roods in consideration of the right of road hereinafter reserved.*

Just a few months earlier, on July 10, 1856, Henry had made out a will leaving his land to his wife Mary in trust for his sons Henry Junior and William. His two daughters were each to receive £50 — a considerable sum in those days.

Perhaps Henry had a premonition that his was not to be a long life. He died of a stroke aged only 54 on October 16, 1864, and was buried in the Symonds Street cemetery. His widow was to live for another 20 years. She passed away in the home of her daughter Charlotte, then wife of Robert Thompson Graham and living in Ponsonby, on July 15, 1886.

As neither William nor Henry Jr could read, the splitting of the block of land was explained to them in the presence of Phillip Francis JP, a Waiheke sheep farmer. Henry received the western portion (leading up to what is now Burrell Road) and William the eastern, each of 134 acres.

These two brothers married two Waiheke sisters: the Hodgson girls who had lived their lives in Omiha. Henry married Mary Ann Hodgson on September 4, 1869, and Sarah Hodgson became the bride of William Brown on October 7, 1878. Ann Eliza Brown married Charles Bell, a boatman of Auckland, and lived for some time on Waiheke where she and her husband started a family.

Henry Junior and Mary Ann had a family of 11 children, eight of whom were born on Waiheke, although only two are mentioned in Coromandel baptismal records: Albert born December 23, 1884, and George on June 2, 1887. The family moved to Rorohara (Pie Melon Bay) aboard the *Henry* on August 8, 1883. They were apparently settled near there in 1884 when Reverend Gould mentions calling in on them on the way to the Careys.

Long-time residents have no memory of a house in the bay, but there was a three-roomed cottage up the hill in the sheltered bush that is now a Royal Forest & Bird Protection Society reserve. Though Henry could not read, his wife could and she taught her children. It is understood that the *Henry* was Henry Brown's cutter and worked the island shores loading shingle.

His brother William had grown up on Waiheke without any schooling but could speak fluent Māori and often acted as interpreter for mainland Māori while they were trading. Once he got involved in a dispute over a purchase of flax and was hit in the leg with a spear— an injury that later caused paralysis.

Known as "Honest Billy", he was a skilled fisherman and gardener. He worked as labourer and shearer on the Kennedy farm and later sold part of the original Brown holding to Kennedy, retaining just 20 acres. On this land a gabled house was built with a verandah along one side and the front facing the sea.

At night the parlour was always lit with a kerosene lamp providing a guide for ships at sea or for anyone walking along the beach. Hung on the walls were old family photos and pictures of the South African War. Off the big kitchen was a storeroom where essential groceries and cigarettes were kept for customers. The local Māori population frequently bought supplies from the lady who later became known to all as "Granny Brown".

Early photos of Sarah Brown reveal a beautiful young woman, small in stature, her dark glossy hair dressed high and held in place with a comb. Her wealthy English grandparents may never have recognised her father's marriage, but Sarah looked every inch a lady.

Famous for her cooking and her skill in wine-making, Sarah would serve grape wine in special glasses and, when older, was never too tired to cook a meal for yachties or a football team. Her custard tarts were a family favourite — one grandson remembers Granny riding side-saddle down to Whakarite carrying custard tarts to the sons and grandsons who were loading sand there.

Sarah was a fearless rider; her silver nickel spurs and riding whip are still treasured by her descendants. She knew and used the old crossing over the Pūtiki mud flats which saved four miles. Though horses were part of their lives, they also brought tragedy. Still in his teens, her youngest son, John, fell off a horse sustaining head injuries that left him child-like and dependent; an older son, Joseph, was killed in a similar accident at the age of 19.

The couple had six boys: William, Richard Stanley, Thomas William, Edward, Joseph, and Henry John. Their father, only able to sign his name with an "X", was determined they should get a better education and initially employed a tutor. The Brown household later became a part-time school, sharing a teacher with Te Matuku Central and Man O'War schools. One pupil remembered school in the kitchen with seven Māori and three Pākehā children seated around a table with a red plush cover, writing with slate and pencils. In 1898 the youngsters were taught by Mr Allison who rode over from Te Matuku.

There were happy family reunions when sons came home at Christmas, anchoring their craft in the bay. The house by the sea had always resounded with the shouts and play of boys and grandchildren spoke of glorious holidays. Their granny often rowed out to the steamer to meet them. In the storeroom hung their bearded grandfather's whips and saddles and they watched him use his whip to flick twigs off the willow tree near the creek.

Waiheke's landscape held no fears for Sarah and she loved walking or riding over the hills. Once overdue on a visit to her friends, the Careys, she was found by her anxious family at night sleeping peacefully in the bush. William, as he grew older, became less active because of the old spear injury affecting his leg, but he amused his young grandchildren telling stories of the old days. He died, aged 67, on March 14, 1917, respected on the island where he had lived all his life.

After his death, 15 acres of the land was sold and both this and the bay then known as Browns were subdivided. In 1921, the first section in the newly-christened Surfdale subdivision was sold. Prices ranged from £25 which could be paid off, interest free, at 8d a day. The names of the surveyors and engineers for Surfdale Seaside Estates, Blake and Burrell, are recalled in street names. A hall, which had started life as part of a tannery at Panmure, was erected by Bert May in 1921 and used for a while as a school. The following year, the new suburb had its own wharf and its own quota of weekenders. In 1929 the last five acres of Brown land was valued at £1830.

Granny Brown became something of a local legend. She was a compassionate woman, always ready to help anyone in trouble. At the age of 83, she was out digging her garden, came indoors feeling tired and died peacefully on June 21, 1941, survived by five sons, 19 grandchildren and 34 great-grandchildren. Her old homestead was later destroyed by fire.

All the boys maintained close connections with the island. The eldest, called William after his father as was traditional in the family, married Kate Walsh who was in service to the O'Brien family of Pūtiki. Kate was born in New Zealand to a young couple who had left their Irish home on board the *Northern Bride* in 1860 because, as first cousins, they were forbidden to marry. The determined young pair, just 17 years old at the time, were married en route to their new home. Fellow passengers were the Gray family who settled at Waiti Bay, so this romantic story became well known on the island.

Kate's husband, William, inherited his grandfather's love of the sea. He became a master mariner and a skipper of J J Craig's boats employed in the shingle and sand trade. He was also part owner of a scow.

One of William's sons, Joseph, recalled coming to Waiheke in the cutter *Lee* and camping ashore. He would run over to Brown's Bay to see his beloved Granny who took the eager boy out in a punt.

This same Joseph also worked on the scows. During the war years he was in charge of the boat regulating the defence boom across Auckland Harbour. His younger brother, Edward, who bought an Onetangi section and built a holiday home there, also worked at sea and became a senior captain in the Northern Steamship Company.

William's two younger brothers, Thomas and Richard Stanley, married two Waiheke sisters, Isabel and Janet (Ginnie) Hooks. Thomas, who married Isabel, went to sea for some time but later returned to live on the island.

Richard Stanley lived on the island all his life. He spoke Māori and bought land for a small farm from Ngāti Pāoa at the western end of Te Huruhi —part of which is now occupied by the Piritahi Marae. He established a garden and orchard there and, in 1903, married Ginnie Hooks.

Richard used to row to Auckland for his supplies, usually returning with a load of fish for sale. His well-planned smokehouse was often in use. As an old man he was still a successful fisherman. The family's comfortable three bedroom home overlooked the shallow waters of the bay near a water supply that Richard used to supplement section holders' tanks when they ran dry. Carrying large milk cans and drums full of water on the back of his horse and cart, he provided the first water delivery service on the island.

Shorthorn and Jersey cows roamed free grazing among the scattered houses and scrub in what is now Blackpool, the bells providing a guide to find them at milking time. They were milked by hand in a shed. Butter made in a cool, concrete block dairy found ready customers. Ginnie opened a small store in Moa Avenue and stocked essential groceries plus kerosene for lamps and lanterns. Because the nearest telephone exchange was at Pūtiki, Ginnie also allowed customers to use her telephone. It was a serious loss to the district when the shop and its contents were lost in a fire before the days of the volunteer fire brigade.

Janet died in 1943. Her eldest son, also Richard Stanley, worked the shingle boats with his Hooks cousins but later returned and lived in a cottage at the back of his father's house. He milked the cows and delivered milk and later served as ticket collector on both the Surfdale and Matiatia wharves in the 1940s-50s.

His son and namesake followed a similar pattern, initially working aboard the scows and later the *Monowai*, before returning to Waiheke. Dick set up business as a painter and gave long and loyal service to the volunteer fire brigade of which he became Deputy Chief before retiring.

William and Sarah's fourth son, Eddie, also made Waiheke his life. Like his elder brother before him, he met his wife-to-be while she was working as a maid at the O'Briens' home in Pūtiki. He was a farm boy there at the time.

Catherine O'Hara was an Irish orphan, educated in a Catholic convent with Gertrude Connell, sister of Will Connell of Connells Bay. The couple were young when they married but it proved a happy union. A studio photo of the young couple shows Catherine looking demure in a dark frock, her auburn hair hidden beneath a smart hat. She holds three arum lilies in her lap while Edward, debonaire in suit and bowler hat, wears a white buttonhole.

Their first home was in the area now called Shelly Beach Road before they settled in what had been the original homestead of Phillip Francis in Belgium St. This, as an Education Board report reveals, was to become Ostend's first school. Initially their son, Cecil, rode some miles to the Te Huruhi School. Records show that on August 2, 1917, three families had applied for the establishment of a half time school at Ostend to be housed in a spare room of the Brown household, "room to be free of cost". However, four years later on, an exasperated Mrs Brown writes to say that *my family is growing up and the extra accommodation, urgently needed, is not available after the 4th July... Mr Aspden proprietor of the boarding house and hall is willing to let the hall for £16 a year to include provision for cleaning and hand washing.*

The Belgium St house later burnt down and the Browns lived for some years in the house and grounds now occupied by the Shepherd's Point Riding School. Eddie was farm manager for Lichtenstein and Arnoldson and, following the sale of newly subdivided sections in Ostend in the early 1920s, he built a grocery store at the corner of Ostend Road and Albert Crescent. Above the entrance was a curved glass panel with the name of his dear wife "Catherine" in gold leaf on the glass. This building has now been enlarged and is a modern supermarket.

A bus service, started by another pioneering family descendant, Allen Day, was later bought by Eddie and Catherine's son Cecil who ran the service for 26 years as well as operating a carrying business and taxi service between Ostend and Onetangi. The garage now in Albert Crescent was moved from Shepherd's Point to its present site.

Cecil was also on call for the local ambulance service in the district. Patients would be lifted onto stretchers and placed on the back of his Chevrolet truck. The driver tried to avoid the worst bumps and in wet weather carried bundles of manuka on the running boards in case the truck got stuck in the mud. This "ambulance" met up with James Kennedy's launch *Dixie* to take the sick or injured into Auckland hospital.

The first school bus service was also run by Cecil who was on the Ostend School Committee. He drove children over from Onetangi in his Model A Ford.

Cecil Brown's bus service, 1930s.

His brother Leslie took over from their father as manager of Lichtenstein and Arnoldson and Eddie then acted as stock agent for NZ Loan and Mercantile Co Ltd, riding round the island, seeking business and drinking tea in farm kitchens.

It was a job that suited his personality and fitted in well with part-time work on Fisher's farm. It was around this time that a young Māori woman called Bella came to keep house and help care for Catherine as her health failed and Eddie lost his beloved wife.

The Browns maintained strong links with the island. One of Eddie's nephews returned in style near the end of the Second World War. Joseph Brown, then Commodore of the Mine Sweeper Fleet, brought all 30 of his fleet into Onetangi Bay where they were promptly given a party in the local hall.

It was Joseph's brother Eddie who had bought an Onetangi section to build a holiday home that was later to be lived in by a fourth generation descendant of Henry and Mary — Noel Brown. Still living on the island that holds memories of some great times, Noel recalled a glorious holiday during the 1949 polio epidemic when Cecil and Leslie had taken their families to camp in the seclusion of Pie Melon Bay. They lived in tents eating local shellfish and freshly caught snapper until school re-opened again.

Noel also contributed to the island community, spending 17 years in the local Fire Brigade, as well as serving on the St John Ambulance committee and as an original member of the Waiheke Boating Club.

As well as contributing to community life, the Brown family have given the island a lasting legacy. When Eddie Brown died in 1958, the trustees of his estate, sons Leslie and Cecil, helped to execute a special clause in his will. This stated that, if possible, he wanted his block of bush-covered land in Onetangi to be bought by the Royal Forest and Bird Protection Society. In the intervening years, the society has developed this land, creating pleasant walking tracks, removing gorse and other exotics, and planting more native trees and bushes. The 65-hectare reserve, which features the only stand of mature kauri at the western end of the island, is now a valuable part of Waiheke's natural heritage.

Pakihi (Day's) Bay

As they stood in line for their daily rum ration aboard the *Lancashire Witch* on the long voyage between England and New Zealand, a young soldier and a little girl would never guess at the extraordinary coincidence that would reunite them in marriage on Waiheke Island more than a decade later.

The Day Family

The soldier was Martin Day, born about 1833 in the parish of Ballinbar, near Castlebar, in County Mayo. Aged 19, he had gone to Liverpool to enlist in the 65th Regiment of Foot, Yorkshire North Riding, popularly known as the "Royal Tigers", and had found himself stationed in Jersey. The little girl, nearly four years old, was Mary Ann Edsal. She was living on Jersey when her mother remarried, to another member of the "Royal Tigers" called Garvey. When the regiment embarked on the *Lancashire Witch* to bolster British forces in the growing conflicts with the New Zealand Māori, among its passengers were Martin Day, Garvey, his new wife and Mary Ann in her maroon cashmere, long white frilled pantalettes and lace-up boots.

After arriving in Wellington on July 21, 1856, the "Royal Tigers" were based initially in the new capital before being sent into action further north under the command of Colonel Gold who was to establish a better reputation for himself as an artist than as a military commander. Ten years and 324 days after he had enlisted at Liverpool, Martin Day was discharged from service at Otahuhu in August 1865. His report noted: *Character good, he is in possession of one good conduct badge* and described him as *Age, 29; height, 5ft 6in; fresh complexion; eyes, grey; hair, fair; trade, labourer; marks or scars, none; intended place of residence, Province of Auckland.*

Martin made his way to Waiheke where he found work clearing bush for Henry Trace and met the Garveys who had settled on the island. Mary Ann, a lovely brunette, was by now entering her teenage years. She fell in love with the young bushman and their courtship ended in marriage in the old St Andrews Church in Symonds Street on October 15, 1867. The church register shows that the bride, then aged 15, signed neatly as Mary Ann Garvey; Martin with an "X".

The newlyweds returned to Waiheke on the 44ft schooner *Vivid*, sailing from Maraetai across to Awaawaroa where their first home, a nikau whare, was waiting for them on Henry Trace's land. Martin continued working for Mr Trace, clearing surveying lines through the bush, while he waited for his promised Soldier's Crown Grant of land. Mrs Trace assisted when the first of ten children, a blue-eyed daughter named Mary Ann after her mother but called Ann, was born in the whare. A studio photograph shows Mary Ann, petite in bonnet and prim matron's frock, holding her first born, bearded Martin standing proudly at her side.

Martin's land grant, when it finally came through in 1869, turned out to be a 60-acre block up north. He decided to sell it and remain on Waiheke. The next year brought a son, John, and a move to Pikau (Cowes) Bay, leased from Finlayson for £10 a year paid quarterly in gold sovereigns, where four more children were born. The next, and final, shift was round the point to Pakihi Bay where Martin had been buying land including 40 acres which he purchased from Duncan Munro in March 1883. There he built a house, probably from his own timber, and established the Day family in the bay that would thereafter carry their name.

A hard worker, lean and active, Martin cleared and grassed his land, selling firewood, some timber and, later, a little shingle or sand. Help with the constant chores of pulling up the regenerating tea-tree and cutting wood for the stove came from his young sons who, with their sisters, were taught to read and write by their neighbour, Duncan Munro, doing their numbers as they sat beside him on a kauri log above the beach.

They were among the first children enrolled at Waiheke's first school, in the Te Matuku Valley, in 1882. The eldest daughter, Ann, now 13, spent two years at the school and the records show that her brother, James, won a book *English Sea Stories* as a prize for his "diligence, attendance, conduct and cleanliness" in 1884. Their mother, who had some schooling in Auckland after arriving in New Zealand, played the accordion and read to her children in the evenings.

The Day home was a plain, unpainted dwelling close to the sea which was a vital source of food. Flounder were speared near the shore, oysters and mussels were collected from the rocks, snapper and mullet were exchanged for bread and butter with passing fishermen. Freed from their chores on the farm, the boys used go fishing on Sundays, pulling in up to 70 snapper, some of which they smoked. Any sharks they caught became manure for the orchard and garden.

Fruit was harvested from the sheltered orchard and vegetables grew in neat rows in the garden. The children collected wild honey and their father made his own special brew of honey mead. Basic stores were delivered by cutter —sacks of sugar and flour, chests of tea, bags of food for the fowls — often the reward of barter deals with Auckland merchants. The only luxuries would come around Christmas with orders for raisins and other goodies, and a merchant might send a festive gift of tins of biscuits and lollies for the young ones.

The children were reared on goat's milk, their mother's preference. The herd of nine goats, each with a little brass bell on a chain around its neck, were young Ann's pets. She would call them home for her brother Edward (Ted) to milk. Like his brothers, Ted helped out on the farm, later remembering one unusual task during a dry spell when feed was scarce and the Days sent some of their cattle and sheep across the channel to "Rabbit" (Pakatoa) Island for extra grazing. The cattle swam, herded along from a rowing boat with ropes lightly tied around their horns. The sheep were taken by boat and Ted Day recalled the trip in later years.

I was about 12 and took a boat load of wethers over to the island. Their feet were tied and they were lying in the boat. A shark followed me all the way across. I waited a long time after I let the sheep go and was so scared as I rowed home again.

The older children were growing up and leaving home, the girls marrying young. The eldest, Mary Ann, known as Annie, married George Pegler from nearby Ōmaru Bay and was carrying her first child at the same time as her mother was expecting her tenth and last baby.

Both babies were due at the same time and, when George was called away on a contract job, Ann was brought by boat to Pakihi where the two women delivered their babies safely. When George returned he was met by Martin Day carrying a baby in each arm. "Which is yours?" asked his father-in-law. George made the correct choice and, with his wife cradling their baby in her arms, he rowed them back to Ōmaru.

Some of the many descendants of Martin Day, at Te Matuku Sunday School 1909. Teacher is Miss Notman.

After only a few short years on his Waiheke farm, Martin Day suddenly fell ill with appendicitis — readily cured by surgery now but so often fatal then. He died on March 12, 1890, aged 57, and was buried, as he had wished, in his bay near a totara tree on the hill. He left no will and the eldest son John (Jack), then 20 and the First Mate on a ship on the Vancouver run, was called back to Pakihi to manage the farm. He was later to marry Margaret Gordon of Awaawaroa and leave the island to farm near Matakana.

Then tragedy struck again. After five years of widowhood, Mary Ann disappeared. After a day in the heat and bustle of the kitchen she had always enjoyed fishing off the rocks. One evening she failed to return and was not at her favourite fishing spot when the boys went to fetch her. Increasingly frantic they searched, calling her name, but there was no reply. The date was July 19, 1895; Mary Ann was only 43.

Again there was no will but the family agreed to stay on at Pakihi until the youngest, Harry, was able to make his own way in the world. Annie and John had married, as had Thomas who, with wife Caroline and infant son Arthur, was working for Andrew Croll at Arran Bay, and Ellen who married John Pegler at Orapiu.

Jane, at 14, took over the running of the house and became mother to George (9) and Harry (6), ably assisted with housework and cooking by Margaret ("Maggie", 12). James (20) and Ted (16) ran the farm and earned money shearing and cutting firewood.

Helped from time to time by their married brothers and sisters, the young Days managed on a very limited income, working hard but enjoying some social life. Popular members of the small coastal community, they visited their neighbours and took part in the regattas at Cowes and the race meetings on Onetangi Beach where Jane rode a horse lent by the Careys of Wairua.

A local woman had taught the locals how to dance at Cowes Bay Hall and, invited to a dance at Coromandel, they decided to try out their steps. With their boat's keel polished with black lead for a smooth surface and their frocks carefully stowed to stay dry, Jane, Maggie and their brothers took turns rowing, hoisting a small sail once they were in open sea beyond the sheltering islands. Next morning they faced the long row back to Pakihi to resume their usual routine.

Maggie's sweetheart, schoolteacher Jim Broun, waited for her while she took over the housekeeping after Jane left to marry Will Connell. Ted went farming near Ōmaru Bay and James farmed in the Awaawaroa valley. George and Harry left the island and, in 1906, John Day and Ellen's husband, John Pegler, were appointed administrators of the estate.

Four years later they sold Pakihi to F W Wilson, the newspaper proprietor and colleague of Horton at Man O'War Bay, and a Mr L Montgomery for £930. In accordance with their wishes, the land on which Martin Day and his sons had toiled so hard was allowed to revert to bush and the farm disappeared as it was quickly recaptured by tea-tree.

The present owners are Mrs Guthrie, a member of the Wilson family, and Mr Guthrie, the son of the noted surgeon, Douglas Guthrie, who also had strong connections with that part of the coast.

The Day homestead, Day's Bay in the 1890s.

Awaawaroa

Site of an early manganese mine, post office and telephone exchange, this quiet rural valley was a lot busier at the turn of the 20th century than it is today. Dominated by Mount Maunganui, the island's highest point and former pa site, its wide inlet, fertile flats and meandering stream have long attracted settlement. One area of coastal farmland claims the distinction of being farmed by the same family for well over 100 years.

The Merrick Family

The first European settler family to establish themselves in the Awaawaroa valley was that of Isaac Merrick, an energetic, broad-shouldered man from the coal mines of Lancashire. Born in 1805, the youngest of six children of a family of miners in Denton, Lancashire, Isaac was determined to lift his children out of the poverty and sorrows that had been his own lot in life in England.

Isaac married Elizabeth (Betty) Hirst in Manchester on April 20, 1823. Over the next seventeen years the couple brought ten children into the world and watched eight of them die — a not uncommon tragedy in early industrial England. The family moved repeatedly around northwest England looking for paid work and healthy (or less unhealthy) living conditions. Finally, in 1840 Isaac saw a way out: the bounty system of emigration to Australia. In October of that year he, Betty, and their two surviving children Samuel and Isaac Jr, boarded the *Margaret* for the five-month journey to Sydney. Betty was pregnant with her eleventh child, and gave birth to a son William during the voyage.

Arriving in Sydney on March 28, 1841, Isaac quickly found work in Parramatta as a foreman of a gang of convicts working a quarry for building materials. Family stories recount how Isaac managed to improve the diet of the convicts by convincing the quarry owners that healthier workers would increase productivity.

The baby William died a few weeks after arrival, but a daughter, Louisa, was born in Parramatta in 1842. The following year Isaac moved his family again to Auckland's North Shore, where he had heard — possibly from John Logan Campbell himself — of the possibility of copper mining. He grew wheat on a farm in Shoal Bay for a year; but mining, not farming, was his real interest and his main talent. Manganese had been discovered on Waiheke Island in 1840, and there were suggestions of copper as well. This caused him to shift one last time to Waiheke.

For a brief 18-month period from late 1843 to early 1845, settlers were permitted to deal directly with Māori for the purchase of land, without going through Crown agents. Isaac Merrick took advantage of this opportunity to purchase what he estimated to be 900 acres of land on the eastern side of Awaawaroa Bay from Hohepa Te Ruinga of Ngāti Pāoa. As was the case with many of these transactions, the boundaries of the land were vague and conflicted with claims of other settlers, particularly those of Robert McLeod of Te Matuku Bay. Disputes flared amongst the Pākehā settlers until the Crown finally resolved the boundaries in 1861, leaving the Merricks with clear title to 368 acres.

Meanwhile, Isaac got busy with mining. In April 1844, John Logan Campbell and William Brown acquired mining rights to land in Te Matuku Bay owned by Henry Tayler, the man who had discovered manganese there in 1840. They immediately hired Isaac Merrick to mine 150 tons of manganese ore; by October of that year he and a small army of labourers had extracted more than three times that much. Although the ore did not fetch the hoped-for prices in Sydney and London, Isaac's reputation as a miner was established.

In September 1844, Isaac contracted to mine for copper on Kawau Island, and in 1849 the governor, Sir George Grey, granted him a 21-year lease of the northeasternmost island of the Hen and Chickens group, also for the extraction of copper ore. That island, still known as Coppermine

Island today, has a Merrick Bay where Isaac set up his operations.

Tired of paying other people to ship his ore to market, in 1847 Isaac built his own schooner, which he named *Providence*, from wood on his Awaawaroa land. He also constructed the Awaawaroa Bay seawall from concrete that he mixed himself on wooden sheets. The *Providence* shipped 18 tons of copper to Auckland before she was wrecked off Tauranga in 1849. The following year Isaac purchased another schooner, *Victoria*. In later years he was owner or master of trading vessels named *Star* and *James*.

In early 1852, Isaac found himself in the midst of gold fever, in a way that raised questions about his own role in the affair. It began with a man named Frederick Mosheim, who had spread rumours that two mariners living on Waiheke had found gold there. Suddenly the island was the focus of a mini-gold rush. As the Rev Vicesimus Lush, of Howick, recorded in his diary of January 12:

> *A schooner ran out of our bay from Waiheke and 20 men rushed into the village to buy spades and pickaxes to hasten back to the "Auckland Diggings", the Gold Fever is beginning — who can tell how frightfully it may rage?*

Nothing was found and Mosheim's rumours were soon debunked, but gold fever had taken hold. On March 6 an Auckland constable delivered a sample obtained from Isaac Merrick, the well-known miner, for assay, and it proved to contain gold. Again the town was in an uproar. Referring to George King, a Māori chief on Waiheke, Rev Lush wrote on March 10:

> *A strong report that Gold is actually found at Waiheke within a dozen miles of Howick. The Chief however, they say, refuses to allow anyone to dig there unless the Govt. will purchase the right for £100,000. They are a powerful tribe and unless the Govt. can find some means of coaxing him into compliance the Chief could no doubt for a long time maintain his lawful right to the island.*

Once again the assay laboratories were busy with hopeful samples, some provided by Isaac Merrick himself from his many mining operations around the Hauraki Gulf, but no further positive results were obtained. A re-examination on March 13 of the original positive sample proved revealing. What Rev Lush had described as a "strong report" a few days earlier he now denounced as the work of a scamp:

The town is in a perfect ferment about the gold finding which many believe, some doubt — and a few altogether deny. £100 has been offered to anyone who should discover a goldfield. A man, a notorious scamp came in great haste from Waiheke with a bag of earth in which sparkled an abundance of particles of the coveted ore — he came to claim the £100. The Committee met — they were at the Mayor's house when I rode into town — assaying the metal. Three policemen guarded the door and groups of anxious lookers on and eager talkers. At last came the news. What was it? Gold? No, all a hoax! When they assayed the gold that glittered in the bag of earth they found it to contain exactly the same alloy as does the gold of a sovereign. Their suspicions were awakened and their golden dream quickly vanished away. The rascal had used a file upon a sovereign, mixed the gold so obtained with some earth and hoped to have so imposed upon the committee as to have bagged the £100, and off to Australia.

Although the "off to Australia" comment could not have applied to Isaac Merrick, it is clear that Rev Lush believed him to be the scamp. No charges were ever brought against Isaac, however, and if he was indeed involved in perpetrating the hoax, its object would more likely have been to drum up mining business for himself rather than to collect the £100 reward — he was much too experienced a miner to believe he could get away with that. Whatever the truth may be, the great Waiheke gold hoax remained a topic of conversation and debate for decades.

Back home at Awaawaroa, Isaac and Betty had six more children, all boys, but only three would survive to adulthood. There was nonetheless much happiness during these times. The two oldest boys married, Isaac Jr (to Mary Ann Boyd) in 1853 and Samuel (to Charlotte O'Brien – apparently not related to the O'Briens of Pūtiki) in 1855, and grandchildren began to scamper around the farm. Relations with neighbours, both Māori and Pākehā, were good, the bitterness of the boundary disputes notwithstanding. Two McLeod children, Jane and Donald, came to live with the Merricks in 1860; Jane remained with them until she married William Gordon (see next section) in 1873. A neighbouring bushman, Thomas Webb, married Wehi Pokai, daughter of Hori Pokai of Ngāti Pāoa and had two children before Thomas drowned in a boating accident in

1855. The Merricks helped Wehi and her children until she returned to her Ngāti Pāoa relatives. Wehi's son, James Webb, married Louisa Merrick in 1860, and more grandchildren arrived.

The days of sorrow were not over, however. A typhus epidemic in 1860 claimed the lives of two of Isaac and Betty's boys, Abraham and David, and a third, John, died in Auckland. The 42-year-old Betty, pregnant with her eighteenth and last child, named him John as well. Son Samuel died in 1864, leaving wife Charlotte with four children. Charlotte moved the family to Auckland and found work as a seamstress, but she herself died suddenly in 1871 at age 33. Then in 1865, son-in-law James Webb was killed by a falling tree, leaving Louisa with three small children and a fourth on the way. Louisa remarried in 1867 to John Colemoss, an Awaawaroa bushman eight years her junior. They had three more children and moved to Kereti on the Coromandel Peninsula.

A curious twist of fate occurred in July 1873. William Castle, a recently-arrived Awaawaroa neighbour, discovered a large manganese deposit on Crown land near the Merrick property. Isaac immediately applied for a mining lease citing his previous experience with manganese on the island, but he was now 68 years old and the lease went to William Castle's own consortium. The mining operation, known locally as the "government mine" because it was on Crown land, became New Zealand's largest manganese mine and produced ore for 23 years, all under the nose of the man who could rightfully claim to be the father of Waiheke mining.

Isaac and Betty Merrick retired to Chapel Street, Auckland (where Aotea Square is now) in 1877; their son Isaac Jr sold the 368-acre farm to Robert McLeod in that same year for £270. Betty died on November 22, 1878, of tuberculosis. Isaac lived on until December 3, 1881, when he too passed away in their Chapel Street home. Isaac and Betty are buried in the Symonds Street cemetery in Auckland. Of their eighteen children, only four survived them.

The Gordon Family

Present farmer Colin Gordon is a direct descendant of William James Gordon, an educated young Irishman who sailed from Liverpool aboard the *Excelsior* in 1858 to arrive in Auckland on March 17 the following year.

His descendants still treasure a prayer book presented to him by the Lismore Church when he left Northern Ireland. A memento of his voyage to New Zealand, found amongst papers at the old Awaawaroa homestead, was a poem he had written for the ship's news sheet after the death of a seaman.

After his first venture in the Pokeno district, 21-year-old William moved to Waiheke, probably in the cutter *Ariel*, in the early 1860s. By 1864 he was shipping firewood from a block beyond the head of Te Matuku Bay; lists show *16 - 30 tons hauled out to waiting cutters, the Jessie, Mary Anne, Julie and others, the best price six shillings a ton.*

Two years later, he recorded the start of what was to be a long history of dairying: *Cow went away to bull... Cow calves in April 1867.*

By 1866 this astute settler had also started what was to be a long tradition of small storekeeping by the Gordon family. He stocked staple items such as kegs of salt beef and salt, 200-pound sacks of flour, tea, sugar, hops, boots and laces, lamp globes, pills, pipes and plug tobacco for sale to island settlers and visitors.

An incentive for successfully establishing himself on the island was Jane McLeod, daughter of Te Matuku Bay's first settler. Although her father did not favour a match between Jane and a man 14 years her senior, the couple were to marry on June 2, 1873, at the home of a Mr Finlayson in Freemans Bay, Auckland. A photo of the occasion reveals William as a handsome and distinguished-looking man who wore his city clothes with a casual elegance.

The couple's first home was built on a bank above the present road. An old magnolia and pink belladonna lilies by the fern grove marked the site; willows and poplars fringe the road. Nine daughters and one son grew up on Waiheke, another son died in childhood.

Stories are told of Jane, a baby under one arm and a toddler under the other, looking for cows in the bush before fences were erected. Always willing to walk over the hills to nurse a sick woman or assist at childbirth, this busy woman nevertheless had time to plant cornflowers, mignonette and lavender in a flower border around her house.

With their growing family, education became a problem and in 1882 the Gordons made a room in their house available for the island's first school which attracted 27 pupils, some already in their teens. Crowded conditions plus the fact that the family could ill spare a room must have prompted some huge sighs of relief when, with the help of a visiting Anglican parson, a proper schoolroom was established in Te Matuku Valley the following year.

One daughter, Edith, passed her 6th standard certificate at the school in 1898. Clever with figures, she later studied bookkeeping in the old "to cash, by goods" method — knowledge that was to prove useful. Early Gordon farm accounts now at the Waiheke Museum precisely record transactions made and money spent: 1895 entries include Lily's dress 7/9, 2 white hats 9d, 2 black hats 1/-, gloves 6d, and elastic and hat pins 3d.

Life for the Gordon family changed when, at the age of 58, William Gordon bought more land — valuation for the 1204 acres was then £1100. The family moved to a new house on the coast and, now much further from the school, employed a governess or boarded the younger girls in Auckland.

Gordon's home in Awaawaroa Bay. The Post Office and telephone exchange are in lean-to at the back.

Their plain but substantial house was built with a wide verandah facing a sheltered beach in Awaawaroa Bay. It included a small room which was to be the first local Post Office and, on January 18, 1900, William Gordon was appointed Awaawaroa Postmaster. If a parson turned up, the house also doubled as a house of worship; Bibles were conspicuous on a shelf in the hall and William had certain rules for the Sabbath. However, the girls also enjoyed dancing lessons and dances were held in the farm woolshed.

This woolshed was also the scene of the family's first wedding when their third daughter, Margaret Grace, married John Day — uniting two of Waiheke's early pioneering families. The ceremony, conducted by the Reverend Dixon of St David's, Auckland, was performed under an arch of nikau and camelias with the bride in a grey dress trimmed with white satin and chiffon attended by her sister Anne and Lily in frocks trimmed with cream lace and ribbon. Seventy guests were there to celebrate the event with a delicious wedding breakfast and more Waiheke folk turned up later in the day for a dance in the woolshed. Wool sacks dragged across the floor gave it a polished surface, piano and accordion provided the music.

As Waiheke became an increasingly popular destination for holiday makers, the woolshed often served as an impromptu guest house. Jane improvised comfortable bedding using the cloth from flour and grain sacks stuffed with hen and chicken feathers or wool; the first beds were made from stretched out wool bales attached to wooden frames. These were later replaced with brass beds and wire wove.

Stuffing the home-made mattresses and pillows was a tedious job: ducks and hens killed for the table were plucked, the feathers were then packed into cotton bags, plunged into boiling water and pegged on the clothesline.

Tariffs for accommodation were low. Much of the food was grown, or caught, on the property and around the shoreline; guests often collected their own shellfish to add to the menu. The guest house became a family enterprise with three unmarried daughters managing the place and married daughters returning to help out in the holidays. There are amusing stories of Lizzie and Ethel Gordon as young women outwitting the first fisheries inspector on the island as they continued to evade the new restrictions on gathering oysters which, at the time, were resented by most islanders.

Some of the Gordon family around 1910. Standing: Ethel, Lily, Annie, Edith.
Sitting: Elizabeth, Will and Jane. Kneeling: Daisy.

Most of the cooking for the growing number of guests was done by
Lizzie Gordon on a stove that measured about 6ft across. Lizzie also
caught most of the fish that ended up on the dining tables. There were two
dining rooms with long scrubbed kauri tables covered in starched white
cloths that were washed in a petrol-driven Beatty washing machine.

Like other Waiheke settlers, Will Gordon initially rowed up to Auckland
for his supplies, later buying a 26ft kerosene-powered launch which was
christened *Mercy*. He still kept staple grocery items which other settlers
called in to buy while collecting their mail. All the Gordon girls learned to

row well; one visiting parson was surprised when he was landed by a boat crew consisting of four girls. It took care, skill and a well-muscled arm to meet and collect supplies or visitors from the paddle steamer *Wakatere* in the channel: it was a long pull back to shore.

Life became easier when, in 1908, the Northern Steamship Co leased an acre of land and a wharf was built in the bay. Its steamers made regular stops as did the Waiheke Passage Co ship, Baroona, in later years. One surprise visit in the 1920s was a member of the Walsh Bros Flying School who flew down in a biplane and landed in Awaawaroa near the woolshed causing great excitement. The pilot's wife stayed with the Gordons; her husband brought mail over and flew back with oysters and fish.

The expansion of the Awaawaroa guesthouse with a new annexe and outside cabins meant that the Gordons ended up catering for around 100 guests. Bedrooms opening onto the verandah were re-booked, at special prices, year after year. Each room was equipped with patterned washbasin, jug and chamber pots, later replaced by an in-door bathroom and two outdoor flush toilets.

An early printed card for the enterprise reads:

Awaawaroa Bay: Private Board and Residence. Splendid sheltered beach, Bathing, Boating, Fishing, Shooting. Northern Steamship Co steamers call three times a week.

Terms: Adult £1 per room, children from 5/- to 10/-. Mrs Gordon Proprietress. Post Office and Telephone Bureau at the house.

An orchard provided peaches, pears, plums, apples, persimmons, figs, walnuts and even Chinese gooseberries (kiwifruit). It is possible that the first kiwifruit sent to the United States came from the Gordon property after an American officer came to visit, tasted the fruit and asked some to be sent over to him in 1944. Some 30 of the fruit were duly packed in a shoe box and sent by Pan American Airways. The Department of Agriculture was apparently suspicious at first, but the fruit arrived safely, was tasted, and voted delicious.

The gardens in the bay produced flowers as well as fruit and bunches of daffodils, jonquils and irises were sent up to Auckland by steamer to be sold through an Indian fruit chain.

After complaints from visitors about the rough path to the wharf, it was upgraded and a wall built with the help of a community working bee and ten tons of cement. Now transport of goods, luggage and cans of cream was much easier.

Dairying was a mainstay of the Gordon farm: shorthorn cross cows were milked and butter made in a huge barrel churn. As the only son in the family, James was responsible for sheep and cattle work and provided table lamb and mutton. Before refrigeration, meat was kept in thin calico bags and hung in a big wire enclosure, shaded by willows. Records show that in 1907 the steam tug *Kopu* took several bales of cross-bred wool from Gordon's farm for NZ Loan and Mercantile Co in Auckland.

With farm and guesthouse to run, there was little time left for entertainment, though one favourite family outing (on a fine day in the quiet season) was a day-long trip up the southeast coast to Waiti and a roast dinner with the Gray family. There were also the family celebrations. Perhaps William's last such family do was daughter Lily's 21st birthday party with wine and cakes for 20 friends and family. He did not live to see another daughter, Daisy Beatrice, married at home to Robert Bowden.

Respected by all and mourned by many, William Gordon died on September 25, 1911, aged 71. Waiheke folk came from miles around and a boat brought mourners over from the city for his funeral at the Pioneer Cemetery in Te Matuku Bay.

James took over the running of the farm, while the women of the family continued to run the guesthouse. For some years the Akarana Yacht Club sailed to Awaawaroa in a cruising race to dance the night away at the local woolshed. Services were still held in the woolshed: one visitor in the 1930s was Auckland City Missioner Jaspar Calder, who would arrive in his launch *Crusader* and bang a kerosene tin to call the locals and yachties to worship.

Apart from supplying his own guests with meat, James Gordon also butchered meat for guesthouses run by Le Roy and McGrevy in Onetangi. Small orders were transported by horseback over the hill; bigger orders had to be hauled out by a bullock-drawn sledge. James also organised stock movements from island farms to the Man O'War saleyards in the 1920s. Travelling up by launch on sale day, he was usually accompanied by sister Lizzie with a load of scones and sandwiches for the hungry crowds. After the saleyards closed, James planned shipment of sheep and cattle to mainland sales with stock loaded from convenient yards on to the scow *Rahiri* whose skipper Jock McKinnon had married another sister, Maud.

Jane Gordon (née McLeod) died on the island that had also been her birthplace on December 21, 1930, aged 76 and was laid to rest beside her husband in the Te Matuku cemetery. Also appearing on the Gordon memorial stone is the name of daughter, Lena, who died at the age of 31 on April 9, 1906. A granddaughter, the three year old child of John and Maggie (née Gordon) Day, was also buried there on February 1, 1916.

Another daughter, Edith, who had served six years as postmistress at Awaawaroa, was the last person to be buried in the old cemetery in 1938, in a grave dug by two other members of Waiheke pioneer families, Ted Day and Jack McIntosh. By then, the centre of Waiheke's settlement had shifted west and the Te Matuku cemetery, like the old schoolroom, fell into disuse. For many years, members of the Gordon family returned to the valley on Boxing Day to tidy and weed the graves as fantails flitted among the tanekaha in that quiet place.

The Awaawaroa Boarding House closed in the late 1930s. Post Office work continued, the telephone exchange there being part of the house complex. Party lines were attached to this exchange and maintained by the owners. All requests for outward calls to other Waiheke districts or Auckland were handled by the operator from 9.00am to 5.00pm. In emergencies, the Gordons would open the exchange after hours.

Bricks from the first farmhouse marked the spot for decades, as well as the ruins of the 19-room guesthouse, but an orchard is all that is left today — that, and the memories of the three "Aunties" who ran the guesthouse. James Gordon's daughter Mavis, who lived on the island for most of her life, recalled growing up tough and shy on a childhood diet of hard work and isolation. The extra work provided by visitors during the annual regattas came on top of a daily regime that would tax the energy of most adults today: up at 4.00am to milk the cows, then breakfast, schoolwork, a lunch break that included gathering firewood for the fuel-hungry copper, then more schoolwork perhaps followed by sheep mustering, help with concreting the woolshed floor, or catching the horse and harnessing it to collect sacks of shingle, then back to the cows...

Mavis was shearing her first sheep with hand clippers before she was 11 and later, working with her husband Farley Scott and fellow islander Johnny Hooks, clipped not only Waiheke sheep but did shearing for most of the gulf islands. Starting the season with a tally of around 100 a day, Mavis worked her way up to a respectable 250 or so — just getting into her stride as the season ended. But her early love was the dairy herd.

After finishing school at the age of 17, she helped build up the herd on the family farm, selling dairy products to an Onetangi guesthouse and, in a flush season, sending up to six eight-gallon cream cans off to the dairy factory in Auckland. This cream fetched first grade despite infrequent transport from the island.

Mavis had met her husband-to-be on a path between their farms after the Scott family started farming what is now known as the Waiheke Station. Although family disapproval of the match prompted her to leave home, and Waiheke, she and Farley later returned to run their own farm on the island.

Life for a young mother on the island was still no bed of roses as she recalled: "You had to take the kids everywhere with you, in the boat or on the back of the horse. Blake fell off and cracked his head open once. You didn't rush to any doctor because there were none to rush to. I just shaved his head and pulled the edges of the cut together with plaster. If it bled too much you'd get some cobwebs to put on it."

Pregnancy was no excuse for stopping work and Mavis was shearing sheep a week before giving birth to her second son. Unlike her mother, who'd had her babies at home, Mavis had her three in hospital, or almost: "Phil was born on the *Philomel* going up to town. They sent down a Fairmile to pick me up but the skipper lost his way. Then I had to lie out on the top deck because they couldn't get me below and it was raining like hell. The baby came about five minutes before we hit the wharf."

As a grandmother, Mavis watched a fourth generation of her family growing up on Waiheke in very different circumstances to her own. She passed away in 1993, and her husband Farley Scott died in 2014.

The Gordon farm still remains in the family. When James Gordon died on November 30, 1952, his only son Colin took over the property, running sheep, cattle and, in recent years, goats. His wife, Wendy (née McNabb), helps manage the farm. Most of the original 638 acres has been sold off for subdivision and vineyards, but about 60 acres are still farmed.

[Colin Gordon passed away at his home on August 29, 2021, while this edition was in preparation.]

The Trace Family

Another early arrival on Waiheke who settled in Awaawaroa Valley was Henry Trace who, with wife Isabella, arrived on the island in the 1860s.

Henry Matthew Trace was born in 1820 in Bristol, and left England as a young man to serve in the merchant navy. Hopes of making a fortune in the Victorian goldfields lured him ashore in Melbourne. Although riches eluded him, he saved what money he earned, married and moved to New Zealand.

What prompted the couple to set up house on an isolated island is not known but early maps show the Trace name on several allotments and the family was to give its hospitality to young Martin Day and his new bride Mary Ann when they arrived on the island in 1867. The couple lived in a nikau whare on Trace land and Isabella later assisted Mary Ann in childbirth.

The former sailor built his home in a valley with no view of the sea. Called "Sunnyside", the house had one attic bedroom reached by a steep staircase. The Traces paid 10/- an acre for land bordering the Awaawaroa Stream which cuts through the island from north to south and, as visiting Anglican parson Reverend Gould observed, was prone to flooding after heavy rains. By the 1880s there was enough land cleared to run a farm.

In February 1882, their only child, Nellie, was enrolled at the school when it opened in a room at the Gordon homestead. The teacher, Mr Hutton, was her uncle, having married Isabella's sister.

The little girl had to climb the steep slope of Maunganui to reach the new school but later rode her pony to lessons. When she was old enough to visit Auckland or Coromandel, this resourceful lass would ride to White's Point at the entrance to Awaawaroa Bay and light a fire to signal to the steamer heading down the Waiheke Channel that there was a passenger to collect.

Her father was tall and lean, a rugged character suited to pioneer life and also deeply religious. He read a chapter of the Bible aloud every night, each one ticked off in the family bible that was later handed down to Nellie. An inscription records:

This Blessed Book presented to Isabella her dear friend, was willed to me by my dear deceased friend and sister in Christ, our Lord and Life, Ellen Battenelli, and now I give it to my dear child Nellie.

Isabella Trace with young Nellie

Religion permeated life at Sunnyside; Church services and Sunday school were often held in the farm house and the Reverend Gould records: *In the evening several met at Mr Trace's and we had singing concluding with family prayer.*

While known for his kindness, this seaman turned farmer could be tough when defending his rights. When miners started digging for manganese on his unfenced boundary, Henry spoke his mind and carried a muzzle loader gun when patrolling the area: the digging soon stopped.

Isabella Trace was of Scottish ancestry, the McPherson clan. Her ladies' tartan plaid was another heirloom that young Nellie was to inherit. She kept in touch with her Scottish relatives as, later, did her granddaughters; a grandson was called Ross McPherson after her clan name.

One young niece who came to stay with Isabella was to remain on Waiheke. Isabella Taylor, the daughter of a Melbourne architect, was 19 when she married John Stephen Hooks in the early 1880s and went to live on the remote Te Patu block on the island's east coast. Separated by rough tracks and kept busy with family commitments, the two women seldom saw each other.

Another relative of Isabella called Painter lived for a time on a block they had bought from Fernandez beyond the manganese mine. A child of this family was also enrolled at the first island school. This particular block of land was later sold to Archibald John Forbes Notman (another relative) and was always referred to as "Notman's".

A 1909 Carey photo (see the section on the Day family) shows Bella Notman, an attractive figure in long frock and hat tied by ribbons, standing beside her Sunday School class in the old school. She and cousin Nellie, in smart riding costumes, both rode side-saddle. To keep the skirt hems down, it was the fashion of the time to weight them by sewing pennies into the lining. Sometimes when Nellie rode up to Gordon's to get mail, she passed an old fellow known locally as "Portuguese Frank" who would call out: "Give me a penny" and Nellie obliged — lightening her skirt hem by a few coins.

This dark-haired, brown-eyed lass met up with James Day, one of Martin's sons and now a crack shearer. Henry approved of this hard-working suitor for his daughter and on April 15, 1901, well-wishers crowded the Northern Co steamer to attend the couple's wedding in Coromandel.

James and Nellie lived in Notman's cottage for a few years but when a cottage was built near Sunnyside, it was easier for Nellie to help her aging parents out. Henry Trace died on 22 February 1908 in his 88th year, followed five years later by Isabella on March 30 aged 82. A burial service was conducted on the hillside near their home; a gravestone marks the site.

In 1914 a spacious new homestead was built for Nellie, James and their growing family. This is now the home of the Philcox family. Nestled in the valley, sheltered from strong winds, it was planned with rooms opening off a wide hall, a big kitchen, and a verandah. Nellie always loved her garden and relaxed there after cooking for the family.

The children, four girls and three boys, attended Waiheke Central school in Te Matuku Valley, walking or riding four up on a pony. Only the boys rode for two hours to reach Man O'War Bay school giving them education six days a week for part of the month.

James Day and Nellie Trace, married April 15, 1901.

Two of the young girls were baptised in their near neighbour Ashwin's house and in 1915 Nellie and James (Jim) took part in a confirmation ceremony which also saw his brother Ted Day and wife confirmed by the Bishop Averill at the Te Matuku schoolroom.

The Days' 640-acre farm included the valley by the stream where shorthorn Jerseys grazed on land top-dressed by hand with fertiliser hauled by horse and sledge. For many years, the 26-strong dairy herd was milked by hand, with daughter Madge (the eldest and first to help) starting the task at daybreak with her father. At best they could milk 13 each in an hour. Then followed the laborious job of separating by hand after which the cream was taken in five-gallon cans down the creek and rowed at high tide out to the Awaawaroa wharf for shipment to the Mt Eden Dairy Factory. To bring supplies back from the steamers, the Days would load their own boat on a rising tide to get as far up the creek as possible; sacks and cases of supplies were then lifted onto a sledge and hauled the last two miles to the house.

In their fertile valley, the Days were never short of water for a thriving vegetable garden and orchard. When wool prices improved, their dairy herd was reduced to two house cows and the farm ran fine-wooled part Merino sheep which Jim would shear with help from his neighbour, Ashwin.

The Day children learned farming and housekeeping skills early and the active life they led kept them remarkably healthy. Their summer holidays were spent camping on Waiheke's beaches — at Careys Bay or even Thumb Point to the east, or northwest over the hill to Pie Melon Bay. A 6ft sledge was loaded up with tents and gear and pulled by two horses.

The Days rode to Gordon's Awaawaroa Post Office for the mail until the 1920s when subdivision at Onetangi saw a post office opened there in 1923. The gradual western shift in the population centre of the island saw the Day girls riding over to Ostend and Onetangi for music lessons and dances. These visits were returned, bringing new friends into the quiet valley to join in farm and family life.

A stronger link to the island's western settlements was forged in the 1940s with the bulldozing of a private road over the hill. Then in his 70s, Jim Day learned to drive on it and was granted his first driver's licence at the age of 73. Nellie was now able to leave the valley by car and the days of saddling up a horse to go visiting were over. Jim and Nellie Day sold their valley farm to Bruce Philcox in 1951 and retired to the Hibiscus Coast.

This branch of the Day family was to retain strong links with the island. Henry, who was named after his grandfather and had inherited the same skills with a rifle, supplemented the family income during the Depression years by shooting rabbits and selling the skins. He was to go shearing for a while in Australia but later returned to the island where he became an active member of the Ostend School Parent-Teacher Association and a member of the Waiheke Roads Board. Asked to give advice on the care of horses, he was to start the first young riders' group on the island.

Allen Day was a member of the first Anglican vestry meeting at Palm Beach on April 29, 1940. He ran the Palm Beach buses and he and his wife managed the store there for some years.

Ross McPherson Day enlisted in the 18th Battalion during the Second World War, serving in Cairo and in the desert 4th RMT before being sent to Greece. In one incident Ross and his mates, attempting to escape, found an untended train. Having had some experience on the railways, Ross was able to drive for some distance before being captured.

Sent to Stalag 88 prison camp in Germany, he slaved in a German paper mill. When the war ended, he was one of many prisoners on the 300-mile walk through Poland — a trek that saw many die en route. He arrived in England weighing under six stone and was nursed back to health by his mother's relatives. His experiences left him very willing to help any ex-servicemen. On returning to Waiheke, he worked as RSA Welfare Officer, becoming the first Waiheke member of the Association to receive the RSA Certificate of Merit at a dinner held in his honour in Auckland.

The Ashwins

Early neighbours of the Gordon and Trace families in the then populous Awaawaroa Valley were William and Mary Ashwin.

William Charles Durham Ashwin had been a member of an English cavalry regiment and probably settled in the valley in the 1870s. He was certainly well established in the early 1880s, just across the stream from Henry and Isabella Trace in a cottage-type home with attic bedrooms.

Mary Ashwin was daughter of another Waiheke family, the Frasers of Waikopou Bay. Her father, John, was one of the original Waipu emigrant settlers from Nova Scotia and she was already well used to pioneer life.

The couple had four children: Margaret, Henry, William, and Lumley. Records show that one of the boys was baptised by a visiting parson in February 1886. Their only daughter, Margaret, was in the first enrolment when the Waiheke Central School opened in 1882.

Interested in music and devoted to the church, William Ashwin was often referred to as "The Deacon".

He was church treasurer and rode over to the valley school to conduct Anglican services every fortnight. He also tried to train some of his small congregation in hymn and psalm singing. Later he held services in his own home.

The Ashwins of Awaawaroa

Henry and William "Bill" Ashwin continued to farm on the island. For a time they worked on the Ōmaru Block on the south coast managing the land for its owner, Beaumont Hotham. Henry married a granddaughter of Te Matuku's first Pākehā settler, Robert McLeod and later managed the McLeod farm.

Young Margaret Ashwin became engaged to Dick Hodgson of Omiha but before they could be married, he was drowned and she chose to remain in the valley, becoming a well-known local character.

She enjoyed the local regattas and in 1902 acted as treasurer for the event which attracted 3000 people. To help supplement her income, she bred ducks and hens and shipped their eggs to city merchants. She became ruthless about the hawks that attacked her birds and searched nearby swamps for hawks' nests, setting rabbit traps for the predators.

Maggie Ashwin also preserved hundreds of bottles of produce for sale in Auckland. Once, while searching for quality fruit, she rode from the valley farm over the range and through the bush to Waikorariki (now Wells) Bay to find laden peach trees in a sheltered coastal orchard. Packing the fruit carefully into tins, she loaded up her pack horse and walked back with enough fruit to keep her working most of the night. Next day the crates of bottles were taken by sledge to the head of the bay and rowed at high tide out to the Coromandel steamer bound for Auckland.

All the boat work had to be done on high tide as the upper reaches of Awaawaroa Bay are very shallow. No wonder that Margaret Ashwin joined other locals in urging the Northern Steamship Co to build a wharf.

Margaret Ashwin's grave lies near that of her parents in the Pioneer Cemetery at Te Matuku.

Her brother, Lumley Ferris Ashwin, survived an early brush with hydatids. He was treated by Sir Carrick Robertson who later used the youngster as a model patient at medical conferences. Lumley served as a lieutenant during the First World War, later returning to Waiheke with a Military Cross and an English wife, Winifred.

Used to town life, Winifred found the muddy, rough roads and isolation a shock, and felt the lack of social life in the valley. Her husband proved to be a progressive farmer, leasing what was later to become the Māori Affairs Block and building the island's first air strip to top-dress his land. This strip, from which Tiger Moths took off with their loads of super, can be seen to the right of Onetangi Road.

In 1928 Lumley was appointed Waiheke's police constable and became a familiar sight patrolling his patch on horseback, using his wartime experience as an officer to help quell local disputes. He continued police work until his retirement in January 1935.

The Ashwins sold out of the Waiheke holding, but the name lives on in old stories, church records and family photos — Mary in dignified black, her daughter in a white dress with only their hands betraying the days of rough work. A fine stand of titoki still shades the little stream near the former Ashwin homestead.

Other early settlers known to have lived in Awaawaroa valley include the McDermott family, William Castle, and Frank Ramsey.

Bernard McDermott, his wife Bridget and son James arrived in Auckland in 1852 and apparently settled on Waiheke for Bernard is listed on the roll in 1855. Nine years later this Irish Roman Catholic family were scraping a living from a five-acre allotment at the head of Awaawaroa Bay. Eight children are said to have been born on the island including Edward, Mary, Bernard, John, Bridget, Catherine, Ann and Chas. Three of the youngsters — James, Edward and John — were also to die on the island as was their father in 1866 at the age of 38. No trace has been found of their graves. Two McDermott sons (James and Barney) became scow masters. Captain Barney McDermott was drowned crossing the Hokianga Bar in 1905.

Their allotment is thought to have passed into the care of a Portuguese known as Frank Ramsey. This dark-skinned old man with his tightly curled white hair told many stories of adventures among the Eskimos in polar seas when he was a whaler. One year, on reaching the New Zealand coast, he jumped ship initially ending up on Great Barrier where he cut firewood for a living.

Frank and his old white horse Polly became familiar figures at the Cowes Bay picnic days. He packed tins of home-grown plums on the quiet beast, walked over to the bay to sell them before riding home. He also carted fruit and veges over to Ostend, selling them to the weekenders who had bought land there.

Unable to read or write, Frank was seen at church carefully holding his hymn book upside down. Still independent as a very old man, he cut firewood on the Jim Day farm while old Polly nibbled on the grass or helped by pulling a light load. Soon even this would be too much for them both.

William Castle lived on the flats beside Awaawaroa Stream in the 1870s, his spacious house with its large parlour and 6ft wide verandah providing the venue for an Anglican Church service held by a visiting parson in November 1881.

He was still listed as a resident in 1884. Belladonna lilies and a Norfolk pine still mark the site where he and his Māori wife lived. She was buried with some of her possessions in the old way, on the hillside near the boundary of Pukeokai.

Waiti Bay

Stony Batter — words that convey several images, all appropriate for the place they name high on the peninsula that commands Waiheke's eastern approaches. Stony Batter sounds like a field of battle, which it was meant to be with its massive World War II gun emplacements; and which it became in a long-running controversy over its ownership. The name could also fit a place battered with stones, such as the huge andesite boulders mysteriously strewn along the ridges like giant marbles. Literally, a batter is a receding slope and the name of Stony Batter actually comes from a place in Ireland, the homeland of the first European owner, Eliezer Gray.

The Gray Family

Born at Moira, County Antrim, in 1831, and reputedly related to Sir George Grey, New Zealand's first Governor, Eliezer Birch Gray and his wife, Mary, were among the passengers on the *Northern Bride* which left Liverpool bound for New Zealand on October 12, 1860. Eliezer's father had intended his son for the legal profession and he was employed for a time by a Belfast solicitor. In 1852, he went to New York where he was in business for a few years before returning to Ireland to marry.

Then New Zealand called and the Grays emigrated with the intention of farming. They bought their first property at Kaipara and later sold it to acquire Waiheke Block No 40 next to the Hooks' land. At Waiti, they built a spacious two-storey home where Mrs Gray often entertained guests from Auckland. With a large orchard, mainly of apple trees, and close to a bay with a good depth of water, the Grays set to developing the farm and raising a family of two sons and two daughters.

The sons, David Sheehan (Davy) and John Hanna (Jack), were to grow into fine young men whose strength, industry and thrift would become legend. Jack was named after his uncle, Thomas Hanna, who had also emigrated on the *Northern Bride* and settled on Waiheke. Jack grew to a height of 6ft 4in, two inches more than Davy, although they shared an equal reputation for their capacity for hard work.

Carrying a lantern, they would both be on the job and ready to start before dawn, returning home at dusk after a day felling bush, cutting tea-tree or fencing. And there was no slacking. They would light a fire to boil the billy for smoko but would not stop work until after a handful of tea had been thrown into the boiling water to brew. Neither was lunch, typically large slabs of cold mutton between homemade bread and butter, a leisurely affair. The brothers would eat quickly and get back to work immediately they finished. This pace they maintained for seven days a week. They cleared 4,000 acres of heavy standing forest in their lifetime, according to the inscription on a memorial in the family graveyard at Waiti. If the area they cleared was not actually as large, there is no questioning the brothers' enduring reputation as efficient and dedicated pioneer farmers.

Davy developed his own method of fencing. He threaded the wire through holes he bored in the posts, many of them puriri, and his fences remained firm and taut for years without battens or staples. As an old man, his brother Jack was out checking the fences and was heard to remark of one post: "Puriri isn't what it used to be. This has only been here 40 years and it's rotted at the bottom."

Eliezer Gray died on June 10, 1903, aged 70, and was buried in the family graveyard. Four years later his sons paid Ted Day and Will Connell 18d an hour to clear a block of about 400 acres between Stony Batter and Ōwhiti. Every tree less than 3ft in diameter was felled. Also on hand was young Arthur Day, then 13, camping in a nikau whare with his uncles and boiling the billy at smoko. He was paid 9d an hour for under-cutting supplejack and scrub. Aged 80, he would still chuckle over the time he gave his elders cheek and they cut down the tree he had climbed to escape from them.

The drive that Davy and Jack piled into their work on the farm had another outlet – at the oars of their 20ft rowboat *Belle*. Their prowess was developed from rowing out, often through choppy seas, to meet the Northern Co vessels in Ruthe's Passage. They each rowed with the usual long oars, their blue boat creating such a bow wave that the steamer skippers, seeing them approaching in the distance, would say "the wee boys are coming".

Dave Gray (left foreground) and Jack, with augur, making a sledge near Waiti woolshed about 1930

Before each Cowes Bay regatta, the brothers would polish *Belle's* keel with blacklead stove polish to smooth her passage through the water. There used to be fierce competition in the paired oars races and the Grays were always keen to win the Settlers' Race from their rivals, the Days and the Peglers.

Four women lived at Waiti: the mother, Mary Gray; her two daughters, Mary Isabelle (Bella) and Jane; and Jack's wife, Dora, the daughter of the widowed Agnes Beckend (née Carey of Wairua). After their wedding, Jack and Dora moved upstairs and it cannot have been the easiest situation for her, sharing her new home with her mother-in-law and two sisters-in-law. The two sisters never married although there is a tale of a brief romance in Bella's life. She is said to have lost her heart to a sailor and had to be persuaded to return home by her father. She was to leave Waiti once again, this time brought back by her two brothers. While Bella's flights of romance are recalled, her sister was known for her copper plate handwriting. Jane kept the farm accounts and wrote cheques on Alfred Buckland forms. Eggs were a woman's pocket money but it is unlikely the hens were aware of this economic arrangement and probably failed to lay their eggs in the right places.

An immense brick oven in the big kitchen was fired up night and day, producing dozens of loaves of bread and scones like dinner plates. The Day twins recalled arriving with the mail and being treated to an afternoon tea which might include a leg of mutton as well as scones, homemade butter and tasty jams, all set out on a long, scrubbed kauri table. The butter, stamped with a thistle pattern, was made in the cool dairy under the orange trees. Elsewhere in the orchard there were rows of apple, apricot, fig and other fruit trees. Sometimes the twins were invited to old Mrs Gray's bedroom — from where she continued to keep a finger on the family's pulse — to see her exquisite crochet work.

Mary Gray died on September 22, 1918, in her 89th year and was buried near her husband, both a long way from their native Ireland. She did not live to see the new house built from kauri felled on the farm, including one monster with a 12ft girth. The logs for the house were towed to Auckland, cut into timber by the Kauri Timber Co and barged back to Waiti Beach where they contributed to a spacious single-storey house looking out across the Waiheke Passage.

Now able to look with pride on their property with its tidy fences, flocks of fine-wooled sheep and herds of cattle, Davy and Jack began to acquire land from neighbouring owners. They bought the Opopo Block, once owned by Thomas Day, and the Huse Bay Block from Bill Hughes, an alert old Welsh veteran of the Crimean War with white hair and beard who lived with only his cats for company.

He accepted the Grays' offer of 10s a week for life for his property and moved his one-room bach to Cowes Bay where he lived free for several years surprising everyone, including the Grays, by surviving into his 90s.

Dave Gray with his bullock team — the last on the island.

A small holding, part of the Webster Block on Kauri Point, is believed to have been purchased from Mrs Wright, a hard-working, no-nonsense widow who ran a small sheep farm with her son. And on the north coast, the Gray brothers are thought to have acquired land from their uncle, Thomas Hanna, and a block owned by James and Harold Cairns, two brothers who were active in the community between 1880 and 1890 and are believed to be buried in the Hooks' family burial ground on Te Patu. By the time they had bought the Man O'War Block from W J Rutherford,

Davy and Jack owned about 4,000 acres. Financially secure, they could afford to stockpile their wool clip through three years of the Depression while they waited for better prices.

Still erect and handsome men, the Gray brothers were beginning to slow down and were unwilling to accept the changes of the time. They were to be seen building a new sledge in the 1930s; not for them the new roads or the vehicles which they could now easily afford. Growing old and set in their ways, they had trouble attracting and keeping farm labour.

Jack died on September 7, 1935, and was followed to the family grave at Waiti by his wife Dora. After all the years they had spent together, Davy must have missed his brother desperately. He had Bella for company until her death. Now old and frail, she had not lost her culinary skills, especially her way with white Irish soda bread.

Allan Insley, who used to bring Davy to Cowes Bay in his launch *Pikau*, remembered him as a tall, striking man, immaculately dressed, a white beard contrasting with his tanned face. No one expected him to survive his brother by 17 years, nor did they predict that he would astonish the whole district by taking a wife, his housekeeper, Grace Stow.

The Japanese attack on Pearl Harbour on December 7, 1941, and the spread of war to the Pacific created fears of invasion in New Zealand. Among the defences hastily erected were three gun emplacements on the Gray property at Stony Batter, part of a ring of fortresses around Auckland Harbour.

The largest of these defence stations, Stony Batter comprised 3000ft of tunnels and stairways, magazine chambers, plotting room, engine room and three oil stores — all to feed the three huge 9.2in guns capable of firing a 150kg shell 45 kilometres over the horizon or at inland targets from Wellsford to Te Kauwhata.

A team of 200 men arrived in October 1942 to build the concrete labyrinth which first required the construction of a wharf at Man O'War Bay and a metalled road up to the site. In vain did Davy's solicitor try to convince the old man that this was his opportunity to use the metal on the farm to build a road down to Waiti. Davy was adamant; there would be no strangers or cars coming down to his home, although he did request use of the new wharf and road from Stony Batter to load stock.

While Stony Batter sprang alive with activity, the rest of the farm was running down. There was talk of contractors dumping loads of manure in gullies instead of spreading it on pastures, paddocks were reverting to weeds and tea-tree, and holes in the floor of the old woolshed by the beach went unrepaired.

In his last years, Davy Gray made contact with a cousin and namesake who was running a top-dressing firm in Perth and invited him to Waiheke, presumably in the hope that he might buy the farm. The Australian David Gray, aged 60 and looking plump and prosperous, arrived with an agricultural expert to look over the land. He was not impressed, saying: "Waiti is tranquil, beautiful — but a hundred years behind the times." His younger cousin's judgment on his life's work must have caused Davy no little pain.

His death in 1952 was followed by a funeral service attended by many local and city dignitaries who were brought to Waiti by launch from Auckland, among them F J C Wilson, the manager of Alfred Buckland & Co which had handled the Grays' wool clip for many years.

Calling at Surfdale, the launch collected well-known locals including Donald Bruce, Bob Burns, Arthur Day and his son, Boy. Jack McIntosh boarded at Orapiu. After being landed at the shingle beach, the funeral party carried the coffin ashore at low tide and laid it on the long kauri table in the kitchen before its final journey to the family burial ground on the rise behind the homestead. Major McCallum, the commander of the Salvation Army establishment on Rotoroa, conducted the service before about 80 mourners. Now the Gray family was together again, mother and father, their four children, and Dora.

Waiti Station was sold at auction; an Aucklander, Dr Harbutt, making the top bid of £38,000. The next decades brought electricity and a road link with the rest of the island, and the property was eventually acquired by John Spencer in 1981.

At Stony Batter, where the guns had long since been dismantled after firing only a few test shots and sold for scrap to, it is believed, a Japanese buyer, a new battle was brewing. Mr Spencer's attempt to persuade the Crown to sell him the 99 acres at the centre of his 4450-acre property sparked a local protest which created national interest and Government intervention. As a result, the gun emplacements now stand within a 45-acre public reserve surrounded by 53 acres of Crown land and can be reached over a public walkway.

Wairua (Carey) Bay

Wairua Bay on the northern coast takes its European name of Carey from the family which settled there in the 1870s and built a home which became a centre of warm hospitality on Waiheke for almost a century.

The Carey Family

The Careys came from Arbroath, a fishing town renowned for its "smokies" (kippered herring) on Scotland's east coast where William Carey was a gentleman farmer. In 1866, he and his wife, Margaret, boarded the *Viscount Canning* bound for New Zealand with six of their eight children. The remaining children stayed behind to look after an elderly aunt while another aunt, Margaret's sister Mary Nicol, joined the family for the six-month voyage to the other side of the world.

Arriving in Auckland, the Careys found temporary accommodation in the Albert Barracks before coming to Waiheke where William Carey had bought land. Long delays in finalising land transactions were not uncommon at this time and, until 1871 when the purchase was approved, the Careys lived on land owned by Joe Hodgson, who also helped out with advice, assistance and cutters to ship their firewood for sale in Auckland.

Cutting firewood was a task for which William Carey would have employed workers back in Scotland. For his three boys, Robert, William (Will) and Alec, the labour of felling trees would have been a new challenge, as the domestic privations of the Careys' temporary new home in nikau whares were for their gently-bred mother, aunt and three sisters, Marjorie (Madge), Elizabeth (Lizzie) and Agnes. The making of a proper home had to wait until well after the Careys moved onto their own land in 1871. Still in makeshift accommodation, the women proved capable homemakers in any situation. *A family named Carey have made a comfortable home,* reported a visiting Anglican clergyman in 1877.

Two years later, after establishing his family on their island farm, William Carey died at the age of 65 on November 26, 1879. His sons carried on, clearing the land and selling wood for an income. In 1882, Rev Gould, doing the rounds of Waiheke settlers on a borrowed horse, wrote:

Rode to the Careys, found the young men busy with the bullock dray loading a cutter with firewood. The cutter was high and dry on the sand and the question was whether she could be loaded before the tide surrounded her. I helped the skipper, Joe Hodgson, to stow away while his mate helped the two Careys. Thirty tons of firewood were shipped. At the last load the bullocks were almost on the swim but the way William (Will) Carey managed those animals was a sight worth seeing.

Will's skill with the bullock team was an inheritance from his father. So was his skill with horses, which was shared by the rest of the family. They rode thoroughbreds, some partially clipped, with ease and confidence. All their saddles and gear were kept oiled and immaculate. A photograph shows Lizzie and Madge, in long dark frocks and white bib aprons, lunging a young horse on Wairua Beach. Diary notes reveal they were generous with their talent, breaking in neighbours' horses.

Will and Alec put the gear on the filly and she was quiet. Madge and Alec took the filly to Long Beach (Onetangi). Hotham visited to get a colt. Filly taken to Owhiti ...

Horses were central to social life on the island. The Careys would ride to Onetangi for the early race meetings, including one in December 1883 for which they and other settlers raised money for prizes. Visits to neighbours were made on horseback, setting off in the morning, catching up with the news over midday dinner, and returning early in the afternoon to milk the cows.

As well as milk, the Careys' herd of Shorthorns yielded cream for making butter which they sometimes sold to the Days, Browns, Castles and McLeods. Lizzie made 18lbs of butter one morning and still had energy to tidy the strawberry bed in the afternoon. Elsewhere on the developing farm, August 1884 brought the arrival of the first lambs.

The Carey family of Wairua around the turn of the century.

Fifteen years after the Careys took possession of Wairua, they started building their home. On February 2, 1886, the cutter Tay arrived with the timber, only to be held offshore for four days to ride out a storm which made the exposed northern beach unapproachable. Meanwhile Joe Hodgson started work on the foundations and, when the sea had calmed, Will yoked up the bullocks to drag the beams from the beach to the building site.

Construction started on February 8 and ceased the next day, being the Sabbath. Monday saw real progress with the erection of the frame; three days later the roof went on. Henry Cairns, a neighbour, arrived to build the chimneys, a task he finished in a week just as Joe was fixing the last of the window sashes. Alec and his sisters could then start on the interior, tacking scrim to the walls before wallpapering.

Within six weeks, by March 22, the house was finished. Behind the verandah facing out to Little Barrier Island were the parlour and spacious dining room. On either side of the central hallway was a bedroom and, in the attic under a peaked roof, two more bedrooms. The long kitchen opened onto a large storeroom, big enough to hold a year's supply of food. To fill it, vast quantities of flour, sugar, oatmeal, salt, tea, candles, matches and other essentials were landed from a cutter which would return to Auckland with the Careys' firewood as payment for merchants ready to barter. Sometimes, Alec would take the opportunity to go into Auckland on the cutter. He would have a lengthy shopping list with special instructions from each of the women. Returning heavy-laden he would land at Huruhe and leave the packages in a cottage, coming back the next day to collect them with a horse and sledge.

In their new home the Carey family quickly gained a reputation for their hospitality. The Watsons, Kennedys, Grays, Days and McLeods all rode over to Wairua on occasions for midday dinners carefully planned by Lizzie whose culinary flair included such refinements as finishing mutton dishes with caper sauce. When a beast was killed it was usually shared with neighbours with some kept for salting as corned beef. Pigeons, wild turkeys and domestic poultry added variety to menus as did fish, in plentiful supply with 25 snapper landed in one day from the rocks in the bay. A creek supplied water for the vegetable garden and an orchard where citrus trees still bear fruit, flourished in the sheltered warmth of the valley, yielding russet apples, peaches and plums. Fuchsias bloomed near the house where a white shell path contrasted with the green lawns and neatly trimmed hedges of boxthorn and tecoma.

Lizzie, so dignified, was happy to maintain the standards the family had observed in their Scottish home. Meals were taken at a long dining table which, with extra leaves, could seat 12 and was re-set after every meal with a starched white tablecloth, each napkin in its initialled, silver holder. The family silver, polished every Saturday, included an epergne with three crystal vases kept filled with fresh flowers. Meals were served on a willow pattern dinner set and guests were offered a choice of India or China tea served in exquisite green and white cups. Will and Alec always drank from moustache cups. After dinner, guests would adjourn to the parlour where Lizzie or Agnes would play the piano.

Their mother, Margaret Balfour Carey, lived to the age of 84. She died on February 1, 1898 and was buried in the family cemetery beside her husband and her sister, Mary Nicol. Of her three daughters only Agnes took a husband, a Captain Beckend whose ship was lost at sea leaving Agnes with a young daughter, Dora, who was later to marry Jack Gray of Waiti Bay. Lizzie managed the home while Madge preferred to work outdoors, capably handling the cattle and sheep, maintaining the poultry run and feeding the native teal ducks.

Alec Carey, around 1921.

Together, the two sisters maintained a striking appearance, dressed in long dark skirts with, perhaps, a blue denim blouse for work and dainty silk one for best. Their slender waists were encircled by Petersham belts, two inches wide with engraved, silver buckles. On horseback they always wore riding habits. In a photograph, Madge looks a magnificent figure in full riding habit, smart bowler hat, buttoned-up riding boots, mounted side-saddle on her thoroughbred, "Twilight".

Madge died in 1929 and was buried near her parents, in the family cemetery shaded by old pohutukawa trees at Matapihi Point on the farm she loved. Lizzie survived all her brothers and sisters, living until 1933, the last of the original Scottish settlers to be laid to rest at Wairua. Will had died in 1922 at the age of 78. In his later years his faithful companion was his cat, "Skipper".

Alec took up a new hobby, photography, at the age of 60 and revealed a remarkable talent, becoming the district's official photographer. A handsome man of distinguished appearance and immaculate dress, especially when off to town, Alec took his camera everywhere, capturing regattas, race days, sale days, local weddings, family groups, seascapes. When he died in 1931, aged 81, he left behind an invaluable legacy — a photographic record of life on Waiheke after the turn of the century. Some of his photographs are to be found in the Auckland and Waiheke museums.

It was up to Robert, the only brother to marry, to ensure the Carey name lived on at Wairua. He had moved to farm a property near Pt Charles after his marriage to Jane Hunter-Blunt. Their son, William, wife Julia and children, Kenneth and Margaret, came to Wairua for holidays and would return in the Depression years to run the farm.

The third generation of Careys also met hardship in the first years at Wairua. Prices for meat and wool were low and, as their pioneer forebears had done before them, they lived a basic life, affording only the necessities of flour, sugar, salt, kerosene, delivered once a year from Auckland by Blue Boat. For anything extra, Kenneth and Margaret rode over to the store at Onetangi. They milked four Shorthorn red poll cows, making their own butter. Their wool was hauled from the woolshed to the beach by horse and sledge, loaded on to a flat-bottomed punt two bales at a time, and taken out to a waiting launch. When William died in 1964, the farm passed into the hands of the fourth generation, his son Kenneth, who

carried on the family ownership of Wairua until it was sold in 1968 —
97 years after the arrival of his great-great-grandfather, William Carey,
from Scotland. Wairua was purchased by Phillip and Diana Goldman,
who farmed the land until Diana's death in 2020. Bruce Plested, owner
of nearby Pie Melon Bay (Rorohara), bought the property in 2021.

The Waiheke Historical Society has books from the Carey estate in
its museum. One set, beautifully bound, is inscribed *Margt Carey* and a
Bible carries the inscription *Mary Nicol, Arbroath, May 29, 1844.*

Ōwhiti Bay: Ryan Family

The broad sweep of Ōwhiti's white sands attracted John Ryan and his
family in the 1880s. Born in 1852, John Ryan was descended from an early
pioneer family. In 1874, he married Sarah Hunter-Blunt, the sister of Jane
who married Robert Carey from their good neighbours along the coast.

Little is recorded of the pioneer days at Ōwhiti. Kauri logs were
shipped out across the beach and a flying fox above the bay was used
to transport manganese from a small mine on the south side of the road
until the metal's low price ended the project.

John Ryan's granddaughter, Rita Dean, is remembered on Waiheke
where she and her husband were caretakers of the Ōmaru Bay property
in the 1940s. The daughter of John and Sarah's eldest son, George, Rita
is well remembered by the community for her many kindnesses and
her creative cake decorating which brightened many a birthday and
celebration.

Rarohara (Pie Melon Bay)

As its name suggests, Pie Melon Bay was once famous for its melons. Made into jam with a little ginger added for flavour and sweetness and spread over homemade butter and bread, melons from the bay provided a tasty afternoon treat for many children on their homecoming from school. Their flavour is remembered better than the identity of the people who planted the melons and named the bay after them.

If there were melons in the bay when John Telford visited in December 1849, they made less impression on him than the people living there at the time. Telford, who worked for the Church Missionary Society in Auckland, had sailed to Waiheke on Bishop Selwyn's *Undine*.

He came ashore at Huruhi (Man O'War) Bay and walked to the bay, then called Rarohara and the site of one of Chief Patene's villages. The men were out fishing and, after pitching his tent, he entered into conversation with the women of the village. His diary records:

7th: rose by break of day ... had service with them and afterwards school... I tried them in native words and spelling and the arithmetic tables ... spoke to them of the sun and stars which evidently afford them great delight. 9th, Sunday: after forenoon service, had school with both old and young. 10th: had prayers again as usual and school ... had a conversation with Patene. Find him to be a most agreeable person. He is perhaps the plainest speaker of the native language I have ever met.

If there were no melons then, they must have arrived in the next decade. A European party of three men and two women, canoeing around the island in February 1858, walked over from Pūtiki (Ostend). According to Elizabeth Stack's *Maoriland Adventures*, they *had a delightful walk to Melon Bay through dense forest . . . and we were invited by William Thompson to help ourselves to melons.*

Then they followed a narrow coastal path to Chief Patara's pa about a mile and a half distant.

Patara was a noble looking man with a fine open countenance and we were honoured by his company back to Melon beach where he held a Maori service which we attended. There were about 20 adult Maori present, all most fervent in their responses.

Although Europeans now knew the bay by its fruit, officialdom preserved the Māori name. When George Graham was allotted the large Onetangi Block (1150 acres) in 1868, he is also recorded as taking the neighbouring 460-acre Rarohara Block at the same time. Its eastern boundary intersected with the Wairua Block of the Careys who used to ride over the hills to gather melons for their summer jam making.

On August 8, 1883, the Careys recorded the landing from the cutter *Henry* of the first European family to live at Pie Melon Bay.

Henry Brown had married Mary Ann Hodgson of Omiha in 1869 and, together with their daughters, Fanny and Ethel, they arrived at Pie Melon Bay 14 years later. Will Carey went over to help them carry their possessions up from the beach and Fanny and Ethel were later to make regular journeys to their nearest neighbours to buy butter.

How long they stayed there is unknown and similar uncertainty surrounds the occupancy of the Thomas Day family who followed them. Meanwhile, the melons flourished. A story by Miss Ivy Smytheman, writing about the first boarding house which Mrs Hindman opened in Pūtiki (Ostend) in 1916, includes a reference to Pie Melon Bay where *in season, the melons grow abundantly... Men offered the proprietress of the boarding house extra horses if they wanted to form a party to go over and get some for jam making.*

Rarohara was to become known as the home of some of Waiheke's resident millionaires. Brendon Whelan, who owned the rights to the

Letraset technology in New Zealand, built a distinctive Spanish-style house beside the beach. Today the property is owned by Bruce Plested, chairman of Mainfreight.

Rore A Maeāea
(Woodside Bay)

This open bay facing Maraetai was, according to legend, the scene of a terrible massacre in about 1200AD. It is said a party of Maraetai Māori, led by their chief Maeāea, accepted an invitation to a feast from the Waiheke people at Ōmaru. They sailed across Te Maraetai (enclosed sea) between the mainland and Waiheke in canoes but, as they landed on the beach they were enclosed in hand-nets and speared — this being the method of attack at that time. Not one returned to tell the tale, but there were later retaliatory raids from mainland Māori. The scene of the massacre is known as Te Rore A Maeāea (the snaring of Maeāea).

Ryan and Kissling

An early map of Waiheke shows an Ōmaru Block on 140 acres with a wide flat and easy access by sea. The first recorded owners of the block were Ryan and Kissling who between them owned 1400 acres. Kissling, a manager for the Bank of New Zealand, and his partner had married two sisters and built identical houses on the block.

Land was cleared for potatoes but the first crop was spoiled by heavy frost. A parson recorded his visit to the bay in 1877 and the kindness shown to him by the Kisslings.

Family quarrels led to the failure of this early partnership and one of the houses was shipped over to Pakatoa Island. The remaining homestead, a plain, square building of kauri with high ceilings and two tall brick chimneys, was restored by a later owner, Peter Lee.

The sea-facing parlour is heated by a large brick open fireplace with a cast iron fender and iron tongs for blazing wood. A family-sized kauri table stands near a window. Across the narrow hall, the master bedroom has a small, ornate corner cupboard built into the wall. In the dining room which is lined by 9in kauri boards, the scrim has been stripped and an inscription reads: *Fred Waitae May 19 1878* — perhaps the carpenter leaving his signature.

In the sheltered valley at the back of a house was a spring near an orchard of which only old figs and plums remain. There are memories of a promontory and small jetty which disappeared when the beach was quarried for shingle in the early 1900s. The house was used as an early post office: Charles Frederick Evans-Kissling is listed in December 1878 as Ōmaru Postmaster. In 1881, Kissling was also elected to the first Anglican Church committee in Awaawaroa Valley. During clerical visits, his front parlour became the venue for a service of up to 25 people.

Beaumont Hotham

The next owner of the property, Beaumont George Hotham, continued the tradition of hospitality to visiting clergy and the task of postmaster, a position he held from 1882 to 1884 when records for Ōmaru end. The son of a lord and nephew of an admiral, Hotham knew nothing of New Zealand farming and employed the Ashwin brothers from Awaawaroa to manage the land.

Toward the close of the century, Lady Hotham, living in England, became anxious about the welfare of her son. She persuaded the son of the local vicar in her home parish to come to New Zealand and report on Beaumont George.

It was a long wait as Francis Woodhouse sailed for Auckland, and the news, when it came, was not good. Shortly after the vicar's son reached Waiheke Island, Beaumont Hotham died.

Woodhouse stayed on as caretaker and later took an option on the land, selling 1100 acres to Judge O'Brien of Pūtiki. After a good sale of sheep he was able to buy the remaining block with the house, and in 1901 he married and a daughter Lucy was born.

When Woodhouse sold to James Rodgers Foster in 1904, the bay initially retained his name but later became known as Woodside.

The Foster Family

A former miller, Foster farmed the Ōmaru Block until 1915. In 1909, using the old shed by the beach and local timber, he built an 18ft cutter christened the *Merry Widow*.

His son, Edward Brunton (Ted) Foster, saw the commercial value of the shingle in the bay. Then a mate on a scow, he negotiated a contract with Ferro Concrete to remove shingle for the construction of Grafton Bridge and the railway wharf in Auckland. He was paid 3d a cubic metre.

The scows *Saucy Kate* and *Janet* were among those that removed the shingle from Woodside Bay before restrictions were placed on the trade. Eventually the shingle bearing portion of the block was purchased by the firm of Winstones.

Ted Foster married Lily May Gordon, daughter of their neighbour in Awaawaroa Bay, and later became well known as the manager of the City Council Transport and the popular Auckland trolley buses. Lily acquired a 77-acre block in Awaawaroa Valley by ballot on November 27, 1914: the bulk of the Ōmaru Block (130 acres) was subsequently bought by James Gordon. Family links to the island remained as their son, Albert (Bert) Foster, who had some vivid memories of early days on Waiheke, was to return to the island when he retired from engineering work in 1949.

Further sales of the Ōmaru Block left the original Kissling home standing in only five acres. Perched on a grassy bank above the beach, this old kauri building has seen more than 100 years of boat traffic down the channel — from Northern Co steamers and shingle-loaded scows to the present-day yachts and pleasure boats.

Frank Annadale

In the small bay just to the east of Woodside, a spacious bungalow was built of totara in 1910 which became home to Frank Annadale. A Scotsman, white-haired and all of 6ft 6ins tall, he was an imposing figure on his big horse as he rode over the hill to Awaawaroa for his weekly mail collection. A friendly character, he enjoyed a lively chat with postmistress Ethel Gordon and became involved in island life, buying shares in the Waiheke Sale Yards and appointed in 1913 as one of the trustees managing the Te Matuku Bay cemetery.

His house, built on a rise above the sea, was about 1500ft^2 in area with a distinctive hip roof and wide verandahs. Big airy rooms opened off the main hall, one lined with books, the others with glorious views of the sea and passing boats. Steps led down to the bay where Annadale moored his boat. The first was a 28ft cutter called *Glengarry* which was later replaced by a launch and moored in a less exposed site in a corner of Woodside Bay.

Stories are told of his "man", a diminutive character called "My Man Friday". Annadale would sit down to a delicious meal, served by his man correctly attired in black trousers and white shirt, a napkin over his arm. Naturally Annadale was desolate when "Man Friday" died, and soon departed the island — one of many interesting characters who found a certain quality of life on Waiheke.

Later owners of this property were the Harveys and Miss Clere who farmed efficiently in a friendly partnership. Enthusiastic members of the Federated Farmers and the Women's Division of the Farmers' Union, they also became a part of the district life.

The Langwell family owned the 170-acre block in the 1970s, and were deeply shocked when the house and its contents were destroyed by fire. The property has since been developed as vineyards.

Oriote (Connells) Bay

History embraces Oriote (Connells) Bay like a warm spell, drifting like the tide around the shell-encrusted remains of an ancient tractor, glowing from polished kauri floors and forever etched into wood where the pupils of Waiheke's first school carved their initials. Once the site of a thriving general store, post office and boat fuelling depot, this quiet east coast bay has now lost most of its bustle, but none of its charm. Cottages built in the 1890s were carefully renovated by a later owner, Warren Fowler. A headland sheltering the bay is still known to older residents as Langs Point after a family that lived and worked in the area for some years.

Lang/McDonald

A Mr Lang was a timber worker who cut taraire from the Ōmaru Block into the usual three-foot billets for haulage by horse sled and destined, it is said, for bakery ovens in Auckland. In nearby Te Matuku Bay he also cut pohutukawa blocks which were squared to size for Calliope Dock. The solid, heavy blocks were estimated to measure about 6ft by 2ft by 18in.

Lang apparently had a working partnership with Robert William McDonald, who was allotted the 46 acres of the Oriote Bay Block 45 in the early 1870s and who was married to Elizabeth Lang. McDonald owned a boat which was used to ship tons of firewood cut from around the Ōmaru Bay area into Auckland. On the 1884 survey map, there is no house shown in Oriote Bay, but "McDonald's House" is noted at Opuihi Bay

171

on the north side of Ōmaru Bay where there was a good depth of water and a sheltered shore. McDonald also owned the 32-acre Block 80 which adjoined his other allotment.

McDonald's House, said to have been built by a marine biologist whose coastline explorations created rumours that he was a spy, still stands. Later it was owned by Berridge Spencer and used as a holiday home. John Spencer, who later purchased the Man O'War Bay Station, spent many holidays at this house as a boy.

One guest was a Mr Allom, an elderly surveyor who noticed the awkward climb locals had into Ōmaru Bay when the tide was in and surveyed an easy gradient over the cliff. Mr Spencer made this available to people walking through his property to and from Connell's store, commemorating the 76-year-old surveyor's work by erecting a "76th Ave" sign on the picturesque track.

The Lang name was to become a familiar one on Waiheke. A son, John Lang, married a member of an old Irish family, Mary Migan, and a descendant, Robert Lang of Palm Beach, surveyed the proposed extension of electricity to the island's eastern end for the Auckland Electric Power Board in 1954, before the road connecting East and West was built. Bob Lang was then overseer of the Power Board staff on Waiheke and had the physically demanding task of surveying power supply routes both to the eastern bays and the southern coast of McLeod's and Gordon's Bays — mostly on foot.

Robert Lang had close family relationships with the Frasers of Waikopou, the Ashwins of Awaawaroa Valley, the McDonalds and Migans. A further link with an old Waiheke family was made when he married a Parris from Park Point — part of the Te Huruhi block on the south coast.

Henry Hewin

The kauri timber cottages that still stand in Oriote Bay were probably built by Henry Hewin in the 1890s. He constructed the cottages with two kitchens so that half could be let to summer visitors and he also ran a small store catering mainly to local fishermen. His name also features in the local regatta.

His five-acre block boasted a strawberry garden from which fruit was sold both locally and in Auckland, and he had enough grazing for a house cow. A resourceful bush carpenter, Henry made use of available trees, trimming them to shape if no sawn timber were available. His work could be seen in several of the island's early cottages where he used scantling of trimmed tea-tree. It was he who built the homestead in Hooks Bay out of locally grown kauri, adding rooms as the family increased, and organised the moving of a cottage on rollers for the Pegler family in Ōmaru Bay. Some of the eastern end holiday cottages had been shipped over from Thames after the gold boom and it is possible that one of the cottages in the bay could have arrived that way and been adapted by Hewin.

Connells Bay, pictured in the early 1900s, is little changed today.

Henry Hewin had three children, Walter, Lily and Mabel, who attended the school in Te Matuku. When he sold the property to William Connell in 1908, both the bay and enlarged store became a hub of activity on Waiheke.

The Connells

The Connell family's history in New Zealand can be traced back to the emigration of a Cornish family in the mid-1800s. "Great grandmother Curley" lived in Auckland and Howick before her husband John, who was with the 2nd Waikato Regiment, was posted to the garrison town of Alexandria (Pirongia). It was here that their daughter, Ellen Curley, was to meet a dashing young Irishman who was then a member of Von Tempsky's Forest Rangers.

Major Von Tempsky was a Polish nobleman who trained in a Prussian military academy after Poland was occupied by Prussia. A professional soldier who learned bush craft and jungle fighting, he was put in charge of a company of Rangers especially equipped for bush fighting during the Land Wars. He was also a friend of the Curley family.

Two Irish brothers, Patrick and Joseph O'Connell, had joined the Rangers and Patrick had just completed a successful mission carrying a message through enemy territory when he went to an Army ball where he danced with blue-eyed Ellen. It was love at first sight and, despite the fact that he was Catholic and she Anglican, it was marriage at the age of 17 for Ellen.

On discharge from the army, Patrick's skill with horses got him a job at an Auckland stables. Later, while working at Huntly, he was killed in a mining accident leaving his widow with seven young children. Ellen's mother, Mrs Curley, took charge of two of her children, William James and Mercie Connell, who moved with her to Waiheke.

When they leased the property at Waikorariki (Wells Bay) from Dr Coates, Mercie was 13 and Will 16. Their new home was in a spacious house close to the sandy bay with its deep-water anchorage; during summer they moved into a nearby cottage, letting the house to visitors. They planted vegetables on the flat and sold fruit from the orchard; cows were milked and butter made to sell at 6d a pound.

As there was little grass for grazing and few fences, cows were turned out to forage in the bush and Mercie would often walk miles searching for them — small wonder this teenager longed to return to Auckland and the excitement of town life where she had enjoyed Fullers Opera and even met some of the singers.

But both young people were to stay on the island. Will met and later married Jane Day, while curly-haired Mercie was to marry Ted Day (see Te Matuku Bay chapter). Will and Jane married in a simple ceremony performed in Dr Coates's study and Will, a young man of initiative who was not afraid of hard work, bought Hewin's block at Oriote, taking over the store and buying about 70 acres of land which they later added to by purchasing 450 acres in adjacent Arran Bay.

Will soon made improvements. He bought and repaired an old boat that had been used as an Auckland water taxi. Christened the *Roller* boat, this 17ft craft with its mast, sails and three pair of oars was used to bring a variety of stores down from Auckland to the much-expanded shop. Later he bought a 26ft launch, the *Miro*, which was powered by a 6hp Kapia engine and did the Auckland run in three hours using a four-gallon tin of benzine for the return trip. As he was on call to transport sick people to the city, Will kept a stretcher in the cabin so patients could lie flat.

Will Connell as a young man; Will and Jane in later years

Apart from running the store, Will with brother-in-law, Ted, often worked on contract bush felling, sometimes staying away for days on end, living in nikau whares and only coming home on Saturdays for clean clothes and supplies. As trips to the city for store supplies were sometimes delayed by bad weather, Jane often had to cope on her own. Once, alone with a baby and other young children, a huge easterly gale brought high tides that washed away the shoreline and flooded a boatshed carrying away all sorts of supplies.

The market for kauri gum was still strong in the early 1900s and Will's son Eric remembers one Māori family who lived and worked on a nearby gumfield coming to trade with his father.

They'd bring the gum into our yard every Sunday, already scraped clean, and tip it out on mats in the yard. Dad bought it and then sold it in town.

Having first ascertained the market price from city merchants, Will would always pay that price.

There were eight youngsters in the Connell family, but tragedy struck in 1911 when little Gladys Winifred, then only two years and seven months old, became ill. The seas were mountainous and the frantic father could not risk taking the boat out. By the time they got the little girl to hospital in Auckland, it was too late. She died of peritonitis and is buried in the island's first cemetery at the head of Te Matuku inlet. Words inscribed on the tombstone eloquently express her parents' grief.

A bud the Gardener gave us
A pure and lovely child.
He gave it to our keeping
To cherish undefiled.
But just as it was opening
To the glory of the day,
Down came the Heavenly Gardener
And took our bud away.

Eric might have shared his sister's fate but for the fact that a Mr Goldie who then ran the Salvation Army launch to Rotoroa was able to take the sick five-year-old up to Auckland Hospital where his infected appendix was removed in time.

In 1915 Jane and Will, as well as Mercie and Ted, took comfort from an Anglican confirmation service in the school room at Te Matuku. It was a unique occasion as the last confirmation on Waiheke was in 1882 but, unfortunately, the rain came down in buckets, drenching Bishop Averill as well as the worshippers who sloshed there through the mud.

This school, to which the Connell youngsters had a steep climb and long walk, had 40 pupils when Eric started, but later dwindled to a roll of just seven and the youngest Connell daughter eventually had to finish her schooling by correspondence. When the school closed in the 1930s, the Education Board put the building up for tender. Because access was difficult, the tender was given to Will and the old windows and weatherboards were used to renovate the family's home. The names of youngsters etched in the wood have been preserved by the present owners.

The children had a busy life growing up in the bay. There were always jobs waiting: cows to milk, washing to be done, vegetable gardens and fruit orchards to be tended as well as helping out in the store. Memories of the bay include the long rows of golden quinces which were picked and packed for Thomson and Hills (Oak jams) earning 3d a pound. There were also supplies to be delivered and boats to be met. "We never seemed short of something to do," says Eric. "There were always other kids around, we had our chores of course, but if you didn't get out of the way and play, you'd get more jobs to do."

The family ran a small farm, supplying fresh milk and separating the surplus to export cream to Auckland. That stopped when the Mt Eden dairy factory closed and milk was then processed too far out of town to make it worth the trip. Apart from the store, they operated an "on demand" water transport service.

In 1913, Will built a barge which was to become a familiar sight in the Waiheke Passage. It carried bales of wool, drums of dieseline, petrol, sacks of flour, fowl food, bags of sugar and other supplies, including heavy goods for farmers and more modest supplies for the weekenders in the various isolated bays. At low tide, a hand barrow minus wheels was used to carry goods ashore or sometimes goods were hauled up the beach by horse and sled, work made easier when the Connells built their own jetty.

One rather startling wartime experience in the quiet bay was when a launch owned by a Mr Wilkinson turned up to buy petrol with a machine gun mounted on the deck and the Army in charge. As Will filled the tank, the owner whispered "Von Luckner has escaped." This German naval officer was under arrest on Motuihe Island at the time and had made off in a stolen boat.

During the epidemic which followed the Great War in 1918, the Connells kept the whole eastern district of Waiheke in supplies as the barge had special permission to enter Auckland Harbour where it was fumigated to avoid spreading the epidemic.

By the 1920s, Waiheke was becoming even busier. Will bought land in Arran Bay in 1924 and sold some sections; cottages were built and let. With more customers living in the district, Will decided he needed a larger boat. Originally built for the Gordons in 1910 and christened *Beatrice* after one of their daughters, the boat was later bought by John Pegler and re-named *Edna* after his daughter. When Will bought her, the boat was again re-christened, this time after his daughter, *Lola*, and was used to collect passengers and goods from the steamer as it plied the Waiheke Passage (the stretch of water between Waiheke and Ponui).

It was a great day when the *Baroona*, a vessel owned by the Waiheke Passage Co, first came on that run. She was already well known to the Connells as she had previously been used as a fishing trawler in the Gulf and the boys used to row out to her to barter for fish. Now the *Lola* was to meet the re-fitted passenger vessel in the Passage to collect visitors who would step off *Baroona*'s lower deck onto the launch. One old lady was overheard to say confidently of this manoeuvre: "Of course, Mr Connell will take care of me."

More and more boats were calling at the jetty to refuel and fill up with fresh water. In summer the bay was alive with activity as yachts and launches anchored in the sheltered waters and people wandered past the big old mulberry tree to the store. City folk were often astonished at the variety of stock the small shop held: you could buy just about anything from a baby's bottle or bootlaces to corks, fish hooks or spark plugs as well as the usual grocery lines. Connell's boats were kept in meticulous order — all brought ashore for scraping and cleaning in the quiet season. The old *Roller* boat was in use for about 50 years and the barge carried more and more drums of dieseline as power plants were installed in the island bays.

After the Second World War, in 1946, Eric Connell and his wife Pearl took over the store and life was easier for the senior Connells who retired to one of the cottages. It was a well-deserved rest for the couple who had raised eight children, run a small farm, developed a store that was known throughout the Gulf and had always been ready to lend a helping hand in the district. Will died in his 77th year on December 12, 1956, and Jane on August 18, 1960, aged 79.

Another of their sons, Les, ran sheep and beef cattle on the farm, sharing the cost of a topdressing airstrip with the McIntosh and Day families. Stock was shipped to and from Waiheke by scow. The family nearly lost one Jersey bull which, offloaded into the water in Connells Bay, decided to head out to the Coromandel with Eric rowing in hot pursuit. Both were fairly exhausted by the time they returned to shore.

The Connells took over what had been the Cowes Bay Post Office on May 29, 1963, but the name did not change until 1966 after complaints that having the Cowes PO three bays distant was just too confusing. "In those days," says Eric, "everyone had their own telephone lines and we ran an old plug-in switchboard. Pakatoa and Rotoroa lines ran through our board as well." Having to be on telephone duty made it difficult for Pearl to leave the house. Before Ponui had its own line, their messages also came through Connells and a flag was then hoisted, bringing the Chamberlins across in their launch. The telephone was used a lot by visiting boaties and in later years a coin-operated box was installed.

The old white house in the bay always exuded hospitality and the spacious rooms were used for church services, family parties, district farewells and weddings. On February 24, 1973, the strains of the wedding march echoed across the bay as Eric and Pearl's daughter Mary was married to Adrian Esdaile. The bride planned her wedding at high tide so city guests could step straight on to the jetty. Captain Fred Ladd (a family friend and MC for the occasion) and wife Mabel arrived in their new Buccaneer seaplane. Other guests came by boat, landrover or by foot over the hills. The last such family wedding had been in 1940 when Edsell and Dixie Day were married.

The opening of a road to western Waiheke gradually lessened the demand for Connell's store and Eric retired in 1981, but the Connells will long be remembered for their service and hospitality in this lovely Waiheke bay. Their name has become part of the island's landscape and the house built by Eric Connell above Arran Bay still serves as holiday home for family members.

Arran Bay

How Arran Bay gained its name is a romantic tale. It represents the little piece of Scotland brought to a distant Pacific island by a young couple whose love match found little family approval at home.

The Croll Family

Mary and Andrew Croll stepped into Waiheke's history in 1888 when they bought 100 acres on the island's eastern coast naming it "Arran" after Andrew's estate in Scotland. Neither of the newcomers quite fitted into the hardy pioneer mould: she was an artist who had never had to keep house, he preferred photography to farming. What brought them to a lifestyle of subsistence farming in an isolated New Zealand bay was the same independent spirit that had led Mary to defy her parents in order to marry the man she loved.

That pioneering spirit had shown itself early in Mary's life, according to the couple's youngest son, Darcy Graham, who recorded the following family history in 1973. His mother, Mary Gifford, was born in 1863, and raised in Edinburgh where her family lived in comfort above a branch of the Union Bank of Scotland. In the days when young ladies learned piano, did embroidery (which she hated), sketched or painted watercolours, Mary was determined to paint portraits in oils — the more difficult medium. After much argument she was allowed to attend still life classes but found them dull and, in a rebellious mood one day, instead attended a life class where the model was an old shepherd. The incident was recorded by Darcy.

181

He sat in a position marked by chalk and every so often he would say 'excuse me' and walk three times around the room, then return to plant his limbs exactly on the marks. Mary just painted what she saw and The Old Shepherd was the best thing she ever did, though many portraits came later.

Mary Croll at her easle

It was around this time, when Mary was 17 or 18 years old, that she met and fell in love with Andrew Croll. The romance was discouraged. Andrew was ten years older, had no apparent career prospects, no money and, worst of all, was her first cousin (their mothers were sisters).

Mary's mother, who belonged to the House of Usher (Ushers Whisky, Ushers Hall, Edinburgh) was after a better match and there was dire talk of malformed children. Wedding banns were forbidden but the couple continued to meet while holidaying at Grantham House near Edinburgh, home of Mary's uncle and the Lord High Provost of Edinburgh, Adam Gifford. In desperation, her parents dispatched her to stay with cousins in South Africa. It was not a good move, according to Darcy.

It was a mistake on two counts. One, she didn't forget him and two, she caught a touch of the sun and warmth from which she never recovered.

Letters were slow and infrequent but, after a year or so, Mary returned to Edinburgh as much in love with Andrew as ever. After further strife, their determination finally won out and they were given parental consent to marry, but no blessings. They married at a Registry Office without benefit of clergy. The ceremony was attended only by Mary's schoolfriend, Gertrude Peterkin and a cousin, Alice Rawleigh.

The newlyweds moved in with Andy's mother, "Grannie Croll", in Glasgow in what, by modem standards, was virtually a slum. Andrew had little in the way of work. Recorded Darcy:

They were short of coal, short of money, short of everything except courage. There, in the cold, sleet and fogs of Glasgow, Mary's first child arrived.

Capturing her firstborn (David Gifford) on film was not easy in those days, so Mary painted a portrait of the baby while he was asleep, covering his hand with the blanket because, she said, a baby's hand was far too difficult to paint. She also did a portrait of Granny Croll — the only way she had of repaying the fine old Scots lady who had so kindly taken them in. Both portraits are still in the family.

The Crolls were able to make a break from their rather bleak life when Adam Gifford (of Grantham House) died, leaving Mary £100. They packed their few possessions in a cotton box which bore the carved date 1886 and sailed for New Zealand. (In the Watson history, one reads that the Crolls were fellow passengers of the Rowbottom family on board the SS *Kaikoura*, arriving in New Zealand in 1886. Treasured by the Watsons is a shell painted by Mary Croll on that voyage.)

Their first New Zealand home was on Mercury Island, off the Coromandel Peninsula where they set up a farm. Despite the fact that Andrew was no farmer and Mary knew even less about housekeeping, they made the best of the situation. While Mary made unleavened bread and homemade butter, Andrew created furniture from packing crates and driftwood. They bought some sheep and a few cows, and supplies arrived by the steamer which called in once a month.

Mary's cooking and housekeeping skills must have been culled from a book which omitted a few basics — like how to add salt or get bread to rise, recalled Darcy.

She certainly didn't know about such things having lived most of her life with servants to do the cooking and housework... When the bed linen got yellow, she tied a rope around the bundle and dropped it down the washing well where it looked lovely and white, but to pull them up again without touching the sides of the well required a stronger arm than Mary's and they finished up green, slimy and muddy. Undaunted, she read about washing blue... and when the steamer next came in she got some washing blue and blued the clothes till they were the colour of the sky.

When a female visitor asked her where she boiled the clothes, Mary reportedly replied: "I don't want to eat them, why should I boil them?"

One other story of Mary's early housekeeping problems concerns a sheep's head. Having read somewhere that such a dish was quite a delicacy, she asked her husband to bring her the head next time he killed a sheep. The experiment, as Darcy recorded it, was not a success.

It arrived: eyes, ears, wool, blood and a ghastly grin with lolling tongue. It was all too terrible, so she shoved it in the oven and slammed the door. When dinner came... she had a headache and didn't want any dinner as she'd had a second look in the oven and the head looked even more ghastly. The wool was all burnt off and the tongue a blackened mess. Later the men rescued their dinner from the oven — and there were hoots of laughter. They shared the tongue, the only edible part.

Thomas Day sledging firewood for Andrew Croll

Their time on Mercury came to an end when it was discovered that the fleeces of the sheep were full of volcanic ash and thus worthless. As the couple packed to leave, the skipper of their supply ship, Captain Herald, gave Mary a present for the baby. Much to her surprise the present turned out to be 50 gold sovereigns. This gift helped them into their new home on Waiheke Island.

By all accounts their life in Arran Bay was an idyllic one. Here the couple had three more children, John or Jack (whose birth in 1888 can be found in Anglican baptismal records), Raleigh, and Nell. In the words of Darcy, they were "supremely happy".

The children were happy and healthy with plenty of fish in the sea, milk, butter and things they could grow plus occasional sacks of meal, flour or sugar. Mary kept house, darned, made and remade clothes. She was experienced and capable by now and found time to do more painting and sketching. She taught the children the three Rs and lots of less tangible things which stood them well in later life.

Andrew became involved in local affairs and was a member of the local school committee (he is recorded as having paid 12/- for firewood for the school in 1892). He employed Thomas Day to help out on the property and was able to spend more time developing his skills as a photographer. His work (now in the Waiheke Museum) provides some valuable insights into life on Waiheke at the turn of that century: here are ladies in long dresses playing tennis, kids collecting seaweed at low tide, regatta day finery, and a disgruntled-looking youngster getting a haircut from mum in the orchard.

Mary left her own mark in the form of a frieze painted at eye level on the bedroom walls: scenes of Waiheke Passage and of Scotland, of Rabbit Island (Pakatoa) which they visited in their yacht and of nursery rhymes.

Arran House itself consisted of a long narrow parlour with an open fireplace and overmantel, two bedrooms, a kitchen and big walk-in pantry. The parlour was in Victorian style with photos decorating the walls, the two attic bedrooms were reached by a steep narrow staircase.

Thomas Day, his wife and young son, Arthur who was born at Arran, lived in a small cottage nearby. While Thomas looked after the gardens, house cow and poultry, his wife helped Mary in the house. Firewood for the kitchen and parlour was hauled by horse and sled.

The Day family recalls the summer of 1895 when Andrew first suggested that the yachts anchored in the bay should compete in a race. He offered a sheep, killed and dressed, as first prize and about a dozen boats competed. The following year, there were local donations of mutton, beef, pork and vegetables; local Māori helped to prepare a hangi, keelers raced and the *Viking* acted as flagship. It was recorded that sisters Mrs Gordon and Mrs Grant won the hotly contested dinghy pair race. Miss Ruthe came over from Ruthe's Island (Rotoroa) for the occasion and residents and visitors had a great time. The island regatta had become an annual event.

By 1897 there was a printed programme and more events. The names of the "ladies and gentlemen donating to Regatta 1897" included Messrs Bloomfield and crew of Viking (Challenge Cup), Messrs C Ashwin, T Brassey, A Chatfield, Coates Bros, C Chamberlin, E Chamberlin, G Chamberlin, F Challis, W Carey, Cruickshank and Miller, J Day, Gallaugher, T Gilbert, W and Mrs Gordon, F Hunt, J A Haslett, H Hewin, S Jeffreys, S Kelly, J Kennedy, W Leatham, G Linkhorn, J M Lennox, W

F Massey, F Moore, Masefield & Co, W Nichol, J O'Brien, HE Parris, G Pegler, J R Parkinson, Mrs Ruthe, G Reid, R Seccombe & Son, Miss Trace, W Wilson, J Wiseman, J J Phillips, J Wilson & Co, H E Partridge, W Phillips, Porter & Co, J Pegler and others. In 1898 the event was called Crolls Bay Regatta. Later the regatta was to move to Cowes Bay.

In 1902, Mary's father, John Gifford, died leaving her £400 a year for life. With this fortune the family left Waiheke and moved to Sydney where they made a home in Stanley Avenue overlooking Balmoral. Later, Andrew started a real estate agency which in the mid-1970s was still being run by his grandson Colin.

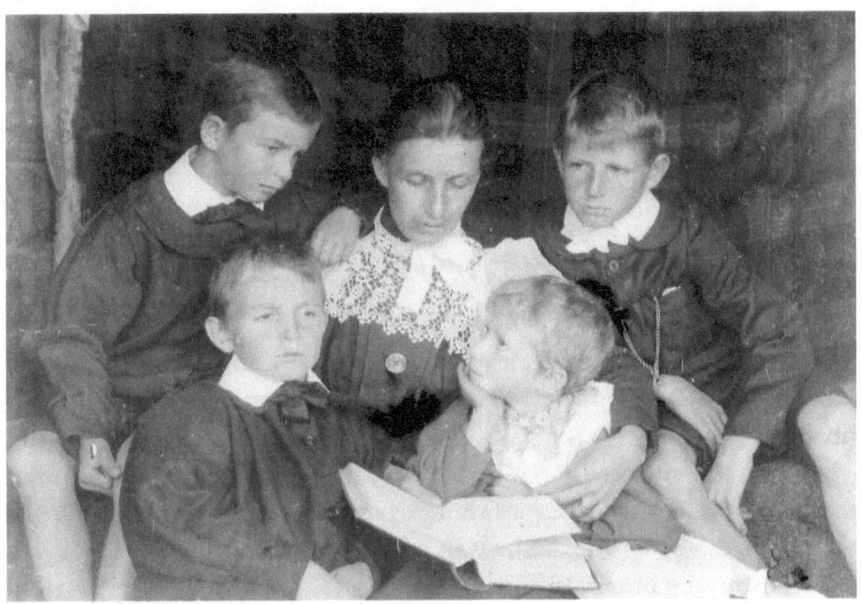

The Croll family from left. John, Raleigh, Mary, Nell and Gifford.

The boys left home or went into business but Mary was happy to stay at home with Nell. At around this time, she bought a portrait by Longstaff called Mignon at Lawson's Auction. She also bought a deck chair from Queen Victoria's royal yacht — the *Victoria and Albert* — because the Queen might have sat in it.

Her contentment was shattered when Nell died suddenly of Landry's Paralysis at the age of 13. At first heartbroken, Mary and Andrew decided to have another child. Time was pressing as, by now, Mary was 47. Finally, on August 10, 1910, the replacement, Darcy, was born. Andrew died of an unknown disease in 1918, toward the end of the First World War, but Mary battled on to put her youngest son through medical school. She died on August 21, 1940, at the ripe old age of 77.

A link with the past was forged when, in the 1970s, a member of Waiheke's Historical Society visited Sydney and made contact with a local land agent, Raleigh Croll. Raleigh had earlier made a trip back to his childhood home and spoken to the Day family. The Croll family made the Waiheke visitor, Mrs Corcoran, very welcome and generously gave her two photograph albums and original glass slides to put in the Waiheke Museum. Mrs Corcoran kept in touch with the family and a widowed Mrs Croll was later able to return the visit and see the house her late husband had told her so much about.

The taped interview of Darcy Croll, its transcription, and photographs taken by Andrew Croll are now in the Museum archives.

The Douglas Family

The Crolls' property in Arran Bay was sold to another Scot, Robert Montgomery Douglas, and the house continued to be a centre of hospitality.

Robert's gentle, well-born Irish wife, Elizabeth Alice Fagan, was used to having the best and was a fastidious, efficient housekeeper, a superb cook and gracious hostess. She welcomed guests warmly.

After buying blocks 46 and 79 in 1902, Robert added to the original purchase until he owned about 500 acres. He was a practical farmer. Land was cleared and fenced and pasture established for sheep and cattle.

Young Arthur Day stayed on in Arran Bay employed as a farm hand. He milked the house cows in a small shed by the creek. When a beast was killed, beef was sold to the Salvation Army Hostel (a treatment centre for alcoholics) across Waiheke Passage on Rotoroa Island. Beef for the house was placed in brine and eaten corned. Any surplus of home-made butter was kept in the brine and eggs were also preserved.

Kauri on the property was cut and shipped to Auckland for milling. With this timber, Robert built two cottages. These were let as holiday homes mainly to professional people — doctors and surgeons who generously gave time and attention to people in the area who needed medical help. In later years, Dr Douglas Guthrie, an eminent surgeon, built a two-storey home in the bay and his willingness to help in medical emergencies is still remembered with gratitude. Holiday visitors were landed in Cowes Bay from where Robert would collect them by launch.

Local residents remembered Robert's love of music. He taught himself to play both the organ and piano. He also bought one of the new Edison gramophones with cylinder discs for £60. This feast of music was enjoyed by many guests, one of whom was Dora Gray who rode over from neighbouring Waiti Station. She was to play nanny to the two young Douglas wards, Kathleen and Lucy, when Robert and Elizabeth went overseas — travel by sea involved an absence of several months.

Robert and Elizabeth Douglas had no children but raised two members of Elizabeth's family as their own. Lucy, nicknamed "Bassie" at school and remembered for her glorious auburn hair, had been orphaned at the age of two. Both youngsters were raised as Catholics. In later life, Lucy recalled her first Communion when, overcome by shyness, she hid in the rocks for hours before meeting the priest who had come to the bay by hired launch for the occasion.

Kathleen was a pretty girl who attracted a number of admirers. Young men from boats anchored in the bay came ashore to flirt with her and one teacher came to play whist at night just to be near her. This young man, Jack Harvey, wrote in exquisite script and a little book in which he wrote quotations in English, Spanish and French illustrated by delicate drawings is still treasured by Lucy's family. Another visiting teacher was Mr Voysey who was later killed in the 1914-18 war.

On April 13, 1913, Kathleen married James Watt-Smith in the flower-decorated parlour of Arran House. The ceremony was conducted by Father Patterson of St John's, Parnell; the bridesmaid was Watt-Smith's niece and among the guests were the Insleys of Cowes and Rene Moore from Rosstrevor Bay.

In Arran Bay there was good anchorage and firm golden sand and, being an astute businessman, Robert saw its potential to fill a demand for weekend holiday sites. In 1909 and 1910, part of Allotment 46 was surveyed by Adam Maxwell Kelly who was well known on the island. Four small sections in the bay later sold for £25 each — a good price for those days— and holiday homes built.

To avoid an awkward scramble over the hill into Cowes Bay, where the private hotel, wharf and post office were situated, a ramp was built for ready access between the bays. The steps came from the Choral Hall in Auckland and the ramp was to last 40 years.

During their time at Arran House Robert and Elizabeth planted a variety of fruit trees including pears, plum and quinces; a lime tree near the house still bears fruit. One wild night an elm fell with a mighty crash, narrowly missing the house, but the row of poplars was unaffected.

Interior of Arran House around the turn of the 20th century. Mary, Andrew, Nell and family friend.

Not long after Robert Douglas left Waiheke to move to the mainland, he went missing on his new property in Mercer. He was found, dead, in August 1917, apparently killed by a tree he was felling. Not regarded as a skilled axeman, he had often been warned of just such an accident by the Day brothers when he was working with them on Waiheke. Elizabeth sold the remainder of Arran Bay land to William James Connell in 1924.

Four years later Connell sold Arran House to Peter Steen, a teacher at Auckland Grammar, and the house remained in the Steen family for many decades. It was considerably altered during that time with the bay window extended right out across the verandah giving a larger (25ft x 17ft) living room, and a staircase in the kitchen removed to make room for a stove. The late Mr Steen was a noted authority on gannets and was involved in banding the young birds. He donated photographs to the Waiheke Museum.

Cowes (Pikau) Bay

In their thousands they came, city folk in their finery on steamers draped in flags and bunting, for a day on Waiheke. The women in sweeping skirts, light blouses and wide hats, men in sober suits or boating whites, children firmly bonneted against the sun, they poured over the gangways and up the wharf, eager to secure a favourable position to enjoy their picnics and watch the events in the bay.

If they were quick they might find respite from the sun under a pohutukawa tree that had not already been claimed by people who had come ashore from private yachts. By mid-morning, as many as 60 yachts and five steamers would have delivered more than 3000 people for the annual regatta that made Cowes Bay a summer Mecca in the gulf during the first decades of the 20th century.

Cowes Bay, already a social magnet with its post office and guest house, grew in popularity after it became host to the New Year regattas, an annual tradition begun at Man O'War Bay in 1882. In the late 1890s, the sailing events were held in neighbouring Arran Bay.

The programme for the Waiheke Regatta on January 1, 1897, lists 10 events including yacht and dinghy races and such novelty events as an open "Blindfold Dinghy Race" and a "Tug-of-War in Dinghies". For readers with an interest in the weather, the first day of the 20th century blew in on the back of a strong southwesterly which, according to a report in *The New Zealand Herald*, gave regatta competitors *a lead to the first mark off Ponui, a smart run round Ruthes and a lead to Rabbit (Pakatoa) Island*. The Gray brothers beat their rivals, the Peglers and the Days, in both the keel and flatbottom boat races; Coffey won £1 for winning the "Race for Māoris in Dinghies" ahead of Mihaka who took the 10/- second prize; and Miss Ruthe was first across the line in the "Dinghy Race for One Lady" with Mrs J Pegler second and Miss Day third.

The Cowes Bay Regatta

To yachtsmen, wrote the *Herald's* correspondent, *the regatta forms a pleasant conclusion to a few days sojourn in one of the picturesque and retired spots which Waiheke abounds in.*

On January 2, 1901, about 2000 people sailed from Auckland for Cowes Bay to see the regatta, now run under the auspices of the Auckland Yacht Club. The event was reported in the *Herald.*

On arrival the sight was one of great beauty. There were fully 60 yachts in the bay and numberless small craft. Both excursion steamers were decorated with flags and the flagship Queen Of Beauty *made an attractive item to the scene.*

Next year, the newspaper headlined its regatta report: "A Record Attendance".

The Wakatere left Auckland with about 1,100 on board and there were so many people left on the wharf that the Northern Steamship Company had to despatch the PS Terranora, the SS Waitangi and the SS Muritai as well. The SS Ohinemuri brought visitors over from Coromandel and some 60 yachts, which made the bay a rendezvous, brought the attendance in all to about 3000. The pohutukawas, with which Cowes is fringed, were aflame with crimson, the bunting-decked steamers were at the wharf and the trim yachts, most of which flew a bit of colour, were dotted all about the sheltered bay. People were thick on the beach and picnicked on the wooded rising ground. Although it was a regatta, it was really more of a picnic.

The *Wakatere* was a paddle steamer which carried up to 1200 passengers and could cover the trip from Auckland to Cowes Bay in one hour 45 minutes. Dressed in flags and bunting, and with a brass band playing, she would lead the convoy of passenger steamers into Cowes Bay and tie up at the wharf.

The other vessels tied up alongside and gangways were laid from deck to deck for passengers to cross to the wharf. With as many as five steamers tied up together, the afternoon departure required careful co-ordination. A gate at the entrance to the wharf was closed once sufficient numbers to fill the first steamer had passed through. The slowest boat, last to arrive, was first to leave and the *Wakatere*, paddles thumping, setting off in pursuit at the rear.

A number of Auckland firms, such as Milne & Choyce, Courts and Sanfords, held picnic days at Cowes. Sanfords ran competitions for singing and dancing, both Highland and Irish, and brought along their own pipers. The Farmers Freezing Co brought a special treat to their picnic day one year — free ice cream, the first that many people had ever tasted.

There was an asphalt cycling track in the bay made by the Northern Steamship Co on which racing bikes, brought from Auckland, would compete. With decorated boats, a band playing, and young people dancing in an open-sided pavilion decorated with punga, nikau and pohutukawa, the normally tranquil bay became alight with colour and activity on such occasions — a mecca for both visitors and locals.

Parris (Parres) Family

The family that had first put Cowes Bay on the map as a tourist mecca arrived there in the 1880s. The arrival of 13-year-old Innes Parres on Waiheke is described in the history of the Hodgson family of Omiha Bay. The young Portuguese sailor made Waiheke his home after jumping ship in the Rangitoto Channel.

He married Jane, the Hodgson daughter who had brought him food when, as a young runaway, he hid in the bush from customs officials, and the couple initially lived near her family in Omiha. It is not known exactly when they moved to Cowes but the first Te Matuku school roll of 1882 includes both Parris and Day children from Cowes Bay. An 1884 map shows the Parris house in Pikau and the Day house in neighbouring Pakihi Bay.

In October 1883, two Parris boys came to fetch the Reverend Gould to see their mother who was suffering a succession of fits. He noted the visit in his diary:

> *...the poor woman knew me but her mind was continually wandering and she had to be watched day and night. About five next morning she was sensible for about an hour, then went off again. In the end she had to be taken to Auckland.*

Jane Parris was just 43 when she died in February 1885. Her grave is on the lonely hill above Cowes Bay. The present road passes near the site but the picket fence that marked it is gone. She was the mother of 11 children, the youngest just three years old, when she died. For some years, her descendants gathered on the hilltop in remembrance.

In October 1886, the Cowes Post Office settled in Pikau Bay with Innes Parris as its new Postmaster. Pikau lost its Māori name and has been referred to as Cowes Bay ever since.

Innes remarried to a cheerful Swedish woman called Bertha who cared for the large family and helped establish the first guesthouse in the bay. Innes (officially known as John) felled trees and built five rooms which were simply furnished with beds and cretonne-covered boxes. With help from local Māori and his sons, Innes continued to develop the site, building a large homestead, more guest rooms and a post office.

These buildings were to stand the test of time, lasting 70 years before being destroyed by fire in the 1950s.

The Northern Steamship Co took a 21-year lease on an acre of the beach frontage and a long wharf with kauri piles was erected and a dance and band rotunda built on the flat. The company ran Christmas and New Year excursions with a return fare of 2/6; the usual fare was 4/- return. The boarding house grew in popularity.

By the turn of that century the Portuguese runaway had established a successful business on his new island home, but he was getting old and in 1902 Bertha took on the job of postmistress until Henry Insley bought the boarding house and property two years later.

While there was, at times, kindly laughter at his broken English, Innes had earned a lot of respect for his hard work and ingenuity. When, in later years, he was troubled by rheumatism, he rigged a bath house on the beach, pumping up salt water through quick heating pipes. One of his specialities was an anchovy paste made by mashing sprats with a mortar hollowed out of pohutukawa. Those on fishing expeditions in the gulf appreciated his provision of a trestle table set up behind a boxthorn hedge on the property to scale and prepare fish.

Although Innes had swapped a livelihood at sea for one on dry land, some of his sons chose the sea. One Parris son, Adolphus, was a well-known captain of the Northern Steamship Co and, for a time, of the Government oyster vessel *Te Waipounamu*. Edward was owner skipper of the trading cutter *Janet* working the shingle on Waiheke beaches. She was a speedy vessel of her type and took first place in her class at the Auckland Anniversary Regatta for six years running. Edward's son recalled summer holidays during which a party of up to 30 would climb aboard the cutter with tents and head out into the Hauraki Gulf to camp above some beach.

The Insley Family

The tradition of hospitality established at Cowes by the Parris family was carried on by its new owners. The Insleys, South Islanders from Dunedin, took over the guest house and established a private hotel which was known for its high standards of service and catering.

Henry Ingram Insley had been a chief steward at sea and understood the importance of proper table settings, spotless linen and superior meals. As he also took on the tasks of local postmaster and police constable, his wife Agnes frequently had to take over the running of the guesthouse as well as caring for their growing family of four sons and one daughter (Henry, Allan, Ada, Charles and James).

Insley's boat **Sunbeam**

When Harry, as he was known, went out on duty calls aboard his launch, *Sunbeam,* he dressed as usual in a sweater and rolled up trousers — the only sign of authority his police hat. Once when transporting a mental patient up to Oakley, he had lent this hat to keep his passenger quiet and reckons he had trouble convincing the authorities as to just who was in charge.

The original hotel buildings at Cowes Bay were gradually enlarged to take more guests. By 1922, they could accommodate 100 guests and were open throughout the summer, employing a chef, housemaids and waitresses.

The farm provided home killed mutton, fresh vegetables and fruit. Pawpaw, figs, peaches and apples flourished in the valley orchard. Older eastern end residents remembered the honey meads and potent wines that Agnes Insley brewed in retirement from mulberries, grapes, passionfruit, plums and guavas grown on the property.

Dinghies were available for guests to catch their own fish and during the Insleys' time at Cowes, the annual regattas and staff picnics made the bay a social centre on the island. The guesthouse also served as an impromptu chapel when visiting clergy from Coromandel stayed in the bay. One such visitor reports *a good congregation at Cowes* in 1907.

The Insley youngsters attended Te Matuku or Man O'War Schools and the guesthouse was sometimes home to the teachers who taught at both half-time. Harry Insley was a shareholder in the Man O'War saleyards and was named as one of the trustees of the Te Matuku cemetery where one son, Charles Shand, was buried in 1937.

Another son, Allan, used to sail in his mullet boat to Matiatia visiting Agnes Croll whose family lived there and managed the extensive Alison farm. The couple later married but Agnes sadly died in childbirth. With his parents' retirement, Allan took over the running of the guesthouse. He married again, and another generation of Insleys continued the tradition of hospitality in the bay.

With reduced staff, the guesthouse also opened in the May and August holidays. Children were always welcome and were given their own Christmas party in fancy dress. During the busy summer season, a three-piece band played for dances in the hall and locals walked for miles to join the fun.

Apart from fishing and swimming, guests could take part in local tennis tournaments or practise their skills on a nine-hole mini golf course. Boaties and visitors could get hot water from a booth on the beach or buy soft drinks or ice cream. A generator provided power.

Flower beds lined the path to the verandah where guests sipped morning and afternoon tea looking across the Gulf to the Coromandel coast. A full-time gardener was employed to provide fresh veges and to milk the cows which kept the guesthouse supplied with milk and cream.

Supplies and mail arrived on a regular ferry service. The mail was sorted in a little post office which was built at the end of the verandah and later housed a telephone exchange.

When Allan Insley decided to sell the guesthouse in 1951, it was the end of an era in Waiheke history. The family ties to Waiheke were not entirely broken, however, and Insley descendants still return to the bay for holidays. One descendant, Alec Pert (son of Ada), was married there in 1951.

The guesthouse continued under different proprietors for some years until the property was sold to the McKendrick family. The old buildings were later destroyed by fire.

Ōmaru Bay

The name Ōmaru has been the source of some confusion in Waiheke geography, as it has been used for two different regions of the island. The Ōmaru Block was a large parcel of land situated on the island's southern coast at what is now called Woodside Bay (see the Woodside Bay chapter). Inevitably, some have used the name Ōmaru Bay to refer to the bay on which the Ōmaru Block was located, even though its Māori name was not Ōmaru but Rore A Maeāea. Properly speaking, Ōmaru Bay refers to a bay just north of Orapiu at the island's southeastern corner.

That this quiet eastern bay was once regarded as a centre of the island's population is evidenced by the establishment of Waiheke's first police station here in 1903.

Although the station, a comfortable house facing the bay, was built on an acre of land purchased by the Government in Ōmaru Bay, it was known as the Cowes Police Station, presumably to avoid confusion with the Ōmaru Block, and because the post office was then at Cowes.

James P Bennett, who was also a fisheries inspector for all gulf islands and the Coromandel coast, was sworn in as first Waiheke District Constable. Since his Waiheke beat consisted mainly of coastal bays and his main mode of transport was boat, the two jobs were complementary. He patrolled the area by yacht and later by launch: the *Albatross,* a small boat with an 8hp standard engine, later the *Nora* — larger at 36ft and with a more powerful 30hp Twigg engine.

With no radio, Constable Bennett communicated by pigeon post. The birds were kept in a pigeon cote at Ōmaru Bay, taken out on the launch during trips that would often last several days, and released if Bennett wanted to send a message to his wife.

Mrs Bennett is remembered for her unruffled calm, as she was ferried by rowboat to bays often several miles distant to help women in childbirth. The nearest doctor was in Maraetai or Auckland.

In a district where settlers had always been free to collect their own shellfish from the rocks, Bennett had the unpopular task of preventing the taking of oysters. There was great consternation when he was appointed fisheries officer as he knew about the local trade in oysters. Rumour has it that he even had a few sacks on hand himself when appointed and, given his new status, found them rather difficult to offload.

Local oyster trade became a game of hide and seek; women hid billy loads in secret niches or beneath their rowboats; skilled locals, able to gather up to a dozen sacks between tides, shipped these off to Auckland at night by cutter. When Bennett got his new launch, his proud son was soon persuaded to describe it in detail to his school mates and their parents were quick to note the descriptions — he was known to change the launch colours. But gradually, Waiheke settlers learned the new rules. The inspector's job later included estimating the number of sacks, arranging pickers, examining damage by oyster borer and even establishing oyster culture at Ostend — a project undertaken by a Mr Turner who skippered the *Tio*.

Bennett retired in 1908 and was succeeded by Henry Insley of Cowes Bay as police constable but not fisheries inspector, the two jobs remaining separate from then on. Insley, who was also postmaster and ran the Cowes guest house patrolled his beat, which extended to the islands of Pakatoa and Rotoroa, aboard the 28ft *Sunbeam*. The two islands were then, respectively, home to female and male alcoholics under a programme run by the Salvation Army, and Insley would be called in to quell any trouble. During the 1918 flu epidemic, he had special duties at Te Huruhi where many Māori families were affected. He would sometimes be called out to settle boundary disputes after early subdivision in western Waiheke, and he also investigated the illegal taking of shingle off some island beaches. Police work in those days didn't include much theft; some quarrels among the settlers made it to court and one who apparently enjoyed litigation was reportedly quite upset when his longtime opponent died.

When Insley retired in 1928, Waiheke's police work was taken on by Lumley Ashwin of Awaawaroa Valley. A lieutenant in the First World War, he had to ride over to enforce law in the new western Waiheke subdivisions until 1935 when Constable Elms started work at Pūtiki, later moving to Surfdale. The police station was finally shifted to Oneroa, the new population centre, in 1942 — a long way from its early base in Ōmaru Bay on land bought from an even earlier arrival in the Bay, George Pegler.

The Peglers

The close family links of Waiheke's pioneer families are characterised by the story of the Pegler brothers who, like others, came to visit but ended up staying to marry into the community and make their own impact on the island's history.

George and John Pegler were born in New Norfolk, Tasmania, where George worked on the wheat farms, spending his days carting heavy grain sacks up into a storage loft. It wasn't an easy way to earn a living and when the brothers, who also had shearing and fencing experience, heard that fencers were wanted in New Zealand, they had little hesitation in applying for a contract with Williams of Waipiro Bay, north of Tokomaru on the East Coast.

When they left in 1878, their mother's parting words were: "George, look after John." Although they were never to see her again, the brothers respected this wish and remained close for the rest of their lives.

George became head fencer for Williams (a former bishop) and in that capacity taught 12 young farming cadets his fencing skills. The brothers remained in this area for some years and in the 1884 Electoral Roll, are listed as living at Waikohu, Gisborne. George was apparently working near Tarawera at the time of its eruption in 1886 and would certainly have been killed had he been downwind of the mountain.

The following year, at the age of 34, George was still working in the Gisborne area when he met and later married Mary Ann Day in Auckland.

Mary, known as Annie, was then 19 years old. According to various reports, the two brothers then walked from Gisborne through to Coromandel where they caught the steamer and were landed at Day's Bay on Waiheke. There John met his new sister-in-law, Ellen (Nell) who was later to become his wife — and the brothers' future on the island was sealed.

The Peglers took on fencing contracts around the island and, a lifetime later, many of their fences of firmly footed grey puriri are still standing. They also helped out with shearing at local farms.

George and Annie Pegler lived initially in Orapiu (see Orapiu chapter for John and Nell Pegler's history), but later bought a 40-acre block in Ōmaru Bay from Holland, shifting a cottage on rollers to the new site with the help of Henry Hewin (of Oriote Bay). With a steep hill behind and a flat facing the sea, this land provided grazing for a few cows and, over the years, was developed into a productive garden and orchard.

Apricot trees, peaches, plums, apples, persimmons, figs, Chinese gooseberries (kiwifruit) and citrus fruit all flourished and visitors came by boat and horseback to buy their fruit and vegetables; their luscious apricots were known throughout the Hauraki Gulf. The Thomson and Hills jam factory in Auckland one year dispatched crates to collect their bumper quince harvest at 3d a pound.

George would row up to Auckland for supplies. Equipping his 20-footer with bailers, a sail and extra oar, he carefully checked weather signs and kept close to the coastline, bringing the narrow flat-bottomed craft back loaded with flour, fowl feed, salted beef and rolls of fencing wire.

Cockles, mussels and oysters were collected in the bay beyond their gate and flounder could be speared in the shallows. Their eldest son, George, had vivid memories of Waiheke Passage alive with fish, and a younger boy, Hugo recalls rowing out to the *Baroona* (then trawling in the Gulf) to barter for fish. Taking a bucket of milk and box of eggs, he would stand knee-deep in snapper to fill his bucket with fish before rowing home. Even their Persian cat apparently caught its own supply of sprats from a concrete sea wall at the bottom of the garden.

Their supply of rock oysters may have dwindled a little, however, when George sold one acre of his land to the Government and a fisheries inspector came to live next door.

The Peglers were to have ten children, six girls and four boys. There are records of three Pegler babies being baptised on Waiheke: Stanley in 1896, Martin in 1898 and Cecilia in 1900. The baptisms were possibly performed at Cowes with the babies tucked up in the boat and rowed to the service.

The third child, Eliza, was to recall her life on the island at the age of 95. She remembered the long walk with her brother and sister to school where at first they learned with slates and pencil, later progressing to copy books, pen and ink. George remembered being taught by Jim Broun, who was later to become an uncle after marrying into the Day family, and by a Mr Hudson.

Days started with a breakfast of oatmeal porridge, sometimes followed by eggs. Then boots were laced, and the little girls' hair plaited before the long walk to school. Eliza remembered being carried on her brother's back over ice covered pools on winter mornings and, in the big and poorly heated schoolroom, having hands so numb with cold she could not hold the slate.

In winter rains, the youngsters wore heavy oilskins kept supple with linseed oil; when winds were bitter they also wore woollen jerseys and caps crocheted by their mother. Ann Pegler had to carefully plan shopping trips to Auckland to buy the yards of blue serge for boys' pants, unbleached calico for lining pants if there were not enough bleached flour bags, and material for the girls' frocks and boys' shirts. All of these garments were made up on a hand sewing machine, usually by lamplight. Skeins of wool were also bought to be wound into balls at home. Hankies were cut from oatmeal bags and hand hemmed.

Saturday was bath night. Water was heated in four-gallon kerosene tins hung on iron bars over the fire and then poured into a galvanised iron bathtub which, in cold weather, was placed in front of the fire. In summer, if tanks were low, the kids would take tins by rowboat to fill at the water hole in the next bay. Used bath water was carefully poured around the garden.

Clean for Sunday school, the youngsters would again walk over the hills to the old schoolroom to hear Bible stories from the young woman who rode over from Awaawaroa Valley to teach them. For Church services, the family would row to Cowes Bay.

George had special memories of Cowes, of regattas whose mementos were the silver cups he won in rowing races and displayed on the old-fashioned sideboard; of school picnics; and of dances held in Gordon's woolshed in Awaawaroa Valley that the family walked to over the hills. He also remembered, as a young boy, seeing a man o' war running aground on a rock in the Waiheke Passage off Orapiu. The same rock caused other problems:

The Stella *went on it with a big tow of logs on a Sunday, so after that they named it Sunday Rock. Captain Bolland of the Government steamer* Hinemoa, *laid a buoy on the south side of the rock with my father directing him.*

The Pegler home faced east with a view through Ruthe's Passage and when the Coromandel gold rush was on, many boats passed the bay on their way there. Sometimes tug masters, seeing dirty weather coming up, would leave a raft of logs in Ōmaru Bay. In 1910, one such raft left kauri logs tethered right across the bay, leaving only a narrow access passage. One little Pegler girl was disappointed because she could not follow her father as he nimbly walked over the logs checking that none had come adrift: the logs were all numbered at the end and chained together. When, after a week, the tug master re-hitched his log raft, he paid George Pegler £2.

The family were enthusiastic gardeners, one daughter even planted a "blue walk" to the next bay; the tamarix or flowering cypress and a hedge used to protect the garden still grow along the shore. Eliza was to leave home at 16 and work, for seven years, as a maid in Madame O'Brien's household in Pūtiki Bay. She told of getting up early one morning there to see Halley's Comet.

The older Pegler boys, George, Stan and Martin all served in the First World War. Martin (named after his grandfather) put his age forward and enlisted for service in 1916. In Flanders he was to meet up with a former teacher, Voysey, who later died there. After surviving two dangerous missions for which he had volunteered, Martin was shot in the heart just a month before Armistice in October 1918. He died in elder brother Stan's arms and it was said that Stan went raving mad killing every German in sight. Martin was awarded the Croix de Guerre and given special honour at his funeral.

Stan, who received the Military Medal, was to return to Waiheke. In the early days of the Omiha (Rocky Bay) settlement, this quiet bachelor met the boat at the wharf carrying luggage and goods with his cart and placid old horse. He retained the family's gardening tradition and was generous with his produce. Stan never forgot the generosity of the RSA who, during the Depression, lent him £3 to get a horse after his old one had died and told him, when he tried to repay it: "That's a gift." When he died, he left his entire estate, worth $10,000, for Waiheke RSA welfare work.

In the Second World War, the Peglers' youngest son, Hugo, then living in Canada, took part in the famous landing by Canadian forces on the shores of France. He survived, returning to Canada and later to New Zealand.

George Pegler died in 1939 but his wife, known to all as "Gran", was to live on for many years, often working in the garden and well known for her gifts of flowers and fruit. She spent her later years with a daughter and died in 1961 aged 92.

The Ōmaru Bay block was sold in the 1940s to Mr Hayman, founder of Tip Top Ice Cream. Fruit trees and vines were planted there to provide pure juice for his products, but he was disappointed with the results and later gave the property to the Methodist Central Mission as a future holiday camp. A caretaker lived in the old cottage and the holiday home was well-used over the years.

Pasadena Bay

Looking out toward Ruthe's Passage, between Rotoroa and Ponui islands, Pasadena Bay commands a glorious view — particularly when the keelers are racing in the Gulf. A holiday home was built here above the sandy beach by city accountant Frederick Moore in the 1880s.

An outgoing Irishman, Frederick was always a conspicuous arrival as, attired in fine frock coat and bell topper hat, he climbed down from the Coromandel steamer into a bobbing dinghy to be rowed into the bay he called Rosstrevor. Frederick was friendly with another Irish family, the Grays, and often rowed round to their Waiti Bay home for a visit — and an opportunity to vigorously condemn the British Government. One of Frederick's grandsons was later named Gray after his Waiheke friends.

The Moore and Day families also saw quite a lot of each other and the friendship extended into the next generation. When Frederick's daughter Ruby took over the music shop he had established in Customs St, Auckland, her Waiheke neighbours were always given a discount on their pianos, and when the local youngsters put on a concert at Cowes Bay hall, Ruby brought a party from town to applaud their efforts.

Frederick, a keen swimmer, one day failed to return from his morning swim and was found floating in the water of the bay he loved so well. One of his sons, George, later returned to the island to work as gardener at Cowes Private Hotel, keeping the grounds there in order for many years.

One of Moore's caretakers, Benjamin Thomas, was buried in the Te Matuku cemetery at the head of Te Matuku inlet.

After Frederick's death, Rosstrevor was sold to William Boucher who renamed the Bay "Pasadena". The head of a city importing firm, Boucher devoted spare time to transforming the property — enlarging and modernising the house and planting exotic trees. As an agent for the Tongan Government, he imported quantities of bananas and pineapples — bounty which the Day and Connell families shared in over the years. Some of the Tongan royal family stayed at Pasadena and Mrs Boucher was deeply involved in the planning of the Auckland Tongan residence and the royal Tongan weddings.

Close to half of the 30-acre estate was planted with exotic trees and an avenue of palms led to Connell's Bay and the store. A stile was conveniently placed for people walking across the property. Here, under flowering trees, grew drifts of golden spring daffodils and, in autumn, pink belladonna lilies.

This delightful bay, with gardens tended by a permanent caretaker, not only became a haven for birds — even snapper would come to the jetty to be fed. Bill Boucher's sudden death, while fishing at Lake Taupo, ended a special era at Pasadena but the beautiful trees still delight visitors who pass by.

Pūtiki Bay

Overlooking the mangrove-fringed inlets of Pūtiki Bay is Rangiona, a hill whose terraced slopes mark it as the centre of Waiheke's once-thriving Māori population. The name of the bay is derived from this pa site which, as legend has it, was part of territory claimed for the Te Arawa people back in the 14th century by a young chief called Kahu Mata Momoe. The hill was named Te Pūtiki-o-Kahu or the topknot of Kahu, and Pūtiki Pa later became an important base for both the earlier Ngāti Huarere settlers and the Ngāti Pāoa.

While the name of the bay recalls its Māori heritage, the road that winds past Rangiona and over the ridge into Omiha (Rocky) Bay recalls early Pākehā settlers who brought to Waiheke a blend of ancient European heritage.

The De Witte Family (by Annie Terlinck)

[The following section has been translated and adapted from an article, "Une famille brugeoise en Nouvelle-Zélande", by Annie Terlinck, a Belgian genealogist and historian, and is used by permission.]

The first European family to put down roots in Pūtiki Bay was not British but Belgian. Charles De Witte came from a long line of well-to-do merchants and shopkeepers in the city of Bruges; at this time they owned the largest and most fashionable tavern in the town. Charles himself was an energetic and adventurous young man, but his enthusiasm sometimes got the better of his judgement, especially in matters of money.

In 1820, at the age of twenty, Charles and his older brother Louis left Belgium for the Caribbean where they set up a trading company. The company operated mainly in Cuba (then a Spanish colony), in the Dutch island of Curaçao, and in the newly-independent republic of Colombia. The brothers purchased two schooners, the *Fingal* and the *Coradino*, but both purchases proved ill-advised. The *Fingal* was impounded by the Dutch authorities in Curaçao for having engaged in the illegal slave trade, and the captain from whom Charles bought the *Coradino* turned out not to have been the ship's true owner, but a pirate who had stolen the ship.

Broke but not broken, Charles returned to Bruges in 1829 — just in time to join in the revolution of 1830, which saw Belgium gain its independence from the Netherlands. As enthusiastic as ever, Charles launched into several projects to build up the new nation: he was one of the founders of the Brussels Stock Exchange and the ill-fated Bank of Belgium; in 1834 he and his younger brother Félix started a company for steam navigation along the Belgian canals (which went out of business in 1841); in 1838 he applied for a patent for a new kind of locomotive engine, a curious combination of a standard steam engine and a steam jet, but failed to find investors to manufacture it.

In 1839, Charles conceived a project of truly Pharaonic proportions. He proposed turning his hometown of Bruges into a major seaport by constructing a canal linking the city to Zeebrugge, on the North Sea. Neither the local nor the national authorities could be coaxed into supporting such a grand scheme at that time. Yet the canal was eventually built — in 1907.

Despite his commercial failure in the Caribbean, Charles had never lost his fascination with overseas adventure, and by 1840 the centre of European colonisation had shifted to the Pacific. England was involved in Australia, New Zealand, Malaya and Hong Kong; the Dutch were in Java; and France was present in Tahiti and New Caledonia (and briefly Akaroa). Why, thought Charles, was Belgium not in the game? In 1842 he wrote to the king and the Minister of the Interior, proposing that Belgium should colonise what is today Papua-New Guinea — with himself as the agent who would make it happen.

I should consider myself happy to be able to embark upon such an expedition in the quality of one of the Government's commissars if it should please you to designate me as such, and moreover I flatter myself that I possess the perfect experience for knowing how to deal with such simple men as the savages, from a four-year voyage that I made amongst them in the savannahs of the Republic of Colombia in America.

The Belgian government declined Charles's project, but that did not discourage him from proposing the Belgian colonisation of Samoa in 1843 and of Fiji in 1862.

While Charles was away in the Caribbean, his family arranged a marriage for him with Adèle Célestine Gilliodts, a beautiful young woman from a wealthy bourgeois Bruges family with aristocratic connections. The marriage took place on April 13, 1831, and their daughter Hélène was born on June 1 of the following year.

Finally, in 1842, Charles succeeded in getting himself named Belgian consul to New Zealand. He, Adèle, 11-year-old Hélène, and three retainers boarded the *Mandarin* in June 1843 to sail to their new life in the Pacific, arriving in Auckland on November 14 of that year.

The list of items that the family brought with them on the *Mandarin* gives an indication of the kind of life they expected to set up in their new home: elegant chairs, tables, beds, and other furniture; a piano, carpets, paintings, decorative clocks, a large library, porcelain, glassware, cutlery, kitchen and garden tools, games, firearms, liquor, and cases of clothes including a consul's uniform for Charles. Adèle supervised the loading of an entire orchard of carefully-crated fruit and nut trees and enough seeds to recreate the luxuriant garden she was leaving behind.

The *Southern Cross* newspaper of December 2, 1843, reports on the opening of the Belgian consulate in Princes Street:

The nomination of Charles De Witte, Esq., as Belgian Consul in New Zealand has been approved; and we were not a little pleased to see the tri-colour banner unfurled before his residence on Sunday last. We understand that Mr De Witte intends to settle and to purchase lands in this colony and we hope this will incite his countrymen to immigrate to our charming islands.

That last statement would find a curious echo a few years later.

The position of consul carried no salary or other remuneration, a fact that must have presented a challenge to Charles, accustomed to being able to draw upon deep family financial resources. He wisely left the management of his household, including the purchase of lands, to the much more level-headed Adèle, and occupied himself with his consular responsibilities. He wrote voluminous reports to the Belgian government on the economic and political situation in New Zealand and elsewhere in the Pacific; he negotiated a duty-free trade agreement between Belgium and the colony of New Zealand, and promoted Belgian exports; in 1855 he was instrumental in exposing the corruption of his nominal superior, Charles Heyvaert, consul-general in Australia, who was recalled the following year.

Although the De Wittes endured a sharp lifestyle change from what they had been accustomed to in Belgium, these were happy years for the family. In November 1844, Adèle De Witte purchased a 207-acre block of land along the north side of Te Whau peninsula from Wiremu Hoete. Its sheltered bays of Wharetana and Oakura were easily reached by canoe or sailing cutter, and the family moved here in early 1845. From humble beginnings — a visitor in 1845 described the De Witte home in Wharetana Bay as "lacking in provisions and the house was in disorder" — Charles, Adèle, and their faithful servant Peter De Norre slowly put together a tidy and comfortable little cottage with orchard, garden and vines. With the help of their Māori neighbours, with whom the gracious Adèle maintained excellent relations, the land was cleared for sheep and cattle.

When Elizabeth Stack visited in 1858, she recorded a most favourable impression:

We got into the canoe and paid a visit to the adjoining bay, where we found a picturesque and more than usually neat little house belonging to a French family of the name of De Witte. They were not at home, but the person left in charge took us over the house, treated us to delicious milk and gave us some almonds grown on the place. The garden was evidently as much taken care of as anything else. Unfortunately, the cattle had broken into it recently and had eaten down the fig tree and vines which, in this country, thrive in the open air. The whole place wore an air of neatness and comfort, both inside and out. The earthen floor was covered with small white shells arranged in patterns, beaten into the clay; they looked cool and clean. We gave a gentle hint, while being shown over the dairy, that our eggs were getting low upon which a dozen were instantly presented to us and a sufficient quantity of flour to make a pie... To complete all, we were given a beautiful bouquet of delicious roses and other flowers. After leaving our cards and thanks for Madame De Witte, we continued our stroll until it was time to return to Pūtiki Bay.

A second daughter, Marie, was born to the couple on March 9, 1846. Her older sister Hélène grew into a beautiful young woman and married Laughlin O'Brien (see next section) in 1856. A treasured family portrait of Adèle De Witte reveals a lovely woman dressed in an elegant gown that she had probably brought with her from Europe.

Adèle Gillodts De Witte in about 1830; Hélène De Witte O'Brien in 1912

Charles, however, had one more spectacular project in mind. In the late 1840s the tragic news reached Wharetana Bay of the European potato famine, which had struck Belgium worse than any other country except Ireland. Why not encourage his unfortunate compatriots to immigrate to New Zealand and establish a Belgian city on Pūtiki Bay? In 1850 he wrote to the governor, Sir George Grey, to inquire as to the rules for Belgian immigration. Correspondence between Charles and his family back in Belgium shows the scale of his ambition: at one point he speaks of up to 200,000 Belgians living on Waiheke Island. Such a number would have more than tripled the population of New Zealand, dwarfing both the Māori and the British population.

The grand project died, as did so many others, for lack of official support. Although Charles was respected and admired in Auckland, it was becoming increasingly clear that the Belgian government did not share that high regard. The death of his dear wife Adèle on May 15, 1864, along with his own advancing years and declining eyesight, convinced Charles to resign his post of consul in 1869. He passed away the following year, on June 3; he and Adèle were buried in the Catholic section of the old Symonds Street cemetery in Auckland. Their graves were moved during the 1960s to make way for Auckland's Southern Motorway.

Charles's plans for a Belgian city on Waiheke Island never came to fruition; yet there is some poetic justice in the fact that Pūtiki Bay today has a Belgium Street and a town called Ostend. Although chosen for other reasons, the names bear an indirect homage to a passionate man for whom no project was out of reach and no dream was too grand.

The O'Brien Family

The O'Brien family after whom O'Brien Road is named has its roots in Ireland. The chief seat for the O'Briens of Thomond is Bunratty Castle which, restored to its 15th-16th century heyday, is now regarded as the most authentic mediaeval castle in Ireland.

Thomond was the birthplace of Andrew O'Brien who emigrated to Australia with his small children after his young wife died, and is thought to have worked as a lawyer in Sydney. When Andrew's only son, Dublin-born Laughlin, turned 16, he was sent to New Zealand to view prospects of settlement. He is understood to have bought a property near Helensville and then returned to Sydney to study law. After qualifying, he came back to New Zealand and set up practice in Auckland where he met his future wife, Hélène Léopoldine Françoise Isabelle De Witte.

Laughlin was pursuing a brilliant legal career in Auckland and sitting as a member of the House of Representatives in what was the young colony's first capital. Andrew lived to see his son become an MP and be married in one of the social events of the year to the eldest daughter of Monsieur Charles De Witte of Pūtiki, Waiheke Island. The ceremony, held in St Patrick's Cathedral on February 4, 1856, was conducted by Bishop Pompallier.

The uniting of these two prominent Roman Catholic families would ensure a friendly welcome for visiting priests — French Marist priests probably visited Monsieur De Witte at Wharetana after ministering to Māori converts at East Waiheke in the early days. Bishop Pompallier visited the family's Auckland townhouse in St George's Road where he would have enjoyed speaking French to the new bride and her parents.

The young couple became regular Waiheke weekenders, sailing down from Auckland in their yacht to share the Pūtiki Bay cottage with the elder De Wittes. Later they owned the cottage which was maintained for some time by the old De Witte family retainer, Peter De Norre. It was a great shock for the O'Briens, on one visit, to find that the old man had died in his fireside chair. He was buried on the hillside past the woolshed, a reminder to the younger O'Briens of the devoted service given to their grandparents. The grave has been lovingly restored by its present owners.

Of eight children born to Laughlin and Hélène, six were to live beyond childhood but none ever knew their cultured European grandmother who died in 1864. A Requiem Mass was held for Adèle Célestine De Witte at the Church of St John the Baptist in Parnell.

The O'Brien family retained their link with Belgium, sending one daughter, Florence Adele O'Brien, to the Belgian Jette Convent for her education. Another daughter went to Timaru College while the eldest son Laughlin Adolphe was sent, at age 14, to endure the vigorous discipline of Oscott College in England.

Back in New Zealand, young Laughlin — who was known as Dolph — complied with his father's wishes to become a farmer in partnership with his brother Eugene (called Jack). The Waiheke holding grew as more land was acquired from its Māori owners (mainly through barter). With the addition of land from the Ōmaru block (Woodside Bay), it eventually totalled 2500 acres that extended through from Pūtiki to Omiha.

Young Dolph remained a bachelor until his mid-30s before proposing to Norah Mulvaney on a moonlit Oakura Beach. The Mulvaneys had emigrated from Ireland via Dusseldorf, where the father had interests in the Ruhr coal mines, arriving in New Zealand aboard the sailing ship *Lady Jocelyn* in 1878. Eighteen years later, in 1896, Norah Mulvaney married Dolph gaining, as a wedding present from Judge and Madame O'Brien, a new house in the bay where Dolph had proposed to her.

Chimneys for the Oakura house were built with bricks made on the site. It was built in the style of the period with rooms opening off a wide central hall and a wide verandah facing the sea. It was to become the family home for three sons and two daughters — one young son died.

By the time their grandfather, Judge Laughlin O'Brien, died in his 80th year in 1901, he had notched up an impressive list of achievements. He had been Registrar of the Supreme Court, Sheriff, Returning and Revising Officer, Judge of the Native Land Court and Native Appellate Court, as well as Sheriff of Norfolk and the Chatham Islands. After his death, his widow decided to move to Waiheke and the house at Wharetana was enlarged. Her younger son Jack lived there with her and she also took on two maids.

Wharetana was a comfortable one-storey dwelling facing the sea with three open fireplaces. The ten rooms included parlour, dining room, a small library lined with books written in French and bedrooms. A verandah went round three sides of the house and was enclosed on the north to form a conservatory for Madame's prized pot plants. There was a large, old-fashioned bathroom, a kitchen with wood burning range, a scullery for washing dishes and the maids' room where Nellie Melville and Eliza Pegler slept.

Eliza, aged 16 and accustomed to hard work at home in Ōmaru Bay, settled happily into this situation, especially when the wages rose to 10/- a week, a generous amount for the time. She was given time off but because there was no transport to her home she spent most of her leisure time at Wharetana. Once, while out riding with the young O'Briens, she fell and was dragged by her bolting horse for some distance. She was unconscious for three days.

Eliza stayed with the O'Briens for seven years and, as an old lady, was to recall Madame O'Brien's kindness and said she had learned a lot from this well-educated woman.

Nellie Melville, who had emigrated from Scotland as a young girl in her late teens, was to remain with Madame O'Brien for more than 20 years. As servants, they lived separately from the family, eating in the kitchen and never thinking of joining family members in the living room. The farmhand had a two-room cottage with very primitive facilities at the far end of the orchard, some minutes' walk from the main house. A narrow path trailed along the edge of a stream to this humble dwelling which was reached, on dark winter nights, with the aid of a hurricane lantern.

The homestead garden, on a wide flat with ample water, was well sheltered from cold winds. Here, the flowering trees, jacaranda and magnolia, still shed their petals where the old Madame once walked. In the orchard grew almonds, walnuts, grapes, figs, quinces, peaches, plums, apples, citrus trees and persimmon. It was, as one daughter of the family recalled in her eighties, "a real Garden of Eden" for the children who trusted that the forbidden fruit was not that of the loquat tree to which they were "particularly partial".

Kathleen O'Brien's account of life in the bay is one of busy and cheerful isolation. While she was growing up in Pūtiki with her brothers and sisters, there were few neighbours. The Kennedys lived at Dunesslin, a two-storey place across the bay from the O'Briens' house. The old homestead in what was later known as Ostend was occupied by various different owners until Lichtenstein, Arnoldson & Co finally appointed Eddie Brown as caretaker. Eddie, recalls Kathleen, had worked on the O'Briens' farm and struck up a romance with "one of our favourite maids, Katie O'Hara" whom he married, settling initially in a cottage on the Kennedy land.

The distance between these homes was covered only by boat or horseback so communication between the families was none too frequent. This was a mixed blessing, says Kathleen, which at least encouraged children to find their own amusements.

A gramophone with its cylindrical records and trumpet horn was a luxury and a curiosity. The sea, the beach, the bush and the hills were our main playgrounds; stories were enacted on imaginary stages out of doors. Grimms, Hans Anderson and Dickens would have felt flattered had they witnessed the naive production of many of their tales.

Sundays were always a red-letter day as we appreciated a sleep-in and a nine-o-clock breakfast instead of the usual 7.00am. As there was no church on the island, the family would gather for a homemade service and a short Bible study or lesson. Both my parents were very religious and regretted that there was no means of attending church services, except on the rare occasions when a priest visited us to stay, usually just one night and day.

It was on one of these occasions in May 1914 that Madame O'Brien, our grandmother, took ill and was grateful to have a priest at her bedside to take the last rites of Holy Church. She died that night.

Hélène, a dignified old lady who often dressed in black with a crocheted shawl around her shoulders, was 82 and did not know that the German Army was soon to invade her homeland, Belgium. Kathleen recalled the almost daily visits to Grannie O'Brien.

Sunday afternoon was a special time when our whole family would walk round the point to Wharetana and spend a couple of hours with her. We children found her foreign accent somewhat difficult to understand, but she was always very kind to us and tried to break down our shyness...

I always picture her as a woman of medium height, about five feet, five inches, I would think, grey eyes and white glossy hair neatly combed back off her face and caught in a bob at the back of her head; she usually wore a long gown with gored skirt, mauve or black in colour, or sometimes just a white, frilly, laced blouse and a long, flowing black skirt. In the years I remember her best, between 1912 and 1914, she was not very mobile and seldom left the house.

After the formal visit to Grannie, the youngsters would scamper off outside.

First to tour the orchard and sample some of its fruit: thus fortified, we would go foraging up the hills for maidenhair ferns that grew in the spring-formed water holes, or gather clematis blooms that clustered vine-like over trees on the edge of the bush.

Baby lambs were always a fascination in spring and many were the pets we had. On other occasions the bush would become our playground. Here we found entanglements of supplejack and bush lawyer, while in the foot of the valley trickled a clear stream where sly and slippery eels darted in and out of rotting tree trunks. A sleepy morepork or two would rustle through the foliage, or a nesting bird would betray its presence by squawking angrily. All nature was at its best even where the bush trailed off into a swamp several chains in length. Here flourished clumps of arum lilies amid the usual raupo rushes with their brown furry reeds which seemed to attract multicoloured dragonflies, so pretty in the sunlight.

From the hilltop above, it was an artist's dream with its vision of bright green heightened by those masses of white blossoming arums which New Zealanders take so much for granted. I remember Nellie declaring they would be worth £1 a bloom in her native land, which gave our empty pockets a yen for a florist trade with Scotland.

Memories of Wharetana include the "poor man's oranges", used only for marmalade and not yet re-christened "grapefruit", and the old man who used to tend the orchard.

Mr Bloomfield, as he was named, intrigued us with his long white beard and his rustic habit of drinking his tea from a saucer at smoko time. This poor chap, on leaving Waiheke, could not get work in the city so apparently decided the next best thing was to obtain board at the Government's expense by breaking into a shop and receiving a jail sentence. No Social Welfare around in those days, but at least his dramatic act drew attention to his infirmities and state of mind.

School was not easy to get to on the island and the O'Brien youngsters were initially taught by their mother who had worked as a teacher before marrying.

Well I remember those mornings of 'lessons' when, with slate in hand, we would trail after mother from room to room as she did the household chores and taught us at the same time. A vivid memory is of struggling with the problems of addition and subtraction of money, sitting on a sack of potatoes in the wash house, while my mother tended the copper and the tubs.

The tuition was thorough, however, and by the time the youngsters went to boarding school at around ten years of age, they were ready for Standard V or VI. School holidays (two months at Christmas and a month mid-winter) provided a chance for family reunions, with visiting school friends swelling the population of this quiet bay.

The sea still ruled the lives of these farming folk. Stock was shipped in on scows with cattle and sheep loaded on or off at a wooden race that ran out from the sheepyards into the sea. One new bull was unceremoniously prodded overboard into the sea a short distance from the beach and directed to swim ashore to his new harem. Scows, recalled Kathleen, were a familiar sight in the first quarter of the century: *and a lovely one at that, when on a calm day like a stately galleon with all sails set, the scow was reflected mirror-like in the calm sea.*

Pūtiki was the first port of call from the city and last from Coromandel — a very open "port" which caused no little anxiety to those whose lifeline it was, as Kathleen explained.

The Northern Steamship Co's ships that served us, the Daphne, Gael, Rotomahana *and* Chelmsford *to name a few, would come just to the entrance of Pūtiki Bay between its string of small islands and Kennedy Point. The menfolk from both sides of the bay had to row out in all weathers to await the arrival of the steamer — never noted for its punctuality. Sixteen and 18ft row boats were employed for this as the seas were often very rough for open boats, so they had to be seaworthy. Even so, it was with no small anxiety that the women would, in stormy weather, watch their husbands and sons out in the bay where merciless white horses tossed the boats over their boisterous crests and troughs.*

The O'Brien farm was becoming one of the best and cleanest on the island, its shearing shed, where local shearers like Ted Day were paid £1 per 100 heavily woolled sheep, noted for its order and cleanliness with a towel at every stand. This shed was near the beach and sometimes old Madame O'Brien would come out to talk to the workers, even speaking a few words in Māori to the delight of the shearers and shed hands. After 1914, Norah O'Brien employed a woman to cook for the shearers now that a big flock of sheep was grazing on the improved pastures.

Scows at anchor in Pūtiki Bay. (Photo by Arthur Breckon)

Jack O'Brien lived on at Wharetana with his wife Blanche (née Peacocke) after the death of his mother. The couple did not have any children. In her will Madame O'Brien left two ten-acre blocks, one of which included Wharetana, three brick-lined wells (one used to provide water for the sheep dip) and — a croquet lawn. Oakura with the two adjacent islands stands on ten acres that was kept separate from the farm.

Like other pioneer settlers, Norah O'Brien was a resourceful woman. Not only did she educate her own children, she also tended to their wounds and ills. When one son was thrown from a horse and his ear almost torn off, Norah stitched it neatly back in place. The First World War brought anxiety for her son Frank who fought at Flanders. She knew, too, that the war had turned her son and nephew into enemies as her sister who had married in Germany to Baron von de Burgh had a son fighting in the German Army. Frank O'Brien was killed.

Another major change to the O'Briens' life in the bay came with the decision in the early 1920s to sell some 250-300 acres of their land in Omiha as sections. The small settlement that developed there had no ocean beach and was dubbed "Rocky Bay". By the mid-1920s a small store had been set up on the site it occupies today.

The O'Briens were indirectly responsible for the naming of another early Waiheke subdivision. Apparently a family friend, Miss Boylan, was staying at Wharetana when Lichtenstein, Arnoldson & Co cut up land for sections. In a contest for names, Miss Boylan entered "Ostend" which she had visited in Belgium. To her astonishment, her entry was the first name pulled out of a bag.

Freda and Kathleen O'Brien both took final vows to become Religious of the Sacred Heart; their two brothers took up farming and both helped out on the farm until Terry enlisted in the Second World War.

He returned, but with shrapnel wounds that he would carry the rest of his life, and married Dorothy, daughter of a well-known stock auctioner, Joe Hardwicke. Dorothy, who was interested in all farm animals and loved horses, was given a horse as her wedding present and the couple moved into the small cottage at Wharetana for two years.

Phillip O'Brien married Olive Grattan who had been a popular hostess on the *Baroona* and they moved into the Oakura home. In 1947 the brothers bought the farm from their father and Uncle Jack. That same year, Laughlin Adolphe (Dolph) O'Brien died on December 20 at the age of 88.

When Terry and Dorothy modernised the kitchen of their Wharetana home, they found remnants of the old De Witte cottage: kauri roof shingles, a strong wall 18in thick and packed with shell, and an old door that still had coloured glass panels. This house became a frequent meeting place for members of the local Federated Farmers (of which both Terry and Phil were active members) and the Women's Division.

For many years, there was no road access to the bay so supplies and guests came and went by boat — so did the schoolchildren. Despite the fact that the long, narrow property often meant that work on the farm took them a long way from the homestead, every school day one brother had to head home, launch the boat and go to pick up the children. It was easier when Ostend wharf was opened but a boat was still needed. Terry used to carry a bag of sand to sprinkle on the wharf steps so that no one would slip.

When a road was put through to Rocky Bay from Ostend, the O'Briens gave eleven and a half acres of land, so it was fitting that the bridge and main road from the junction to the Rocky Bay store was named O'Brien Road.

The property was finally to pass out of O'Brien hands in the 1960s, partly due to the destructive invasion of a sedge called Carex Longifolia. This had started appearing in paddocks during World War Two when Terry was away at war and farm labour was in short supply. Possibly it came in early grass seed (before the days of seed testing), or it may have come embedded in the fleece of rams imported from Australia.

However it got there, the sedge spread rapidly and stock would not eat it. As finances tightened, the struggle to keep the pasture clear became too much and the brothers decided to sell. While many farmers were wary of the sedge problem, the 2500 acres was sold in 1963 to Robert and Maurine Rothschild of New York, USA. The farm was later sold to the Reeve family.

Terry and Dorothy moved to Howick while Phillip and Olive retired to Shelly Beach Road. The O'Brien name is remembered not only on Waiheke but in Auckland where the De Witte name is prominent in old newspapers and historic documents. A memorial window in the parish church of St John the Baptist in Parnell is inscribed in plain glass: *Of your charity pray for the souls of Laughlin and Hélène O'Brien.* On another memorial window to servicemen who died in the 1914-18 war, the name Frank O'Brien is included.

It was in this church that Sacred Heart Sister Kathleen O'Brien was to repeat family history. Then in her eighties, she read the lesson at Sunday Mass in May 1982 during the anniversary celebrations for the birth of St Francis, almost exactly 120 years after her grandfather Laughlin O'Brien had read the address of welcome from Catholics to Bishop Pompallier who blessed this new church in Parnell.

Phillip Francis

An early Pūtiki settler about whom little is now known, Phillip Lloyd Francis appears on official records as master of the Waiheke Post Office in November 1876. He was apparently the original owner of the land that now includes the villages of Surfdale, Ostend, Palm Beach and Onetangi.

An early report on Waiheke to the Anglican Synod records that "the only official institution on the island is the Post Office kept by Mr Francis at his residence in Pūtiki Bay." It is known that Phillip Francis gave hospitality to a visiting parson by lending him a horse and guiding him to the neighbouring station. It is also known that a baby was baptised at a service in his woolshed and that in 1881 some 25 people assembled for worship there. In November 1881, Francis was appointed a member of the first Anglican church committee following another service held in the woolshed. It is this same woolshed that, relocated to Onetangi Straight, was restored by the Waiheke Island Historical Society as a museum.

His homestead was on the rise somewhere near the present Council offices and there was also a brick-lined well. The Carey family, who rode from Wairua to attend service, often stayed to dine here. The Francis family left the island in 1883 and, a little later, it was to this house that Captain Kennedy, his wife and son came to start what was to be a lengthy Kennedy association with Waiheke.

The Kennedy Family

The Kennedy story starts with a letter to Scotland written by one Hunter Brown of Hawkes Bay. Brown had purchased a Waiheke property from Phillip Francis which totalled some 4500 acres and took in an area from what is now Surfdale to Burrell Road, Palm Beach, Ostend, Onetangi and Pie Melon Bay. He wrote to urge his cousin, Captain John Brown Kennedy, to come to New Zealand to see this run.

Kennedy, a captain in the Royal Scots Fusiliers, was a man of courage and initiative who studied medicine in Edinburgh and had ventured into farming on the plains of Patagonia in South America. He both spoke and wrote Spanish.

Returning to Scotland, Kennedy married Jessie Gillespie, a tall, dark-eyed girl who had enjoyed a life of culture and some luxury at her parents' Dublin home. The couple set up a home with an indoor staff of four in Scotland and there John Kennedy farmed for about seven or eight years.

Brown's letter was to change all that. Kennedy decided to head for

New Zealand and he, his wife, and eight-year-old son James set sail on board the *Doric* to make landfall in the self-governing colony in 1883. After a look at the Waiheke property his cousin had acquired, he decided to buy it.

Arrival on Waiheke was a shock for Mrs Kennedy. She was badly frightened climbing down from the cutter into an open boat bouncing around in a choppy sea and, while landed without mishap, never really recovered from this initial unnerving experience. The family furniture, silver and treasures that had come with them from Scotland, were unloaded in Pūtiki Bay to be hauled up a slippery bank by teams of bullocks.

In January 1884, a New Year greeting from the Carey family must have warmed the hearts of the new arrivals. Lizzie, Madge and Alec Carey, who had ridden over from Wairua, could supply some much-needed advice about ordering supplies and other housekeeping problems Mrs Kennedy now faced. By 1885 Kennedy had assumed the post Phillip Francis had filled: that of official postmaster for Pūtiki Bay. This task involved regular trips in the 18ft, double-ended whale boat to convey mail bags to and from the steamers that passed down the Waiheke Channel. The heavy boat needed two rowers to get it out to the mouth of the bay in both rough and calm weather. A flag flying on a pole erected on what is now Kennedy Point was the signal for a bag to be collected but boats were frequently late or failed to heed the sign. Later, when the Kennedys built a new house, a special office with a side entrance was included for sorting mail into pigeonholes.

The new house, built of kauri in 1888, was an imposing two-storey residence with handsome marble fireplaces. Its site, on the eastern side of Kennedy Point, was carefully chosen to be sheltered from the cold southerlies. It was christened Dunesslin — "the house under the hill" — and remained a landmark for 70 years.

With spacious rooms designed for gracious living, Dunesslin was, at that time, Waiheke's finest house. It had a gabled roof, deep windows and wide verandahs; off the entrance hall was a huge drawing room which featured a fireplace of black marble streaked with grey, a finely-carved kauri table, a solid oak sideboard, and a matching oak table that could be extended to seat 20 and was an impressive sight when set with damask and silver.

Dunesslin, the Kennedy home in Pūtiki Bay, built of kauri in 1888

Two downstairs bedrooms had open fireplaces surrounded by pretty tiles; an attractive winding staircase with walnut handrail led to the upstairs bedrooms, and along a narrow corridor lay the kitchen and maids' room.

While Jessie Kennedy found life on Waiheke very different from what she had been used to, she was determined to keep up the standards — with the help of local girls. These girls, accustomed to the tough pioneer existence were, in turn, able to learn about the trappings of a more cultured world as they helped lay out the fine china and silver cutlery for a dinner party.

The Careys, also emigrants from Scotland, were frequent visitors. They rode over for midday meals and might sing ballads of home, around the piano, before riding home to milk the cows. A special treasure the Kennedys had brought with them from Scotland was a model yacht, 6ft long, lead-keeled and in full sail. It was later given to Billy Brown (Kennedy's right-hand man for many years) who cherished the gift which was handed down through his family.

The captain proved to be a practical and progressive farmer, employing local labour to clear the land, but maintaining stands of native bush as well as pohutukawa which he also planted to help beautify the landscape.

He ran shorthorn cattle and when drafting would still use his skill with a lariat that had been learned in Argentina. His first sheep were wild blackfaced Shropshire which were bred with rams imported from England. The sheepyards were sited near the present Ostend beach reserve. Before the wool auction system was set up in Auckland, wool was shipped off to England fetching prices of around 8d a pound in 1900.

Although Jessie Kennedy enjoyed riding, sidesaddle and dressed in riding habit, she never got used to the difficulties of climbing from a small pitching boat up into the steamer— the necessary pre-requisite for a trip into Auckland. When the family had been on the island nearly 15 years, she fulfilled her desire to make a much longer sea voyage, back home to Scotland. Dunesslin was left in the care of Tom Day who lived in the farm manager's house near Shelly Beach.

On the return voyage, their boat, the *Paparoa*, was able to sail close enough in around Cape Horn to allow Captain Kennedy to photograph that notoriously treacherous bit of coastline. The trip had an unsettling influence. While the Kennedys took up Waiheke life again and James became the new postmaster of Pūtiki in 1902, the family did not stay long.

In 1904 they sold their land to the Bayley brothers and again set sail for Scotland, this time for good. That could have been the end of the Kennedy connection with Waiheke, but the island call was too strong, especially for James who had been reluctant to leave. He was an enthusiastic yachtsman, owned a 41 ft yacht named the *Lady Wilma* and from 1896 had been a member of the Royal Yacht Squadron.

Two years later, the family returned to New Zealand to find their property back on the market. So in July 1907, they bought it back again. The captain was upset to find that a number of pohutukawa had been cut down in his absence. James Kennedy took up his old position as Pūtiki postmaster — a task which Frank Bayley relinquished along with the land. The Kennedys were back and this time, they stayed.

When Waiheke was connected to the Auckland telephone exchange in 1908, Dunesslin became the local exchange with a phone that, cranked up, had to be yelled into in order to get a message through. James retained

responsibility for both exchange and mail until a post office was opened
in the new settlement of Ostend in 1916.

Interior of Dunesslin, Pūtiki Bay

James married Elizabeth Caroline Dyer and the young couple moved into Dunesslin while the captain and Jessie went to live in a smaller and more manageable cottage. This house, which stood further up the hill, was enlarged and an annex built. The captain became an enthusiastic orchardist growing Bon Chretien pears, bottling peaches and a luscious eating peach called Sea Eagle. A tin shed was built to pack the fruit which was sent off to the city markets on board Kennedy's launch *Dixie*.

When the captain died at the age of 78 on November 6, 1923, he was cremated in Auckland's first crematorium, to which he had donated funds. His ashes were returned to Waiheke on board his own launch and three Scottish pipers played a lament as the procession of mourners moved up the hill to his grave above Pūtiki Bay. His wife, Jessie, died five years later, on October 9, and was buried beside him.

The extensive run was gradually being carved up. In 1911, the captain had sold Onetangi and part of the Pūtiki block to Commander Newton who, in 1915, disposed of 2900 acres to Lichtenstein, Arnoldson & Co. Much of this was subdivided during the First World War, creating new settlements in Ostend and Onetangi. In 1916, a wharf to cater for the increasing number of visitors was built.

Much of the Surfdale area — from present-day Burrell Road — was sold to a Mr Rutherford who then sold it to a syndicate which subdivided the land in the early 1920s. Inspired by the speed with which the Surfdale sections were going, James Kennedy decided to subdivide the farmland around Palm Beach. He did most of the work himself.

"That was in 1923," recalled his son Jack. "I was still at school and when I came home in the holidays, it was already under way."

Photographs of Palm Beach at this time show grassy headlands with only a few trees dotted here and there in the gullies. The palm that gave the subdivision its name still grows there, now lost amidst the growing profusion of trees and houses.

James encouraged Bradney and Binns to start a ferry service to Ostend wharf and this helped to sell the new sections. The farm was eventually cut down to about 1100 acres, a more workable size for a couple of people to handle.

Then came the Depression years during which James and Caroline Kennedy became known for their willingness to help out those in trouble. James gave firewood and mutton to pensioners in Pūtiki and Surfdale.

Needy folk received cakes and puddings made by Caroline Kennedy who also visited anyone who was sick, often taking soup.

The Kennedy launch was called on by District Nurse Tribe to carry the sick or injured into Auckland Hospital; it was also used by the Police when needed. With farm prices at rock bottom, James sold pine trees which were taken to Auckland for milling.

James and Caroline had two sons, John (known as Jack) and James (Jim), who schooled in Havelock North and at Wanganui Collegiate. With the boys away from home, the elder Kennedys decided that Dunesslin was now too big for them and, like his parents before them, moved into the smaller home on the hill.

Jim joined Union Airways as a pilot and later shifted to Air New Zealand where he became a senior pilot until retiring at 55. Jack was keen on farming and returned to work on the Waiheke property. In 1940, a new farmhouse was built in the bay for Jack and his new wife, Mary. Now unlived in, Dunesslin fell into disrepair. Built too low to the ground, its piles and flooring were rotting. Because the cost of repair was too high, the old house was sold for demolition. Some of the timber was used for fenceposts, other pieces were made into broom handles at an Erua Road factory. Some of the antique furniture and fittings were bought by Fred Alison of Matiatia.

James Kennedy died in 1964 at the age of 88 and was buried in the family plot at Pūtiki. Jack continued farming and carried on the family tradition of community service as a member of the Roads Board for 14 years and an active member of Federated Farmers.

He and Mary made their own butter and got fresh bread from town twice a week. Electricity didn't arrive until the late 1950s. That, recalled Jack, was a great day.

"We were one of the last places on the island to get wired up. My wife was so excited that she ran round turning everything on. No more lamps to trim and clean, no more chopping firewood for the stove — she thought it was great."

The land was farmed until 1973 when Kennedy Point was sold for subdivision along with 100 acres adjoining Wilma Road, 60 acres along Junction Road and the 300-acre Thompson Point farm. The home his parents lived in has been renovated as part of the Goldwater vineyard (now called Goldie Estate and operated by the Wine Science programme of the University of Auckland). The deep red blossom of the pohutukawa that still thrive on the headland makes a colourful welcome to the hundreds of summer visitors who now pour across the Kennedy Point vehicular ferry wharf.

Jack Kennedy continued to live on his 16-acre farmlet, enjoying a view across the peaceful inlet that had changed little since his grandparents first looked out on it more than 100 years earlier.

Pūtiki Bay around 1900. (Photo by Henry Winkelmann)

Ostend: The Birth of a Village (by Ivy F Smytheman)

[Dixie Day's note: The firm of Lichtenstein, Arnoldson & Co were gum merchants who in 1905 owned and occupied the building in Quay Street which in later years became the Ambassadors Hotel. One of the properties they owned was named Horsham Downs, and at around the beginning of 1915, they exchanged part of this block, just out of Ngaruawahia, for Commander Newton's 2900-acre block on Waiheke. In later years, the firm also owned land at Patumahoe and Rotoiti. Ivy Smytheman's father was their accountant, a job later taken on by his son. When the last of the old firm, Mr Lichtenstein died, the Waiheke farm (Pie Melon Bay was the area they still owned and worked) and Rotoiti Block were sold; Patumahoe having been sold some years earlier. This chapter is taken from the memoirs of Ivy F Smytheman, written in 1948.]

It was about the beginning of 1915 when Messrs Lichtenstein, Arnoldson and Co purchased from Commander Newton approximately 2900 acres of land on Waiheke, comprising all the present Ostend and Onetangi districts. An Order in Council dated January 12, 1915, gave the firm licence to occupy a part of the Pūtiki Bay foreshore as a site for a wharf.

The wharf was built during 1915 and was completed before the first group of sections in what had been called the Ostend Estate went up for auction in February 1916. It was not a very successful day as not more than 30 sections were sold, at prices ranging from £10 to £21.

My father, who was the company accountant, bought the one on the high corner known in later years as Steedman's. That was the beginning of our family's long connection with Ostend. His parents bought a

section on either side of ours and my other grandparents, Mr and Mrs J
Hindman, bought the area opposite to build the Ostend Accommodation
House and store. This building was commenced almost straight away
and was open for guests by Easter.

A twice-weekly launch service had started up and we went down to stay
in the Accommodation House for the holiday week. On Easter Monday
there was a big excursion: The Northern Company had been prevailed
on to run the *Wakatere* (a paddle vessel which was on the Auckland/
Thames run for many years), and she brought hundreds to the island.

In 1916, the first road was built from Ostend to Onetangi via the hill
route. A second road linking the two areas was started the following year
but took longer than expected because of a large culvert filling required
at one end of it. The plan name for the first road was Sea View Road,
but it was never called that. These two routes were respectively known to
everyone as the High Road and the Low Road, names that were still in use
when our family's connection with the island ended in 1935.

My father's parents had their cottage completed in time for Christmas
1916 but ours wasn't sufficiently advanced to occupy, so we "bached" in a
marquee beside it. The cottage was finished by the following Easter.

During that first Christmas holiday on the island, a party of us went
for a picnic to Onetangi — by farm dray. I can still remember several of
us having to get down as the long hill climb commenced and walk behind
the dray to lighten the load for the horses.

It is strange, now, to remember Onetangi as we first saw it. It was the
largest bay on the island, its fine ocean beach over a mile long, and not a
building anywhere. We had the whole beach to ourselves.

In those years, there were horse races held on this beach every
summer with crowds gathering to watch various island farmers competing.
I remember our excitement when Lichtenstein and Arnoldson's farm
manager, Eddie Brown from the Ostend homestead, came first.

The Pūtiki Post Office and Telephone Bureau were opened in the
Ostend Accommodation House at the same time as the Ostend Store, in
early 1916. The store was at the front of the Accommodation House and
the post office was in a separate room behind the store with mail handed
out to customers across the store counters. A telephone booth was in a
small lobby at the end of the verandah but getting through to Auckland
was often a frustrating business. I remember hearing my grandmother's

voice calling out distractedly as she tried to get a clear connection through. Although both the Accommodation House and store had been named after the new resort, Ostend, the authorities insisted that the post office and bureau use the name Pūtiki.

The Accommodation House at Ostend with the wharf in background

The environs of Pūtiki Bay looked somewhat different in those days. The undulating land around it was not yet built on and there were more, and larger, tracts of bush. On the sandy strip of beach nearly opposite Pūtiki Road stood a white boatshed with a red roof that normally had a boat anchored near it. Close to the shed was a rustic sheep and cattle race which remained there for many years.

On the other side of the mudflat behind the sandy strip, on a tongue of land round which the little Ōkahuiti Creek runs, stood an old, dark red woolshed surrounded by fences where sheep were mustered before being driven to the beach, through the race and on to a waiting scow to be taken away. It was common to see a scow lying in the channel waiting for high tide: In earlier years, it was usually the *Wanderer*, a very old vessel, later it was the *Wendel*.

Across the same end of the bay was a row of posts marking the way for those walking to or from Huruhi Bay. It was a muddy, unpleasant bit of track which had to be crossed at low tide. I have vivid memories of mud squelching nearly to our knees, of sitting on the grass afterwards cleaning the worst of the mud off with wet rags carried for the purpose. Stories were told of a man lost through being sucked down into the soft mud because he had tried to cross the bay without following the sticks that marked the "safe track".

One of the most familiar figures to be seen on this old mudflat route was a fine old Māori who used to bring fresh fish, and sometimes kumara, from Te Huruhi to sell to my grandparents at the Accommodation House.

We got our milk from the homestead which was then in Belgium Street and occupied by Eddie Brown and his family. Meat had to be ordered from Auckland and came twice a week by launch. Bread and supplies came twice a week on board the Cowes steamer which was met by rowboats out at Pūtiki Point. Rarohara (Pie Melon Bay) provided jam; there were always large quantities of melons there in season and a small party would ride over with pack horses to bring back a load of the largest ones.

In 1917, because the Accommodation House was now fully booked every holiday season, a separate annexe was built out the back. At about the same time, a cottage was built by F Lipscombe just above the annexe. This was owned and occupied for some time by a man called Keesing. Many years later it was to become the Pūtiki Post Office.

The regular launch service continued for two years, familiar vessels including the *Redwing*, *Sterling*, *Jumbo*, *Sambo*, *Red and Black*, *Olivene*, and *Olive Jean*. Around 1920 a large launch named the *Muriwai* was purchased, renamed the *Ostend* and made our regular launch. She was still on the run when Northern Company boats started calling at Pūtiki twice a week but was withdrawn because of reduced patronage.

The Northern boats only called in on their way to Cowes Bay if there were passengers to drop, and on the way back if a signal flag showed there were passengers for Auckland. With the increase in holiday population they became more regular callers. Infrequent callers included the *Wakatere*, *Ngatiawa*, *Clansman*, *Aupouri*, *Waimarie*, *Tasman*, *Rangitoto*, *Ngapuhi*, *Waiotahi*, *Gael*, *Kotiti*, *Manaia* and *Taniwha*; more frequent callers included the *Waipu, Kawau, Hauiti, Omana, Daphne* and *Waiuku*.

The *Daphne* soon became our regular vessel and was popular as her usual sailing time from Auckland to Ostend was a bare hour-and-a-half. She flew her company's "greyhound" at her masthead, declaring her their fastest steamer and, occasionally, when wind and tide were with her, was said to have done the trip in one hour twenty minutes — she was always carefully timed by some of the passengers.

The Ostend Hall was built in the latter part of 1918 and was opened on October 26, a Labour weekend Saturday. It was a day of special celebrations. Crowds came down, including a band which played during the afternoon on the Accommodation House lawn. A flag flew all weekend at the top of the new hall's flagpole. A marquee erected on the flat beside the beach served soft drinks, ice cream, sweets and afternoon tea.

The opening function was that evening; hundreds of printed invitations had been sent out for this occasion which culminated in a Grand Ball. There was another equally memorable ball a few months later when New Year festivities served as a celebration for the ending of the First World War.

(Other early island residents remember the Saturday evening dances held in this hall. Don Croll and sister Agnes rode over from Matiatia crossing the tidal creek with their good clothes held high to avoid mud splashes. Edna Peet, whose parents had a little house above the Ostend wharf, recalls the Labour weekend dances when it was easy to spot those who had been outside to look at the moon — evidence of sitting on a sheep-grazed hillside was speckled on their light-coloured summer clothes. Piano music was frequently provided by Harry Garrett.)

There was no regular transport in the early days and supplies were brought up by the ferry on a large sled with wooden runners made by my Grandfather Hindman. Later, when the road was metalled, the runners were replaced with four big iron wheels.

The first bus on the island ran from Ostend to Onetangi, via the low road. We children used it once or twice, for novelty, but ordinarily despised any kind of transport and walked everywhere. We generally used the high road to Onetangi because it was more interesting though the low road did have its attractions — like the culvert where we sometimes fished for tommy cod, or an old deserted quince and fig orchard near Stony Hill.

On the high road, boy scout camps were held at Christmas in Brinsden's Bush. I remember once, when a party of us were returning from a night walk to Onetangi, we listened to their singing, watched the bright glow of their campfire and laughed with them at the way our voices echoed round the hills as we and they called out to one another.

Once the steamers began calling in at Ostend, a big party of us local holiday residents went to Cowes Bay for a day picnic, which was eaten in the large dance rotunda on the flat. Other bays we often walked to for picnics were Onetangi, Whakarite, Oneroa, Matiatia and Huruhi Bay.

In 1920, my grandparents, having found the running of the house too much for them, sold out to the Aspdens who also took over the store and post office. In 1921, the first motor car appeared on Waiheke — a dubious-looking Ford which was used for driving prospective purchasers to view distant sections.

At about this time, the *Daphne* was taken off the Ostend run and replaced by the *Waiuku* — spacious and comfortable in fair weather, but a bad sea boat, having originally been built for river work. Her crew, Captain Vann, Miss Warren the stewardess, and Mr Fagan the engineer, were very popular with the Ostend people and there was quite a lot of competition connected with inviting them to midday Sunday dinner.

This pleasant side apart, however, the steamer service to Ostend was becoming increasingly unsatisfactory and did not improve despite many complaints. Finally, something had to be done.

A few years earlier, my uncle, Mr W Hindman, had chartered the *Onewa* (a Bradney and Binns vessel) to bring a big excursion party to Ostend. These gentlemen were now approached to see if they would consider running a regular "Ostend only" service.

After discussions, James Kennedy, who had started subdividing land in Whakarite (later Palm Beach), and Lichtenstein, Arnoldson & Co bought about £150 worth of fares as an encouragement for the company to begin this service. Thus the *Onewa* started 20 years of faithful and popular service to the growing community. She was small and slow but solid and dependable — a good sea boat. Her engineer, Ernie Binns, won peoples' hearts with his cheery friendliness, not to mention the cups of tea and biscuits he laid on: 6d a cup and free repeats.

To old Ostendites, the picture of the *Onewa's* cabin, crowded with people being served from the little wooden table by Mr Binns while he exchanged greetings with all and sundry and kept up a cheerful patter, is one never to be forgotten.

In September 1917, a school was opened in a cottage at Ostend, with seven youngsters attending. The teacher, R J Martin, taught there in conjunction with the Te Huruhi School, each having three days a week. The Ostend School closed again on July 31 1921 for lack of suitable accommodation and remained closed until April 1 1922 when it was conducted at another cottage by R J McKenna under the same three day a week arrangement.

This lasted until the following year when, in February 1923, a school building was erected in Ostend consisting of a large classroom and small porch. The roll was then 18 with Mr McKenna still teaching half-time there and half at Te Huruhi. The latter was closed a few years later.

Onetangi was also being developed. The private hotel was built there shortly after Ostend was established, and in 1919 Mrs Taylor built and opened up the first store and post office in the bay. Later, she and her husband, both cultured people, ran a fine guest house. I remember their library of good books and collection of classical music.

Although we spent a lot of time around Ostend, bathing, rowing, playing tennis on the Brinsdens' court, or joining friends in the Hall on wet days to amuse ourselves playing the pianola and dancing, we were also accustomed to venturing far and wide visiting the then deserted beaches.

Toward the end of 1921, the eastern part of Huruhi Bay was cut up and sold, and given the name Surfdale. A year later, James Kennedy cut up a large area at Whakarite which was named Palm Beach. Apart from a children's holiday camp of the City Mission, Oneroa remained untouched until after our contact with Waiheke had ended.

In the 1920s, despite openly expressed opinion that it would prove a failure, a wharf was built at Onetangi Beach. The *Waiotahi* was put on to this run and some doleful episodes peppered her career there. One day after disembarking her passengers, she was forced to cast off from the wharf and move out to a safe distance because a strong sea had come up. Unable to return, she left a crowd of disgusted picnickers to be taken to Ostend in a series of hastily arranged bus trips and picked up from that wharf. Another time, the vessel arrived at Onetangi and, unable to berth, had to return to Auckland with all her passengers still aboard. Finally, as many had foretold, the wharf was destroyed in a winter storm.

The Ostend Road District was formed in 1921 with a board of four members. The district had no funds, so these members each guaranteed £100 each until they could strike and collect rates. The first plant purchased was a wheelbarrow!

Truck owned by the Kennedy family, early 1920s

During the depression, the Ostend Accommodation House became unoccupied and the Pūtiki Post Office was transferred up the road to Mrs Brown's store, later run by Mrs Hopkins. When she moved into Mr Keesing's old cottage above the annexe, the post office moved with her to its third home. At around this time, the annexe was moved to Palm Beach.

In December 1930, the Ostend Development League was formed and during holidays its members held working bees to clear the woolshed reserve and plant trees along the boundary. One member, Norman Brinsden, drew up a comprehensive plan for the reserve's layout and development, including swimming baths and a general play area. These plans never eventuated.

In January 1932 some boys from the Auckland Community

Sunshine Association were brought for a few weeks to Ostend, staying in the deserted Accommodation House. My father and I rehearsed them for a concert which was given in the Ostend Hall and, with the proceeds, prizes were provided for a gala sports day for them on the new reserve — its first formal function. The depression interrupted fulfilment of plans for the reserve and caused the break-up of the League as many had to leave their Ostend holiday home.

We leased our cottage to various Ostend schoolteachers for a few years and later sold it to Mr L Steedman who had married Eddie Brown's eldest daughter, Mabel. My grandparents Smytheman had both died in 1934 and their cottage was sold to Eddie Brown's elder son.

It was nearly 11 years before I returned to Waiheke and saw Ostend briefly through the windows of the "Round Trip" bus during an Easter holiday spent at Oneroa. It felt strange to be sitting there instead of being a part of it, and to look at the cottage that had been ours for over 18 years.

Many old landmarks had gone: the boatshed, sheep race and old woolshed, the annexe, the old homestead in Belgium St (burned down), and the sticks on the mudflat track. I was told the old Accommodation House was now flats. Ostend in 1946 appeared to have almost forgotten the Pūtiki of 1916.

Selling Ostend

Advertising booklets written in the 1920s outline some of the delights of the new subdivisions on Waiheke for prospective customers. The Ostend booklet, much of which could equally well have been written today, was worded as follows. Copies of this and a similar booklet advertising Palm Beach are kept in the Auckland Public Library.

Auckland, the Queen City of New Zealand, is destined for a great future. Its population is increasing so rapidly and congestion becoming so great, that the natural tendency is to extend the residential area to the various bays and islands handy to the city. Of the seaside estates near Auckland, none gives greater promise of soon becoming an integral part of the city than OSTEND.

OSTEND is situated on the harbour side of Waiheke and extends from

Pūtiki Bay to the magnificent Onetangi Beach. It is 15 miles from the city and is well served by a regular steamer service, the trip taking one-and-a-half hours in smooth water.

Although a newly opened seaside estate, the growth of OSTEND has been phenomenal. Over 800 sections have been sold. 120 houses have been erected. Over 16 miles of good roads have already been made.

To keep pace with the development of the estate, OSTEND has been formed into a Road District, and the Ostend Roads Board is fully alive to the interests of this splendid resort.

A Post Office, Telephone Bureau, two accommodation houses and stores serve to fill the requirements of visitors to Ostend while the motor-bus service makes a pleasant run from the Ostend Wharf to the ocean beach at Onetangi.

OSTEND gives ample opportunity for the pleasures of the seaside. The pretty Pūtiki Bay, so nicely sheltered, affords ample facilities for bathing and boating while there is no finer spot in New Zealand for surfbathing than on Onetangi Beach with its one-and-a-quarter miles of beautiful hard sand.

Good shooting and fishing. Quite a little hive of industry has already sprung up at Ostend and experienced strawberry growers state that nowhere around Auckland have they found land more fitted for the cultivation of the strawberry than on this estate. Early potatoes, tomatoes, peas and in fact all vegetables thrive at OSTEND; the absence of frost permits of gardening being carried on all the year round.

The ONETANGI BEACH PRIVATE HOTEL, probably the finest seaside hotel in the Dominion, has attained great popularity among tourists and pleasure-seekers.

Pretty houses are springing up everywhere, and week-enders and visitors are well catered for by the Hotel and by the Store on the beach.

Nowhere in the harbour can prettier views be obtained than from the hillocks at Ostend. Here truly we have nature at her best, the fresh bracing air giving new life and vigour, in great contrast to the sultriness so noticeable in the city areas.

For the information of those likely to build, it might be stated that there are several builders resident on the estate and a timberyard has already been established at Pūtiki Bay. 102 homes already erected at Ostend.

In laying out the OSTEND ESTATE many picturesque spots have been set aside as public reserves. Some of the finest Native Bush has been included in these areas, and with the development of OSTEND these breathing-spaces *will be treasured by residents and holiday makers alike.*

To those desirous of taking up small holdings for poultry farming, bee keeping, fruit growing and intensive cultivation, areas of from 5 to 50 acres can be had; while for graziers and others, larger areas are available. Owners of seaside cottage at Ostend have been enjoying their week-end trips throughout the year, Summer and Winter, the Northern SS Co catering specially for this traffic. During the Summer season, the steamer runs five days a week, and with the ever-increasing popularity of Ostend, the service to this resort must soon become a daily one. As an investment, nothing more attractive can be shown than OSTEND.

Its growth has been remarkable, and its future as an extension of the residential area of the City is assured. Already large profits have been made by purchasers, and it requires no special vision to see that new investors must reap the benefit of the increased prices which will inevitably follow the progress of the estate.

The attached plan is a new subdivision just opened and many sections command most magnificent views of sea and land. Each section is reported on in the price-list sent to enquirers.

Sections are available from £20 on the most extraordinary terms of

£2.10s per section deposit,

balance £1 per month,

no interest

These terms make it possible for one and all to secure a section and commence building a seaside home at any time without waiting till the section is paid off. There is no obligation to build.

Intending builders, speculators, and others are advised to take a run down to OSTEND to convince themselves as to its tremendous prospective value, and have a chat with some of those who have already bought. Sections originally sold for £20 have been resold up to £100. For further particulars, price-list, and report on each section, please write or call on:

T R Smytheman,

Imperial Buildings,

Opp. Smeetons,

44 Queen St, Auckland.

Matiatia

As pioneering families were starting the task of turning eastern Waiheke's bush clad hills into pastureland in the mid-1800s, the most western reaches of the island remained a predominantly Māori settlement.

Had a Crown intention to create a 2100-acre native reserve on the island in the early 1800s been fulfilled, that might still be the case. When the newly-established Māori Land Court investigated titles to Māori land on Waiheke in 1865, the 2100-acre Te Huruhi block, 2800 acres to the south which included the Awaawaroa and Okoka blocks, and a further 800 acres at Mawhitipana were the only tracts of land left in Māori hands.

Early maps show the Te Huruhi block set aside as a reserve that would have given its tangata whenua, Ngāti Pāoa, ownership of most of Oneroa west to Matiatia. The reserve was never formally created, however, and gradually the land was sold.

Early purchasers were boat owners whose vessels worked the gulf shoreline or anchored in the sheltered waters of Matiatia. The first non-Māori owner of an 11-acre block on the Matiatia flat was the Royal New Zealand Yacht Squadron; this block later passed into the hands of the Devonport Steam Ferry Company and was bought by company founder Alix Alison's son, Alfred.

This block formed the basis of what was to be an extensive farm as Fred Alison gradually purchased more than 2000 acres stretching from Matiatia through to what is now Surfdale.

At this time much of the land was already under cultivation with its Ngāti Pāoa owners growing kumara, potatoes, rock melon, watermelons, corn and other crops for sale in Auckland. A native school had been established at Te Huruhi in 1911 with a roll of more than 30.

The Croll Family

The first Pākehā family to settle in Matiatia was the Croll family who moved there in 1911 to manage the Alison property. John Croll had worked for the Alison family for many years on Browns Island where he ran a thoroughbred stud farm and later as ticket collector on the ferries.

John, his wife Mary, and family were then living in Devonport but had earlier connections to the island as Mary's mother, Mary Regan, had been born in Man O'War Bay in 1841. Her father was employed cutting kauri rickers there for use by the English Navy. Mary had eventually left the island and married Lieutenant Colonel Henry Parker who was first fishery inspector for the gulf and also customs officer for many years. He owned land in the area that is now Hobson St in Auckland.

John and Mary Croll had six children but the older three were to remain living and working in Auckland. The following extracts from the memories of their fourth youngster, the late Don Croll, provide an interesting look into the past of what is now the island's most populous settlement.

> My first glimpse of Waiheke was as a lad of ten years.... I was sitting on top of a house which was to be my home being taken there by the scow Mabel owned by Fred Alison. Also on this scow was a dray and horse box which carried a horse named Mary Moran.
>
> The house, then 40 years old, had been standing where the present Travel Lodge is and had been the dock keeper's house. It had been taken from the graving dock to be erected in Matiatia. The carting of all the building was done, of course, with Mary Moran and the dray.
>
> I remember on one occasion, they found it necessary to move the scow along the beach and decided to do it by attaching a line from the scow to the axle of the dray. This had the effect that when the horse moved forward, it lifted the dray off the beach, flipping both horse and dray completely over. Luckily no damage was done to either.

The Crolls' house was rebuilt by Auckland building contractors Sam White & Sons. John stayed to help and act as cook, and Don spent a week there "thoroughly enjoying myself, and missing school of course". He records that one day, while everyone was working, pigs from one of the Māori settlements found and ate most of their food supplies leaving them with little to eat until Alix Alison arrived in one of the ferry boats. The family finally moved over to their new home in October 1911.

The day we moved in was not the best, with a hard sou'wester blowing. We were taken down with all our household goods on the Ferry Co's paddle steamer Takapuna, calling into Browns Island for a cow we promptly called Red Wing.

It was very rough trip but my sister Agnes and I loved every minute of it, watching the waves wash over the sponsons and into the cabin. This steamer had very little free board as it was a real old timer. On arrival at Matiatia, the furniture was ferried to shore in a dinghy, the cow swimming of course. Everything was placed on the grass from where the horse and dray were to do their job, but no Mary Moran could be found, so my father had to shift everything on his back. He was unwell for some time after.

With the older Croll children, David, Linda and Hilda in Auckland, the family on Waiheke consisted of John, Mary, Don, his sister Agnes and baby brother Albert. Mary Croll is described by her son as a "very capable, very gentle, loving person who could do everything but ride a horse" and, despite her boating background, did not like boats.

As she became known to the Māori, they loved her very much and called her affectionately by her Christian name.... My father, too, was a very capable man with a great knowledge of stock, boats, gardening, and a good all-round sportsman.

The older children were regular visitors, often coming down in friends' yachts as there was no regular boat service to the island. The younger ones went to the newly opened native school in Te Huruhi, as Don recorded.

The day came when Agnes and I had to go to the school which had only been opened six months and was situated in the southwestern end of Te Huruhi Bay (now known as Blackpool) — just two miles over the hills from our place. On this occasion, our first day at school, it being a beautiful spring morning, my father decided to row us all round, including my mother and baby brother — at least four miles there and four back again.

We arrived at the school feeling like every child does on their first day to find we were the only two white children. The school had a roll of 30 Maori children and we two Pakeha. Our teacher's name was Mrs Smith and she also had an assistant, Miss Hill. Mrs Smith taught us till after the Christmas holidays after which we had a new teacher by the name of Miss Jamieson who was an excellent teacher and very fine person. Her assistant was Miss Dickson.

Every morning as soon as the bell had been rung by one of the boys, we all had to line up for fingernail inspection and woe betide anyone who had dirty fingernails. Before we started the day's lessons, morning prayers were said.

On one side of the schoolroom was an open fireplace where we had many a log fire burning in the wintertime. Surrounding this was a mantelpiece on top of which was placed rows of half-gallon jars, each holding different types of medicines such as cough mixtures, blood purifier, laxatives etc which were periodically given to the Maori children as at that time TB was rife among the Maori population.

Each day we had singing lessons and could those Maoris sing! The Maori songs we learnt then are still sung. Those were all sung in the Maori language but unfortunately this was forbidden out in the playground and English was the only spoken word.

Spending a lot of time with the Maori at school, at play and in their homes, it was not long before Agnes and I were speaking their language quite fluently. So much so, that we were able to hold quite a conversation with one another around the table at home which exasperated the older folk at times, not knowing what we were talking about.

I remember one occasion when an elderly Maori lady who was visiting Waiheke Island from the Miranda, heard me speaking and offered them 400 acres of land if they would give me to her. It was customary in those days to do that sort of thing, but my parents refused of course...

The four years of attending the Native School were happy ones except that for the first couple of years when, each afternoon after school, I had to fight a different Maori boy to prove who was the best, Maori or Pakeha. Needless to say it was more friendly than hostile and at the first sign of a bloody nose the fight was over.

Although my father earned only £2 a week, we lived very well. We had plenty of homegrown fresh vegetables, milk and farm eggs, all the fish we required as well as shellfish and, as there were a number of rabbits on the farm, braised rabbit and delicious rabbit pie were often on the menu.

Fish was in abundance those days and it was nothing for my father to go for a couple of hours fishing, bringing home between 50 to 60 snapper as well as kingfish. He was also an expert at making fishing nets and spent many evenings, often sitting up all night, to make these.

As well as snapper, we would have mullet and green-boned butter fish — the latter being a real delicacy. Some we ate fresh, others were smoked. To smoke the fish we would first gut them, then clean using a small stiff brush, but not scale. Heads were cut from the snapper but not the mullet. Snapper were split leaving the backbone; mullet were opened from the back, the heads being split as well.

The fish were then dried and salted using coarse salt, left for two hours, well rinsed in fresh water to remove any blood and then hung in the smoke-house to drip dry all night. The following morning, a fire was built of tea-tree or dry pohutukawa — never boxwood or kauri or other such wood producing a black smoke that would taint the fish.

The fish were then cooked until such time as one could insert a finger easily between skin and flesh and then the fire was covered with either white tea-tree, sawdust or green pohutukawa leaves, and the fish smoked till a nice golden brown. After all fire and smoke was removed, the fish would be painted with egg white to give it a nice sheen and left to dry. The result was truly delicious. Also outside was a cookhouse which had an open fire with a bushman type chimney about 10ft wide. My mother had several camp ovens on this fire in which she could cook bread, all sorts of stews, and roasts. In summer, she did most of her cooking out there as the cookhouse had no sides, only a roof and was cooler. Often we had our meals out there...

In those days our nearest Pakeha neighbour was Grannie Brown who lived in Okahu Bay (Surfdale) and kept a small store of unperishable provisions for sale in the kitchen of her home therefore becoming the first shopkeeper on that part of the island.

The next white family were people by the name of Rutherford who lived in Okahu on 650 acres which was eventually sold to Fred Alison. The homestead and 40 acres around it was sold to Johnnie Hooks who farmed Hooks Bay. The block Mr Alison bought later went to a syndicate called Surfdale Estates. Captain Kennedy was also a neighbour though he lived five miles away.

Most of the bays on the western end of the island were the homes of Maori belonging to the Ngati Paoa tribe who were all very fine people. We got to know them well and grew very fond of them. There was a woolshed in Matiatia and a Maori whare where two brothers named Tamati and Ngaeiho Kepa lived, two sisters named Bella and Ngaronga Araoma and a family by the name of Werama.

In Owhanake Bay, north of Matiatia were several Maori families including the Mihakas, Kawhis, Kihis, Rawiris and the Linkhorns... In those days the Maori families cultivated the whole of Owhanake Bay, Church Bay and Te Huruhi Bay.

Owhanake was a shingle bed which at that time was in the process of being sold to J J Craig who later removed all the shingle which was taken to Auckland by scow. It is well known that half the city of Auckland was built from the shingle beds of Waiheke. All the Maori families ran a few sheep, cows and pigs, had their own horses and did their own shearing with blades.

On the southwestern side in Church Bay lived a family named Rehutai Karaka who had a woolshed and a very comfortable home which was later shifted to Matiatia Valley where two of my sons lived in it at different times.

Another Māori family by the name of Kepa lived in Wharau, and going east past Wharau cemetery over the hill was Graham's Gully which was home to Piwaka Graham and family.

The cemetery there contains the remains of a number of Maori who were originally buried in Owhanake but were shifted to avoid being disturbed as the shingle beds were taken. There were also a number who died during the 1912 smallpox epidemic, among them a 16-year-old schoolgirl, Iritana Tehihi. Past Graham's Gully on the western shore of Te Huruhi, past the school, were several homes belonging to the Thompson and Hepo families. They were very fine people. Along the eastern end of Te Huruhi where the new school was eventually built lived the Taipu family.

In 1916, most of the Maori families left Waiheke and settled in the Miranda district, as they had sold their land. It was not long after this that the Native School was abandoned.

At the age of 14, Don Croll was helping to milk Eddie Brown's cows in Pūtiki Bay and he remembered watching the Ostend Wharf being built and the roads being formed by Tom O'Brien.

The present woolshed in the bay now known as Matiatia but whose original Māori name was Ahipaua was built by Fred Alison, John Croll and a builder named Les Vosper in 1914. The original framework came from the old New Zealand Insurance Company's building in Queen Street and was pre-cut in the Devonport Ferry Company's shed close to their slipway in King Edward Parade, Devonport. The lining of thick-heart kauri came from the cabins of old ferry company paddle steamers. At one end were temporary living quarters used by the Alison family until they brought their own house across to the island in 1916. The woolshed has since been converted into a holiday home.

The Alison home, later renovated and operated as a restaurant, brought its own history to the island when it arrived at Matiatia in sections on board the scow *Mabel*. The spacious, two-storey dwelling had originally been built near North Head in Devonport by Captain Isaac James Burgess.

Burgess (1824-1906) had trained as an officer at the Greenwich Naval School before sailing to New Zealand where, in 1850, he became pilot and acting harbour master for the port of Auckland. He was later promoted to chief harbour master and retired in 1894.

The captain had bought several acres of land overlooking Cheltenham Beach on the North Shore, where he and his young wife initially lived in a nikau whare. Here pit-sawn kauri timber was stocked to season for two years. It was around 1850 when the couple moved into their new house with its kauri-shingled roof. An upper storey of four rooms was added later. One guest entertained there was Bishop Selwyn who had crossed over from Mission Bay in a whale boat rowed by young islanders to attend a church service at Devonport.

Neighbours included the Duder and Alison families. After the Burgess children married and their parents died, the property was sold and subdivided. The house was bought by neighbour Fred Alison.

Don Croll, then 15 and working on the Alison farm, got the job of carting all the material up from the beach by horse and dray. The firm of Sam White was again used to re-erect the house and the Alisons moved over to live on their now well-established farm.

The woolshed had been completed in time for the farm's first shearing in October 1916. Cattle yards had been built down on the flat and a race to ship stock out on the scow. The farm shipped its own stock using Alison's twin-engined launch *Makora* as tow boat and a stock scow, *Rita*. At that time Alison was also farming Browns Island, on lease from the Devonport Ferry Company as Don Croll recorded.

In the spring we would ship our cattle and sheep off to Browns Island for topping off, leaving them there for between six to eight weeks before shipping them off. We took the sheep up the Tāmaki River and unloaded them on to the Panmure Wharf from where we drove them on foot to a holding paddock which was situated halfway along what is now known as the Mt Wellington Highway.

That same night we would walk back to the launch returning at dawn next morning to drive them on to Westfield to be sold. The cattle we would ship up to a little beach at the foot of a cattle track, which is now the approach road from the waterfront drive up to the Savage Memorial. They were then taken over by one of Alfred Buckland's drovers who would take them on to the saleyards at Westfield.

During the years from 1916 to 1921, Mr Alison and I had many trips back and forth to Browns Island, spending a week or ten days there each month, as he ran 900 breeding ewes and 35 head of cattle on the island, employing an elderly man to take care of things there between trips.

Browns Island had little water and it was while prospecting for a spring there that Alison and Croll came across an old volcanic slab-lined well which they later discovered had been built by Sir John Logan Campbell. They reopened this and built another on the eastern side of the island.

The year the Alison homestead was barged over to the island, the old three-masted sailing ship *M A Doran* was also towed over and beached. Originally an American ship, registered in Seattle, the *Doran* had served as a coal hulk for the Ferry Company which also kept an emergency stockpile of the black gold on Browns Island. At one time the old ship had 600 tons stored away in her holds to keep the ferry steamers running should a miners' strike, or other emergency, affect coal supplies. The hulk was a landmark in the bay for several years until its rotting decks became a danger to the visitors who scrambled over it. After stripping its copper bolts and sheathing, Alison and Croll burned the hulk.

By 1923, with subdivisions at Surfdale and Palm Beach already under way, work was started on a wharf that would eventually change Matiatia from an isolated farm bay to Waiheke's gateway. Alison and Croll took soundings and the Matiatia wharf was built. Don Croll had the job of carting survey pegs for the Oneroa block as he had done for the earlier Surfdale subdivision. The island was starting to change, recalled Croll.

More people started coming to the island... More frequent boat services began to Ostend, Surfdale and Matiatia. As the island became more populated, the peace and quietness seemed to disappear and the island started to lose some of its charm for me.

Agnes Croll married Allan Insley from the Cowes Bay private hotel. A union which promised much happiness was short-lived however and Don lost his loved sister and constant childhood companion when Agnes died in childbirth.

When Don Croll's mother died of diabetes in the 1920s aged 53, he left Waiheke to live in Wellington where he married Florence Holway on November 16, 1927. After a few years, a letter arrived from the Alisons asking if he would return to manage the Waiheke farm. They wanted a break from the island and intended spending winters in the city.

This we did, taking our baby son with us, going back to live in the same old house again, and so another generation of Crolls began life on Waiheke. We had a daughter and two more sons, the boys all eventually working on the farm as they left school.

Although an uneasy sailor, Flo adapted to island life. She learned how to use the wood-fueled stove and to make butter but, like her mother-in-law before her, never learned to ride a horse. The four youngsters, Don, Bruce, Jean and Ian, enjoyed a happy childhood in the bay.

The 1930s on Waiheke saw more ferry services running, and good schooling and entertainment for the teenagers began. The oldest son started his schooling in the Surfdale Hall and all of them later went to the newly-opened school in Blackpool.

In 1933, a firm called Watkin Wallace started a ferry service with what Don Croll described as "the best steamer that ever ran to Matiatia": the *S S Duchess.*

The Captain of this ship was Eddy Wann, a great skipper and a very fine man. Sunday, of course, was gala day and the Duchess *would arrive bedecked with flags and carrying as many as 900 people. I had the job of seeing that Matiatia wharf was dressed in bunting...*

The Duchess *was known as 'The Lady of the Gulf', a very appropriate name for her, as a 'Lady' she certainly was and one could not have wished for a more comfortable boat to travel on.*

On Fridays the *Duchess* ran a day "shopping" trip from Matiatia to Auckland, leaving the island at 7.00am and returning at 7.00pm. She then went on to Mansion House Bay in Kawau, a further 27 miles, called into Matiatia on Saturday morning at 7.00am (to pick up the Saturday shoppers) and returned to the island again at around 2.00pm with the weekend visitors. Return fare from Auckland to Matiatia was then 2s/6d for adults.

During the Second World War, the *Duchess* was taken over by the navy as a patrol ship and mine sweeper and was not used to carry passengers again. She was finally laid to rest on the northern side of Rangitoto.

During the Depression years farm incomes on Waiheke, as elsewhere, shrank with returns as low as 3/- a head for prime 4-6 tooth wethers. Croll and Alison decided to start slaughtering their own meat on the island.

For a start, we built a safe about 8ft by 6ft and erected it in the shade of a big plum tree. The sheep were killed there and hung in the safe. We also built a yard where the sheep stood during the day to fast, and in the cool of the evening, very often after dinner and a day's work on the farm, by the light of a benzine lantern, I would kill between eight and ten sheep which I would break up and deliver next morning.

Delivery was done in a Model T Ford. Eventually this meat delivery became very popular as the meat was good and prices very reasonable: 4d a pound for forequarters and 6d a pound for legs and loins, 6d for frys and 4d for flaps. On top of selling the meat, we sold pelts to the wool stores, all this proving much more profitable than sending the stock to town.

Eventually a proper slaughterhouse was built, and Fred Alison bought a zinc-lined butcher's van with gauze-lined louvres to allow air circulation. By now Croll was butchering between 15-20 sheep a week with the tally rising to 50-60 during the six weeks over Christmas. On top of normal farm work it made for long days with Croll often starting work at around 2.00am and not finishing until 10.00pm.

The growing number of visitors to the island brought its share of problems to the farm. People left gates open so that stock became mixed up, or climbed fences springing the staples out and, worst of all, they brought dogs to the island and did not always take them home again. These dogs became sheep worriers, sometimes leaving up to 80 sheep killed or badly mauled in one attack.

During his years of farming on Waiheke, there was one experience that was to leave a lasting impression on Don Croll — one that he was to record for the first time in his late seventies.

I am now going to relate something which my eldest son and I saw one day when we were mustering and I doubt very much if any other white person has seen this before or heard about it, as up to now I have not spoken about this to anybody and to my knowledge, neither has any other member of my family. I am not going to mention the locality of this sighting as I don't want this interfered with in any way.

This day, as we were mustering sheep, my son happened to look down and see this strange formation on the beach. We'd had a terrific storm the night before and the sea had washed the beach clear of shingle exposing this complete Maori burial ground.

It was a most remarkable sight. It measured about 30ft by 40ft in area and consisted of row on row of skeletons ranging from children to adults. These were laid out on tea-tree sticks which were absolutely uniform in size, approximately the size of a wooden peg and about 5-6ft long. On top of these were woven flax mats and both sticks and mats looked to be in perfect condition, though I guess if they'd been touched, they would have disintegrated. The skeletons were more or less imbedded in the sticks and mats.

We looked at this some time in awe, but having much respect for the Maori tapu, we did not touch a thing. Next day we went back, but the incoming tide had covered it all over and they were left in peace once more....

In 1950, Don and Flo's daughter Jean was married in Oneroa and a little later their eldest son, Don, also married and in time re-settled in Matiatia with his wife and little daughter, making a fifth generation of Crolls on Waiheke. Their second son, Bruce, also married and returned to Waiheke where he worked for the Alisons until the farm was sold in 1963.

In 1955, Don Croll's life of hard work took its toll and ill-health forced him to leave the island. When he wrote his account of life on the island in 1979, the memories were happy ones.

I am very pleased that I had the opportunity to live and spend my youth on such a beautiful island and now, at 78, I look back on many happy days spent there, doing all the things a young lad loves to do such as swimming, fishing, boating, and shooting plus horse riding and breaking. I am pleased I was able to give my family the chance to share my experience in the same way. I know that they, as well as I, will always have many golden memories of Waiheke Island.
  Haere-ra Waiheke Tuku Motu Kaianga.

The Alison Family

Alfred R Alison, known as Fred, was destined for a life centred on the sea and shipping. His father ran the Devonport Steam Ferry Company and he was apprenticed to a boat builder gaining valuable yachting experience on his father's 75ft keeler *Volunteer* which, at that time, was the largest yacht on the Waitemata. Fred's own ambition, however, was to be a farmer.

It was perhaps inevitable that these two somewhat conflicting strands of his life eventually led him to become a farmer of two Hauraki Gulf islands. In early years, Fred ran his own fleet of scows and did a lot of work for the Auckland Harbour Board. He started his farming career by leasing Motukorea (Browns Island) and was soon looking for more land.

Waiheke was a popular destination for yachties and the *Volunteer* was a regular visitor. Used for entertaining guests, including many overseas visitors, this vessel came equipped with a piano and had its own English-made ceramic dinner service. Some of this elegant set was later used in the Alison home. One notable guest was the Governor-General, Lord

Ranfurly, who was very interested in local history and, in 1903, visited the island where he examined Māori fishing nets in Church Bay.

Because Matiatia was such a popular destination for yachts, the Royal Yacht Squadron bought 11 acres there from Chief Tamati, fencing the flat and planting trees. After being taken over by the Devonport Ferry Co, this land became Fred Alison's first Waiheke property.

He soon expanded his base, buying from Māori owners until he had around 900 acres including what is now Oneroa and land to the north and south of Matiatia. Later he bought 600 acres in Surfdale, 360 acres around Owhanake Bay and a further 500 acres around Park Point, bringing the total acreage to around 2360. As there was multiple ownership and at least 38 titles involved, many years passed before the settlement was finalised.

As Fred had a troublesome back injury suffered during a boat building accident, he relied on the Croll family to do much of the heavy farm work. However, he was a good stockman and proved a successful farmer.

A nephew has vivid memories of early days on the island, including an exciting controlled burn-off of dry danthonia grass from Little Oneroa through Oneroa and over to Te Huruhi. He also recalls a big swamp, alive with eels, that had to be drained and the efforts to build a track up the valley the road now runs along.

Where the road now crosses the Matiatia swamp, one crossed on horseback or a sledge (in dry weather), or got bogged up to mid-thigh. When Croll, Fred Alison, George Kawhi and another worker were shaping a bend in the road below the Alison Reserve, they used picks, shovels and a scoop drawn by a black draught mare called Nancy.

Near where the road now passes the carpark was a stock yard. A rough track led across the rocks to the site of the present wharf where there used to be a rickety jetty just strong enough to accommodate a big dinghy or small boat. There was no track round the bluff to the right and the only access to the woolshed was past the stockyard and over the hill at the back. Alison and Croll blasted a track just wide enough to move stock cattle, one at a time.

When the Burgess house was rebuilt on Matiatia flat, a garden was planted featuring banks of hydrangeas, beds of roses, dahlia and other blooms protected from westerlies by a lawsonia hedge and kept immaculate by a gardener. Quick growing macrocarpas and pines were planted as shelter on each side of the avenue. A nephew recalls bringing young trees to Matiatia during the 1930s in his school bag — the surplus from a tree-growing project at Kings College. Gums were planted and a magnificent Moreton Bay fig still provides welcome shade for visitors.

A flagpole erected near the house was originally the mast of a big yacht named *Iona* which had helped in the rescue of survivors from the wreck of the *Wairarapa* on Great Barrier. In the early 1920s, it was moved to Matiatia from Devonport after the death of Alix Alison on whose waterfront property it had stood for many years.

In the 1920s and 30s, when roading around Auckland was unsealed, rough and dusty, Matiatia was a popular destination for city notables who arrived by pleasure craft or ferry and were often guests at the Alison homestead. Sir Ernest Davis was a family friend who enjoyed the gracious hospitality of the Alisons in their Victorian-style drawing room, sheltered garden or on a croquet lawn that was later converted to a putting green. One overseas visitor he brought with him was celebrated actress Vivien Leigh.

In the 1920s, Alison sold land in what is now Surfdale to a syndicate for subdivision. The surveying company of Blake and Burrell laid the town out. The first section was sold in 1921 and the opening celebrated with a marquee on the beach and a champagne lunch for VIPs. Oneroa Beach was sold the same way a year later with Alison giving road access to Matiatia to the Auckland syndicate which bought it. Mr Blake, of Blake and Burrell, who again surveyed the new block, lived for a while in the Alison home.

Early holiday visitors to Oneroa were the youngsters who stayed in a children's holiday camp run by the Rev Jaspar Calder. City missionary during the Depression years, Calder was also a close friend of Fred Alison and started the camp on an Oneroa section in 1924, initially in tents and later in a boarding house built on a donated section. The Jaspar Calder Lodge continued to provide cheap holidays for needy families up until the 1980s.

Fred's wife, Anna Fanny Alison, who, because of her natural dignity, was aptly named "The Duchess", originally came from Scotland and, in

1939, the Alisons returned there for what proved to be an extended stay. The outbreak of war made it difficult to get a ship home and eventually they had to travel via the United States.

In later years, the Alisons spent winters in a city apartment near Princes Street, Auckland. When they sold the property in the 1960s, they retained a house site above the bay where a nursing couple cared for them into their nineties. The family name is remembered in Alison Park, a piece of land opposite the present Oneroa hall that was given to the community when Oneroa was subdivided.

Te Wharau Bay

One of the first Pākehā purchasers of land at the western end of Waiheke was J J Craig who owned and operated a number of sand and shingle boats in Hauraki Gulf as well as cutters and scows that carried supplies around the Hauraki Gulf. In 1908 Craig owned the following boats: the *Clio, Huon Belle, Irene, Lee, Lizette, Rimu, Mona, Nellie Mason, Ida, Lark, Gem, Stag, Saucy Kate, Three Cheers* and *Puka Puka.*

His property had a frontage to Te Wharau Bay and included several broken gullies and steep ridges, some 148 acres altogether. In 1916, its management was taken over by William Parris, the son of a young Portuguese sailor who had made Waiheke his home after jumping ship. (See the Hodgson and Parris family stories). The farm was stocked with fine-wooled sheep and shearing was done by hand.

The original house near the beach was poorly constructed and shabby, the kitchen lined with pictures from the *Auckland Weekly News.* The Parris family lived there in some discomfort for two years until, one stormy night, they heard a terrific thump and the house slid off its foundations. Unhurt, but frightened by the incident, they moved into the Te Huruhi schoolhouse

A new house, soundly built, had three bedrooms, a kitchen and sitting room, a wash house, and verandah running along the front. The concrete floors of the dairy could still be seen there many years later.

The Parris family were near neighbours to the small pa on Te Wharau Point. Take Kaihe Ranginui was then the much-respected elder of this pa; one of the young Parris girls who often visited his whare recalls him telling her that "the Māori language is like a gently flowing stream."

When the flu epidemic struck New Zealand after the First World War, there were about 20 Māoris living in the area. William nursed the sick at Te Wharau and his wife, Alice, made soups and custards for the invalids.

Because the illness was highly infectious and there was no medical assistance, William had a disinfectant bath in which he also dunked all his clothes each time he came home. He also smoked a pipe with strong tobacco all the time. He helped dig graves for those who died at Te Wharau. His own family were luckily spared the sickness which had killed so many on the mainland as well as Waiheke.

William proved to be a resourceful medic when his own son disobeyed orders by playing with the axe and managed to sit on the sharp end. The boy was stitched up on the kitchen table and carried the scar on his bottom for the rest of his days. The Parris children went to the Te Huruhi Native School which, by this time, had more Pākehā than Māori children attending.

Only some of the Craig land was cleared and William worked on clearing out big stumps and keeping the pasture open for sheep and cattle. The land was also used as a holiday home for the draught horses Craig used to haul heavy loads in Auckland. They were brought over by scow and given a spell of freedom on the island hills before returning to their work in the city.

Every three months, William headed for Auckland with a shopping list of supplies which, as well as staple items, included sweets for the children and a whole sugar bag of broken biscuits. These supplies were brought back to the island on his brother's scow.

William's health was eventually affected by the heavy work of hauling stumps and the Parris family left the island in 1922. An old water trough bearing the inscription *T E Parris Feb 26 1916* is a reminder of his time there. One Parris daughter, Wynne, returned to the island to live at Palm Beach for a few years. She had married Robert Lang, another pioneer descendant, who was employed on Waiheke by the Auckland Electric Power Board.

After the Parris family left, Craig considered the possibility of subdividing the land described as Huruhi No. 2. At one point, Jessie Craig leased 12 acres of this block to Kaihe Ranginui at 5/7d per acre. A letter in the family records from C F Bennet, a land agent, suggests that the option of subdividing was not economic. Broken gullies and steep ridges made it a "difficult proposition", as did the lack of access, he reported.

I estimate that 60 sections, at an average of £50 per section would be obtained, and a further block of 40 sections at an average of £35, this giving a total of £4400. To secure this sum a wharf would have to be erected, costing, I should estimate, at least £1000 and roads constructed.

Costs would be approximately as follows: Wharf £1000; Roads £350; Surveys £150; Engineering £55; Advertising £250; Transportation £100; Legal & Contingencies £250; Commission, about £700; Total £2850

The land was later sold to Fred Alison.

Opopo Bay

Opopo Bay, tucked into the southern coast of Kauri Point, was bought in the early 1900s by Thomas Day. Most of the £200 deposit for the 139-acre block came from the sale of the kauri gum he had dug up in Te Matuku Bay. Every three months he would row his wife and family round to the Orapiu home of the previous owner, John Pegler, and pay off the balance with carefully hoarded gold sovereigns.

Tom and Caroline Day

Thomas, son of Martin Day, had spent his childhood in the bay that still bears the family name. After marrying Caroline Beesley, he moved to Arran Bay where he was employed by Andrew Croll. Tom worked on the land and Caroline helped with the heavier housework in Arran House. Their son, Arthur, was born in the farm cottage in 1893. Later the family moved round to the northern coast, living for a time in a nikau whare in Rarohara (Pie Melon) Bay, before Tom was engaged in 1898 by Captain Kennedy as caretaker of Dunesslin in Pūtiki Bay while the captain took a lengthy holiday overseas.

Arthur, showing an early interest in the sea, was fascinated by the 6ft model of a yacht in full sail in Dunesslin's drawing room. He began his formal education with seven Māori and two Pākehā children around Granny Brown's kitchen table under the instruction of red-haired Mr Allison. A rugged independence was a characteristic of Arthur's which he demonstrated on a visit to Grandmother Beesley in Auckland, a trip which could become quite complicated in those days. Accustomed to running around barefooted, he set off in new boots to walk from his home to Kennedy Point where he was rowed out to meet the steamer *Chelmsford* en route to Cowes Bay and thence to Coromandel. Arthur took his bag into the saloon and was served a dinner of stew while the ship rolled its way across the gulf. The weary little boy slept while cargo was loaded at Coromandel in the dark and through the voyage back to the arrival in the early hours of the morning at Auckland. Disoriented, he almost walked off the end of the wharf before he saw the city gas lights and turned round to make his way to Constitution Hill where his anxious grandmother finally welcomed him into her home at 4.00am.

Although they had a free cottage, meat, milk and firewood, the family struggled to live on Tom's low wage. When one quarterly grocery bill arrived from an Auckland merchant, Tom said to Caroline: "This last bill is nearly £6. Could you go a little easier, dear!" After Captain Kennedy refused a request for a small raise, they packed all their possessions into their mullet boat. With Tom at the oars, rowing in big sweeps through a calm sea, they followed the coast round to Te Matuku Bay. Patiently probing the ground with a heavy gum spear, Tom began searching for the soft kauri "gold". After several months he was so good at finding gum deposits that people said he could smell it in the ground. Within two years and with Caroline's support, he managed to accumulate £200, a large sum then and sufficient for the deposit on Opopo Bay.

The property was commonly known as "The Slip" because a bank had fallen away where the Grays of Waiti had made a bullock track to bring logs down to the sea for shipment. Tom set about clearing the land for grazing sheep and cattle, cutting firewood for export to Auckland. When grazing was short, he rowed sheep across to Rabbit Island (Pakatoa) for a few weeks. Tom also managed Mr Bruce's neighbouring farm at Man O'War Bay and still had time to tend a vegetable garden and orchard with damsons, greengages, apples, peaches and a pear tree that continued to bear fruit for knowledgeable yachties in the 1940s. Down by the rocks is a clear water spring which may have attracted one famous seafarer centuries earlier. The chart of the *Endeavour* records that Captain Cook, on his way up the east coast of the North Island, obtained water from a place he described as "The Black Rocks" in 1769. The possibility that it was the Opopo Bay spring, allowing Waiheke the privilege of claiming a landfall by the great explorer, will always remain one of history's imponderables because it appears in no other documents or records.

Living at Opopo, Arthur was able to attend school every three weeks in four, spending one week at the Man O'War Bay School, and two at Te Matuku Central, a seven-mile walk in bare feet up steep Nelson's Hill and along rough bullock tracks which turned to cold, slippery mud in winter. One morning, when he was 12, he was awakened at 1.00am by his father. "Son, your mother is taken bad. Go and get Mrs Bennett" — the midwife who lived miles away at Ōmaru Bay. After alerting Mrs Bennett, he crossed the hill to Orapiu where he borrowed a boat from his uncle, rowed back into Ōmaru Bay to collect the midwife, then up the Waiheke Passage to arrive home about 10.00am. Shortly afterwards, Caroline safely gave birth to twin girls.

The sturdy twins later followed in their brother's footsteps as they walked to school at Man O'War Bay, taking their flounder spears when the tides were right to catch fish on their way home. Twice a week they would deliver mail, brought to school by children from Cowes Bay, to the Grays at Waiti and were rewarded with sumptuous afternoon teas. One teacher, Jim Broun, boarded with the Days for a time and later married one of Tom's younger sisters, Margaret. Around the annual centrepiece of the Cowes Bay regattas, when the girls could wear their best frocks and flower-trimmed hats, their social life was dominated by school and visits by Orapiu Peglers. The appearance of the Peglers' boat in the channel would be their first and only warning, time for Caroline to get a roast in the oven and prepare a big plum pudding, filling fare for about 14 men, women and children, all with hearty appetites.

Around 1918 the Days sold the Opopo property to their neighbours, Davy and Jack Gray, and moved to a new home up the Wairoa River at Clevedon. Several years later, Arthur was to return to Waiheke to take up the threads of the family's association with the island. It proved an ideal place for someone who had made boats his life.

Wanting to go to sea, he signed on as an ordinary seaman with the Northern Steamship Co on the *Rotomahana*, doing the Coromandel-Auckland run. Next, he joined the barquentine *Ysabel*, running under sail to the Friendly Isles (Tonga), carrying cargoes of corned beef, saloon biscuits, and kerosene. This was a tough experience with poor food and conditions on board. He later worked with the Richardson Co in

Napier where he knew the danger and excitement of unloading stores in surf boats on the open beaches of the East Coast and loading up again with wool hauled to the beach by bullock train. He gained his Masters Certificate for coastal boats and established a stevedoring business in Napier. However, after sustaining heavy losses as a result of the Napier earthquake, he decided to return to Waiheke.

Back on the island, he soon saw the need for a boat service to the eastern bays and began this, in a small way, with the diesel-powered launch *Hauraki*. On her first trip, Labour Day 1934, she carried 24 passengers. Arthur's next purchase was the 40ft *Waiheke* which was powered by a 44 hp Twigg engine and carried 80 passengers. The boat left Auckland at 1.15pm after Saturday morning shopping and returned the following day. It was popular with guests going to Cowes for a weekend's fishing. During weekdays, the launches were used to tow barges loaded with shingle from McCallum's quarry on Pakihi island.

In 1936, eastern Waiheke and Ponui settlers provided finance to start the Waiheke Passenger Service Ltd and the *Baroona* was purchased. From steam trawler used for seine fishing in the gulf, she was converted to a ferry powered by a six-cylinder direct reversing Fairbanks-Moore diesel engine. The *Baroona* ran from Auckland up the Waiheke Channel calling in at Rocky Bay, Awaawaroa, Orapiu, Cowes, Ponui and, if necessary, Man O'War Bay. Skipper was Arthur Day. As well as passengers, the ferry carried cargo including animals. In 1939, the *Tangaroa* joined this service which later became the Waiheke Shipping Co under the management of Leo Dromgool.

Arthur continued his involvement with transport in Oneroa where he ran the Oneroa taxis and operated a bus service. The family were active supporters of a local fire service whose first call-outs were all taken at Martin (Boy) Day's garage.

Life ashore had its share of tragedies. Arthur and Anne's son, Douglas Ross, died in the last polio epidemic in 1949, daughter Gilda was killed in a motor accident and their last son, Arthur Martin (Boy) died in hospital. Despite the sad family losses, there was always a cheerful welcome to the couple's house in Waikare Road in Oneroa. "Skipper" Day was always ready to tell a story and was proud of being a grandson of one of Waiheke's early pioneers. When he died, three years after his wife, in 1977, he was returned to Waiheke aboard the *Baroona* — still a mainstay of the gulf ferry services. A large crowd paid their respects as he was buried beside his family at the Ostend cemetery.

Days on Waiheke: Dixie's Story

My life on Waiheke began in 1940 when I married Edsell Day in his family homestead at Ōmaru Bay. It was not unlike some of the early pioneer weddings with guests arriving by horseback and boat, and the Reverend Castle, who officiated, having to travel over from Great Barrier Island.

I had some qualifications for my new role as farmer's wife in an isolated bay. I was an experienced bookkeeper and our family excursions around the Gulf meant that I could row well and swim. But my real education began when I nervously sat beside our gentle Jersey cow, Silver, and put fingers used to tapping typewriter keys around her teats. Hopefully squeezing, I managed to get the milk flowing into a bucket.

I learned how to make butter, working on a bench by shady trees. The milk was left to set in the dairy until the cream could be skimmed off and put in the butter churn. During the war, gifts of our home-made butter were much appreciated by city friends. As we had no fridge, the butter was stored in big crocks of brine in the dairy.

Summer visitors bought our milk until a stranger arrived to announce that he was the milk inspector and that we were breaking the law. When wool prices were low, we shipped cream off to the Mt Eden Dairy Factory. This was taken by boat to Orapiu for collection and the empties brought back on board the *Baroona*. Our sturdy 12-ft clinker dinghy handled well in rough weather, though it could sometimes be a bit alarming. Lifting heavy cans from a bobbing boat wasn't easy — but we never lost one overboard.

With no vet handy, we often ran into health problems with our finely bred Jerseys and dreaded the milk fever which attacked them. I used to mix a preventative medicine of calcium chloride and molasses — a nauseating brew which I poured through a funnel into the cow's mouth. The cows weren't too keen on it either, and sometimes sent it whooshing straight back, leaving me covered with the sticky stuff. However, this medicine did seem to be effective.

We also had a treatment for milk fever that was administered on the spot — and it could almost be guaranteed that the cows who fell victim came down in the most awkward of muddy places. The pretty frocks and dainty shoes I used to wear while working at a legal office in the city became a memory as I wore any old clothes — in those years, rationing was a fact of life and jeans had not yet been invented.

Because we now separated the milk from our small dairy herd, we needed some pigs to drink the skim milk, and piglets were bought from the Rotoroa Salvation Army farm. These thrived and we butchered them on the farm. I found an old English recipe for pig's head brawn which was delicious. Sides, kept for bacon, were soaked in spiced brine with brown sugar and turned in an immense kauri box. I also devised a number of recipes for mutton. Despite lack of refrigeration, the meat kept well when cooked and stored in spiced brine.

Apron fat was rendered down — and how I hated that smell. During the hungry years of rationing in Britain we packed fat in carefully soldered tins to send to relatives and friends. Gifts of fat were also taken to friends in Auckland. One, like me, made it into soap. Surplus eggs were rubbed with Ovoline to preserve them and stored in the cool dairy.

I was not a true pioneer because we had a telephone line strung across the hills and a little Delco plant for electric lights and radio. Candles were only used when the plant broke down. Although we had water laid on to the wash house, I did our main wash in the old way, boiling up whites in the copper, rinsing and wringing in blue water. The worst job was washing men's work clothes — the woollens, work shirts and heavy saddle tweed trousers that had to be scrubbed on the washing board which was hard on the knuckles.

Rising wool prices meant some improvements in our life — a new 230-volt Lister Diesel generator that ran the milking machines, separator and shearing plant; and a refrigerating unit set up in a concrete room that was lined with Portuguese cork stuck on with boiling pitch. What a day of celebration when we were able to hang our first carcass in it— no more problems with keeping food fresh. We were also able to eat our first home-made ice cream.

Holidays always brought unexpected visitors, who walked in over the hills or scrambled around the shoreline from boats anchored in nearby bays. Some became friends, and most were thoughtful. A few, however, were not and there were often problems with gates being left open, dogs worrying sheep and people lighting fires in the bay.

I remember the awful beauty of our own fires against the backdrop of blue seas when we burnt off the danthonia grass which in summer grew too long for the sheep to graze. For this task, I became a fire lighter, carrying a long pronged wire which held pumice to be dipped in kerosene. First we burned fire breaks; the beating out was done with green tea-tree. Despite the warmth, the men wore woollen shirts and after my cotton one caught alight, so did I.

Once the firebreaks were safe, one lit with joyous abandon. If possible we planned our fire to back into a breeze for a sudden gust of wind would send flames racing up the hills. I remember the time when, after beating a firebreak on the farm boundary, I went into a steep-sided gully to see if my husband needed more kerosene. He did not hear my calls but when he saw where I was he yelled: "Get out, I've lit down there." I had stumbled, my clothes were wet with kerosene and the only way out of the gully was up a steep face. The roar of the fire behind me was a great spur and I crawled and scrambled my way up with heart pounding until, with great relief, I felt cold ashes beneath my hands.

One of the delights of our farm was the abundant bird life: the pied stilts that strutted the bay, the heavy whoosh of a wood pigeon's flight, the chattering fantails and melodic tuis. I never learned to ride but enjoyed walking over the farm checking the stock during lambing or before the once-yearly shear when a heavy fleece made the sheep more vulnerable to blowfly strike or getting cast. Etched in my memory is the picture of an early morning muster when the sun's rays edged the first ewes and lambs with gold as the bleating flock came toward me over the curve of the hill.

It was always a relief when shearing began and wet weather which stained the wool and left yards muddy made us edgy. I worked as a fleeco and felt a sense of personal pride when our Waiheke clip was declared "best in war years" by the *New Zealand Herald*. The price of 25d a pound was the highest in the country.

I often did my shopping and mail collection by boat and enjoyed heading round the coast into Connell's Bay, looking across the channel to the islands of Pakatoa, Rotoroa and Ponui with Cape Colville in the blue distance. I might see gannets diving or a school of porpoise romping through the Waiheke Passage and at the end of the trip, there was always a welcome cuppa in the Connells' kitchen.

To brighten winter months made lonely by bad weather and muddy tracks, we women of the southeastern bays met regularly in each other's houses, preparing elegant afternoon teas. No matter that we arrived in drenched oil coats and muddy gumboots, beneath this rather shabby outer layer were our pretty frocks and our best jewelry. I remember one of our social evenings at Cowes hall with guests making their way there through choppy seas in a freshening nor'easter. We enjoyed the dance despite our awareness of the rising wind but ended up having to stay the night. Unable to return by boat, we clambered home along the shoreline in the early morning, my evening finery tucked up around my waist to avoid the mud and salt water.

Transport was a problem for the occasional Federated Farmers meetings held at one or other of Waiheke's scattered homesteads. We formed a Women's Division and travelled to meetings by tractor, horseback or boat. Once I attended a meeting in Auckland where members were astonished at the way Waiheke women travelled to Division meetings and admired us as pioneers.

With the difficulties of getting to the mainland, sickness or injury was always a worry. Saturday was the best time for an accident as a doctor might be down on the island for a holiday — the eminent surgeon Dr Guthrie was always very generous with his help. In emergencies, neighbours helped each other out. I remember an incident when I helped ferry a neighbour's teenage girl, suspected of having appendicitis, around to Connell's store in search of a doctor. We found that one was staying in Boucher's Bay. He was fetched and we took Connell's launch to Orapiu where a phone call could be put through for an ambulance to come to Maraetai and meet the launch. The doctor arranged for a bed at Auckland hospital and the girl was operated on that night. When Captain Fred Ladd started his amphibian service to the island in the late

1950s, his mercy flights changed our lives. Fred also kept us in touch with mainland news — by air-dropping our copy of the *NZ Herald* which came adorned with his funny scribbled rhymes.

Dixie, her hands full with just one of the prize Waiheke fleeces

Our isolation was much reduced when the P & T installed lines that gave us toll-free contact with Auckland, and by the construction of our first road from western Waiheke. Even before this arrived at our gate, the Power Board arrived with truck and sheerlegs to connect us to electricity. We had to learn how to cook on an electric stove, and housekeeping became much easier.

Edsell's father, Ted Day, was never to drive along the route he had traversed by horseback so many times as he became too ill to travel. After being nursed at home for six months, he died peacefully at the age of 86 on January 18, 1966. A few weeks later, my husband collapsed from exhaustion and this, combined with a wool-price slump and higher wages, reluctantly persuaded us to sell the farm. The years had taken their toll, but we could not leave our island home and settled in Oneroa.

Looking back now, I wish we had known more about the value of our wetlands — the mangroves that are nature's pantry. But we had cherished some fine stands of native trees that can still be enjoyed by tourists who pause to admire the view across Ōmaru Bay.

References

Arran booklet by K Guthrie.

A Story of the Anglican Church on Waiheke, by Colin C Banfield.

Church Missionary Society Letters and Journals, Anglican Diocesan Office Auckland.

Church Gazettes, Diocesan Office, Auckland.

Cultural Values Assessment, by Mahuika Rāwiri and Morehu Wilson

Diary of John Telford, Diocesan Office, Auckland.

Further Maoriland Adventures, J W and E Stack, published by A H and A W Reed.

New Zealand Shipwrecks 1795 to 1960, C W N Ingram and P O Wheatley, published by A H and A W Reed.

Remembrances 1823-1876, James George. Auckland Public Library.

The New Zealanders Illustrated 1846, George French Angas, published by Thomas McLean, London. Auckland Public Library.

"Une famille brugeoise en Nouvelle-Zélande", by Annie Terlinck.

Waiheke Island: A History, by Paul Monin.

Waves on the Shore, by Jack Watson.

Alexander Turnbull Library and National Archives.

Anglican Baptismal Records Coromandel Parish, Diocesan Office.

Auckland Education Board.

Auckland Museum and Institute Library New Zealand Section.

Auckland Maritime Society.

Auckland Outdoor Education Association.

Auckland Public Library.

Catholic Diocesan Records.

Department of Education.

Lands and Survey Department. Maps Waiheke Survey District.

Public Relations Officer, Post Office Headquarters, Wellington.

Waiheke Island Historical Society Archives.

Waiheke Police Historical Data.

Waitangi Tribunal reports:

  No. 10, The Waiheke Island Claim (1987)

  No. 686, The Hauraki Report, volume 1 (2006)

Index

286

287

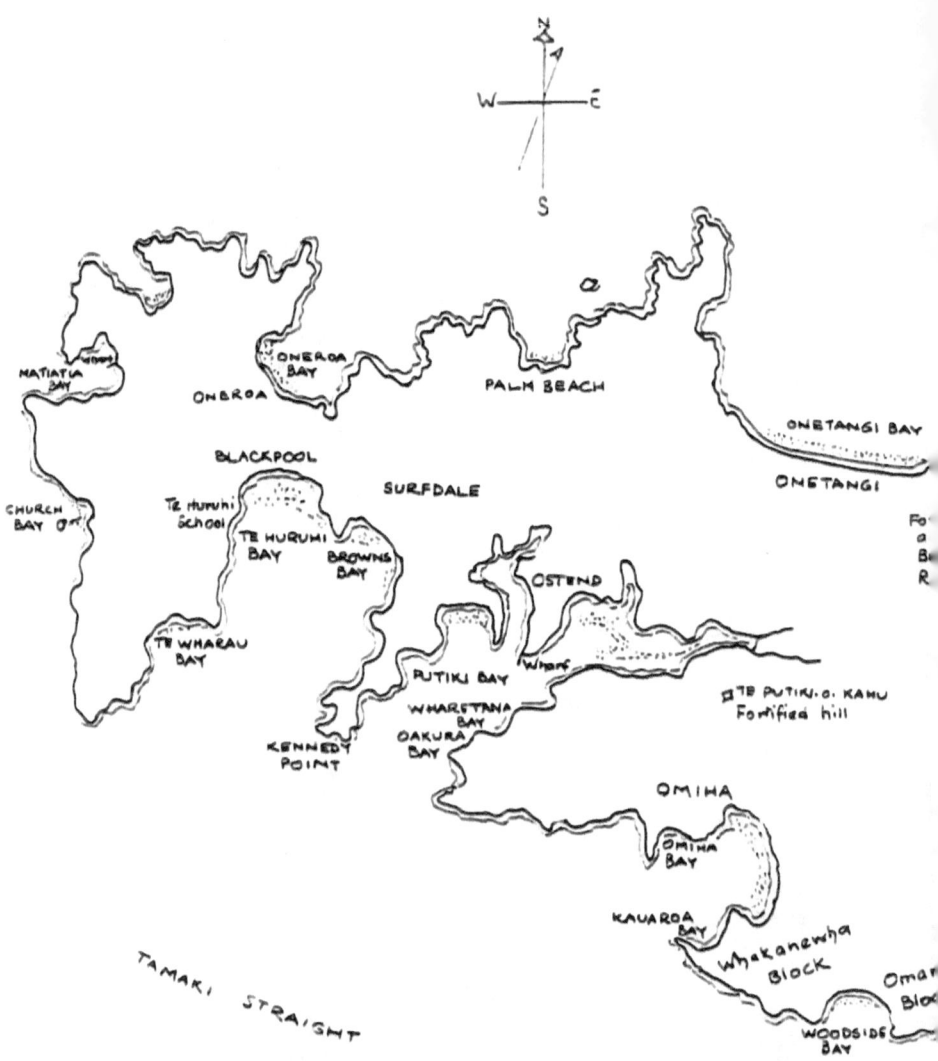

N
W E
S

MATIATIA
BAY
Wharf

ONEROA
BAY
ONEROA

PALM BEACH

ONETANGI BAY
ONETANGI

BLACKPOOL
SURFDALE

CHURCH
BAY
Te Huruhi
School

Fo
a
B
R

TE HURUHI
BAY
BROWNS
BAY

OSTEND

TE WHARAU
BAY

PUTIKI BAY
Wharf

☒ TE PUTIKI·O· KAHU
Fortified hill

WHARETANA
BAY
OAKURA
BAY

KENNEDY
POINT

OMIHA

OMIHA
BAY

KAUAROA
BAY
Whakanewha
Block

Oma
Bloc

TAMAKI STRAIGHT

WOODSIDE
BAY

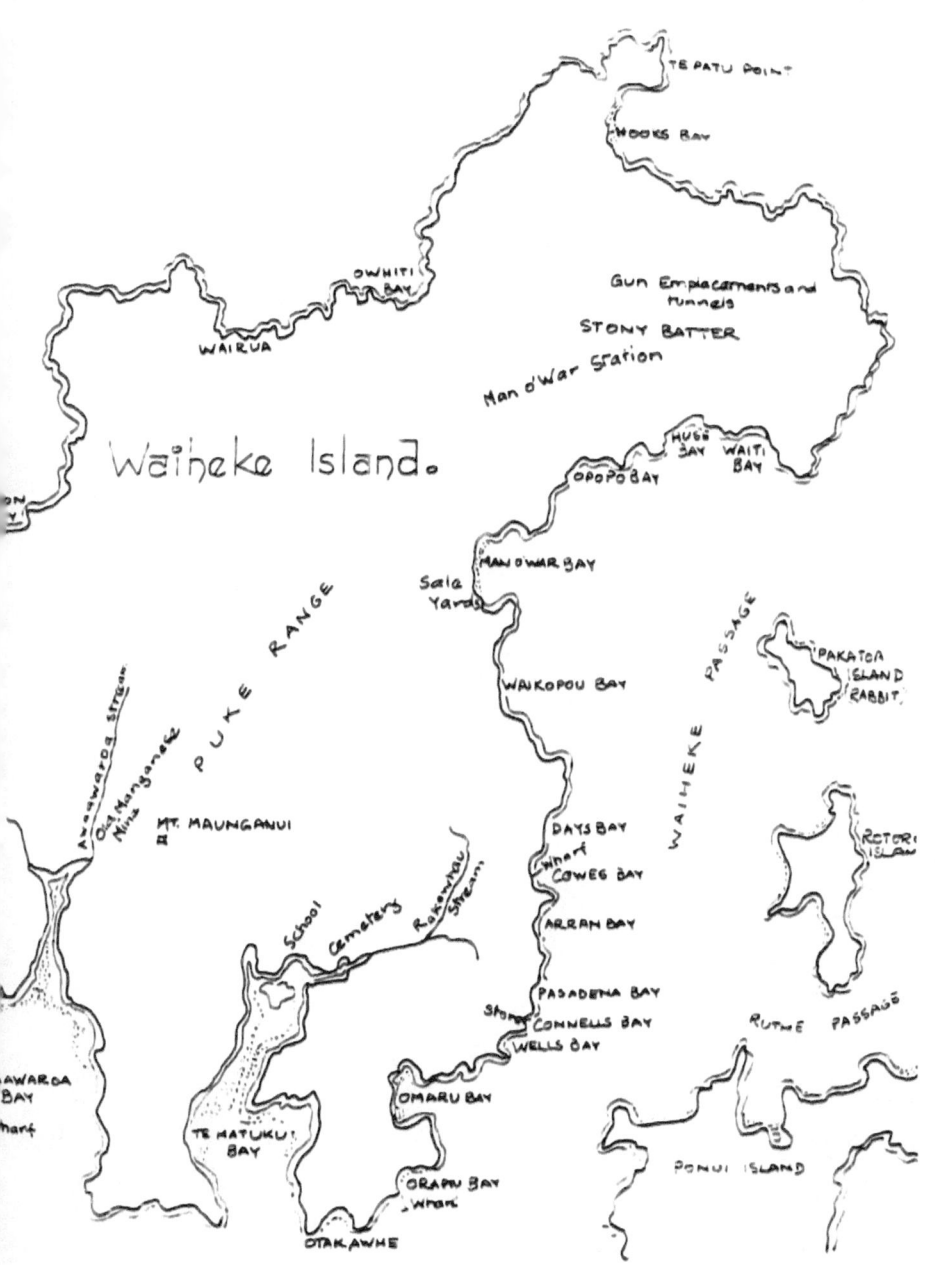

Waiheke Island.